Domestic Partner Abuse

Kevin Hamberger, PhD, is a Professor of Clinical Family and Community Medicine in the Department of Family and Community Medicine, Medical College of Wisconsin. For the past $13^1/_2$ years, he has conducted a program of treatment and research for domestically violent men. For the past several years, Dr. Hamberger's research has focused on the characteristics of and treatment outcomes for domestically violent offenders and the interface of these variables with policy making. More recently, Dr. Hamberger has begun exploring different gender-related contexts and motivations for the use of violence against partners.

In addition to his clinical research work in domestic violence, he has chaired the Kenosha Domestic Abuse Intervention Project's coordinated community response to woman abuse. He is presently Chair of the Society of Teachers of Family Medicine Group in Violence Education and serves on the editorial boards of the *Journal of Family Violence* and the *Family Violence and Sexual Assault Bulletin*. He has been a guest reviewer for several other violence-related journals, and a consultant to the National Institutes of Mental Health. He has published over 50 articles and chapters, and 2 books.

Claire M. Renzetti, PhD, is a Professor and Chair of Sociology at St. Joseph's University, Philadelphia. She is also the editor of the international, interdisciplinary journal, *Violence Against Women,* and coeditor of the Sage Book Series on Violence Against Women. She has published 8 books and numerous book chapters and articles primarily on the topics of same-sex partner abuse, women's use of violence, and violence against women. Among her ongoing research projects is a study of domestic violence in Australian Aboriginal communities.

Domestic Partner*Abuse*

L. Kevin Hamberger, PhD

Claire Renzetti, PhD

Editors

Springer Publishing Company

With the exception of Chapter 7, materials in this volume were previously published in the journal *Violence and Victims,* Volume 9, Number 2, 1994.

Springer Publishing Company, Inc.
536 Broadway
New York, NY 10012

Cover and interior design by Tom Yabut
Production Editor: Pam Ritzer

96 97 98 99 00 / 5 4 3 2 1

Library of Congress Cataloging in Publication Data

Domestic partner abuse / L. Kevin Hamberger, Claire M. Renzetti, editors.
    p. cm.
    Includes bibliographical references and index.
    ISBN 0-8261-9090-1
    1. Family violence—United States. 2. Abusive men—United Staes—Family relationship. 3. Abusive women—United Staes—Family relationships. 4. Gay male couples—United Staes—Psychology. 5. Lesbian couples—United Staes—Psychology. I. Hamberger, L. Kevin. II. Renzetti, Claire M.
HQ809.3.UTD63 1996
362.82'92—dc20   95-31331
                                                                                   CIP

Printed in the United States of America

To Nancy, Heidi, and Alex

L.K.H.

Contents

Contributors

Steven Adelman, PhD
Addiction Medicine Consultant
Harvard-Pilgrim Health Care
Boston, MA

David H. Avery, MD
Director, Inpatient Services
Harborview Medical Center
Seattle, WA
Associate Professor
Department of Psychiatry
and Behavioral Sciences
University of Washington
School of Medicine
Seattle, WA

Vallerie E. Coleman, PhD
Adjunct Faculty
Antioch University
Los Angeles, CA

Donald G. Dutton, PhD
Professor of Psychology
Department of Psychology
University of British Columbia
Vancouver, B.C. Canada

Kenneth E. Fletcher, PhD
Assistant Professor of Psychiatry
University of Massachusetts
Medical Center
Worcester, MA

Steven K. Hoge, MD
Associate Professor in the Schools
of Law and Medicine
University of Virginia
Charlottesville, VA

Jennifer Langhinrichsen-Rohling, PhD
Assistant Professor of Psychology
Department of Psychology
University of Nebraska
Lincoln, NE

Patrick Letellier, MA
Counselor and Advisory
Committee Member
Gay Men's Domestic Violence
Project
Community Against Violence
San Francisco, CA

Ronald D. Maiuro, PhD
Director, Harborview Anger
Management and Domestic
Violence Program
Associate Professor
Department of Psychiatry and
Behavioral Sciences
University of Washington School
of Medicine
Seattle, WA

Susan L. Miller, PhD
Associate Profesor
Sociology Department
Northern Illinois University
De Kalb, IL

Theresa Potente, MSW
Private Practice
InterConnections
Kenosha, WI

Alan Rosenbaum, MD
Professor of Psychiatry
University of Massachusetts
Medical School
Worcester, MA

Dina Vivian, PhD
Research Assistant Professor
Department of Psychology
State University of New York at
Stony Brook
Stony Brook, NY

William J. Warnken, PsyD
Assistant Professor of Psychiatry
Law and Psychiatry Program
University of Massachusetts
Medical School
Worcester, MA

Introduction

Expanding Paradigms for Understanding and Intervening into Partner Violence

Great strides have been made over the past 25 years in clarifying and expanding our knowledge about violence in intimate relationships. Once thought to be a rare, aberrant phenomenon (Macoby & Jacklin, 1974), partner violence is now understood to affect at least 2 million married couples per year (Straus & Gelles, 1986). Similar rates of violence have been estimated for nonmarried couples (Stets & Straus, 1989) and gay and lesbian couples (Island & Letellier, 1991). Awareness of the problem of intimate violence has increased in medicine (American Medical Association, 1992) and law enforcement and criminal justice (U.S. Department of Justice, 1994); in March, 1995, President Clinton inaugurated the new Violence Against Women office within the Justice Department. Within academic disciplines, too, attention to the problem of intimate violence has increased substantially. In 1994, for example, the American Psychological Association established a Task Force on Family Violence, charged with summarizing the state of the art on domestic violence and providing recommendations for education, research interventions, and policy.

Along with these positive gains, the field of domestic violence has also been characterized by recurrent issues or themes that have been the subject of considerable, at time contentious, debate. These include the role of psychopathology in battering, whether battering has biological or physiological underpinnings, and the challenges posed by women's use of violence to feminist or patriarchal theories of partner abuse. Given that these issues and a number of others continue to resurface or lack resolution, it is the goal of this book to revisit and reanalyze them. This continued analysis is itself controversial. Current theoretical and popular notions will be challenged as well as supported. Our ultimate goal, however, is to stimulate further research that expands the horizons of our thinking about partner violence. In anticipation, we provide here an overview of the topics to be covered and raise several issues that merit attention but are beyond the scope of this book.

Several contributors address the question of the relationship between psychopathology and battering. Early theorizing suggested that battering was caused by battered women's psychopathology (Snell, Rosenwald, & Robey, 1964). This view was refuted and laid to rest by subsequent research (Kuhl, 1984). Although other studies showed many battered women to exhibit signs of psychopathology (e.g., Rosewater, 1987), this research demonstrated the need to interpret psychological assessment findings in light of the overall context from which they were drawn. The psychopathological symptoms exhibited by battered women are typically the product, not the cause, of the abuse. Saunders's (1994) research, for example, indicates that a large percentage of battered women exhibit symptoms of posttraumatic stress disorder (PTSD), a finding of particular relevance to practitioners to whom these women may turn for help. As Hamberger and Potente show in chapter 3, battered women who are court mandated for treatment because they used violence against their abusive partners usually exhibit high levels of compliant, submissive, and startle behavior. These women benefit from programs that develop assertiveness skills useful in effectively interacting with their abusive partners, establishing social support networks, and successfully navigating the maze of social service agencies.

The question of psychopathology among batterers has also been controversial. Various researchers have identified particular personality problems common among batterers (Hotaling & Sugarman, 1986; O'Leary, 1993). The most frequently reported are the borderline, antisocial, and compulsive personality disorders

(Bernard & Bernard, 1984; Hamberger & Hastings, 1988; 1991), and what Walker (1984) calls the violence-prone personality. In his review of this research, however, Gondolf (1993) raises the criticisms that it is based on small, clinical samples and is fraught with contradictions. In studies in which control groups are utilized, few differences are found between batterers and the general male population. Although abusive men in treatment appear to have more personality and alcohol problems than do nonabusive men, the research has failed to establish a *causal* link between psychopathology and battering. Gondolf concludes that there is no definitive profile of the batterer. Others who are critical of the psychopathology model argue that battering is *socially* caused and that focusing on individual factors diverts limited (and dwindling) resources from societal-level interventions (e.g., Adams, 1988).

Although Hamberger and Hastings (1988) as well as Hamberger and Lohr (1989) have argued that the social and psychological perspectives are not mutually exclusive nor necessarily incompatible, the debate is not likely to be resolved soon. Indeed, it may be unresolvable if we continue to frame it in either/or terms. A number of authors in this volume argue for an integrated theoretical approach—one that incorporates psychological, social, and in some cases, biological factors. In chapter 6, Dutton for instance, makes this argument in his critique of feminist analyses of wife assault, which emphasize the role of patriarchy over other causal variables. Dutton suggests that psychopathology may combine with cultural norms about women and gender roles to produce the outcome of violence in particular men. In his view, while patriarchy may play a role in the etiology of domestic violence, it is an indirect one, providing personality-disordered men with the values and attitudes they need to justify or rationalize abusive behavior. Both Letellier (chapter 1) and Coleman (chapter 4) also call for a theoretical perspective that assesses the psychological health of individual batterers but also places their violent behavior in social context. Although Letellier's chapter offers a review of the literature on both heterosexual and same-sex domestic violence in support of his position, Coleman draws largely on her clinical experience with lesbian batterers and their partners to make a case for a multidimensional theory of partner abuse that incorporates both individual personality factors and sociocultural variables.

If the debate surrounding the role of psychopathology in domestic violence has been heated, that regarding the possibility of a biological or physiological basis for domestic violence has perhaps been more so. Biological theories of partner abuse have been roundly criticized (Dobash & Dobash, 1987), but some observers, such as Maiuro and Avery (in chapter 7) maintain that too little research in this area has been undertaken to completely rule out biological factors. Rosenbaum (1991) argues that biological factors have been almost completely neglected in research on battering. Some early studies (e.g., Faulk, 1974) showed that at least some batterers exhibited organic-related problems. In one recent laboratory study, Jacobsen (1993) found that a small number of the batterers in his sample (20%) appeared to be vagal reactors; that is, these men exhibited decreased heart rates and other physiological symptoms during arguments and fights, which indicates that their behavior is dissociated from physiological reaction. Jacobsen's study suggests that for at least a small subgroup of batterers, violent behavior may be related to defects in the autonomic nervous system (ANS). However, research on ANS abnormalities in various groups of violent offenders have yielded inconsistent or contradictory findings (Bartol, 1980; Kraska, 1989).

Maiuro and Avery review a substantial amount of research that has examined biological bases for violent and aggressive behavior, especially those that have been amenable to psychopharmacological treatment. Many of the symptoms exhibited by subjects in these studies are also those exhibited by men who are in batterer treatment programs for having abused their intimate partners. Maiuro and Avery speculate on the potential use of various psychopharmacological treatments to lower the incidence of domestic violence among particular subgroups of abusive men. However, as the authors themselves note, there has been too little research on such applications with batterers to allow for much confidence in drawing conclusions about their feasibility. Moreover, the research that is available is plagued by numerous methodological problems. At the same time, Maiuro and Avery emphasize that there is no "magic pill" to end abusive behavior; domestic violence must be understood in the broader context of institutional as well as individual causal factors.

A number of other biological and physiological factors have been implicated in the etiology of domestic violence. Rosenbaum and Hoge (1989), for instance, reported that batterers are more likely than nonviolent men to have a history of head injury. Their study, however, is only correlational and shows no direct causal relationship between head injury and partner abuse. Warnken, along with Rosenbaum, Hoge, and other colleagues (chapter 5), again take up this issue. Although they identify several risk markers for domestic violence and marital conflict that may follow a serious head injury, they did not find that head-injured men were more physically abusive towards their female partners than were a control group of men with no history of head injury.

Harway and Segal-Evans (in press) contend that researchers' and practitioners' focus on "the batterer"—be it the batterer's psychology or physiology—as the phenomenon in need of explanation is misplaced. Instead, they advocate redirecting attention to the dynamics of battering behavior. Several authors in this volume speak to this issue by considering women's use of violence in intimate relationships. Vivian and Langhinrichsen-Rohling (chapter 2), for instance, show that although women may use violence against their intimate partners, their motives and the consequences of their actions are different from those of men who aggress against their partners.

It is Dutton (chapter 6), however, who most vociferously takes up the issue of women's use of violence in intimate relationships. He points to domestic violence in lesbian relationships and studies showing comparable rates of violence for male and female partners as evidence that women are as violent as men in refutation of feminist theories of domestic violence. Though provocative, the research cited by Dutton is not without serious problems. Research on same-sex domestic violence is still so new that the conclusions that may be drawn from it are tentative at best. Particularly problematic are the methodological weaknesses in these studies, which rely on nonrandom, self-selected samples. Moreover, the vast majority of this research has focused on victims of same-sex domestic violence, using their accounts to construct second-person, retrospective profiles of batterers (Margolies & Leeder, 1995). DeKeseredy (1995) delineates numerous methodological difficulties in research on heterosexual intimate violence as well, including the fact that we should not be surprised that reported rates of aggression for males and females are comparable since men are more likely than women to underreport engaging in violence toward their partners.

In the, it is likely that Dutton's chapter, as well as the others in this book, will be most valuable not because of the definitive answers they provide, but because of the additional research and debate they provoke. Indeed, each of the chapters generates a multitude of issues that warrant attention in their own right and are sure to generate future books. This is one of the purposes of the two commentaries that conclude the book. Miller and Renzetti each evaluate, from a feminist perspective, the challenges posed by the work of the authors that precede them and highlight directions for future research. In Chapter 9, for example, calls for additional study of how gender intersects with race, class, sexual orientation, and age as central organizing variables in domestic violence perpetration and victimization as well as institutionalized responses to the problem. She also asks researchers and practitioners to examine how women's survival strategies, including fighting back against violent partners, are criminalized. Miller, in Chapter 8 raises, among other critical issues, the need for additional cross-cultural research. Several recent cross-cultural studies indicate that how aggression is expressed, the meanings attached to it, and reactions to it vary across societies as well as between women and men. For instance, "From around the world, the diversity of women's responses to violence against them bespeaks the diversity of their experiences" (Burbank, 1994, p. 190).

To continually sharpen our focus and deepen our understanding of the vexing problem of partner violence, we must confront difficult issues. By doing so, the field will expand and evolve. This book constitutes one collective contribution to this effort.

— Claire M. Renzetti and L. Kevin Hamberger

References

Adams, D. (1988). Counseling men who batter: A profeminist analysis of five treatment models. In M. Bograd & K. Yllö (Eds.), *Feminist approaches on wife abuse* (pp. 176–199). Beverly Hills, CA: Sage.

American Medical Association (1992). American Medical Association diagnostic and treatment guidelines on domestic violence. *Archives of Family Medicine, 1,* 39–47.

Bartol, C. R. (1980). *Criminal behavior: A psychosocial approach.* Englewood Cliffs, NJ: Prentice Hall.

Bernard, J. L., & Bernard, M. L. (1984). The abusive male seeking treatment: Jekyll and Hyde. *Family Relations, 33,* 543–547.

Burbank, V. K. (1994). *Fighting women: Anger and aggression in aboriginal Australia* (p.190). Berkeley: University of California Press.

DeKeseredy, W. S. (1995). Enhancing the quality of survey data on woman abuse: Examples from a national Canadian study. *Violence Against Women, 1,* 158–173.

Dobash, R., & Dobash, R. (1987, July). *Theoretical underpinnings of family violence.* Paper presented at the Family Violence Research Conference for Practitioners and Policymakers, Durham, NH.

Faulk, M. (1974). Men who assault their wives. *Medicine, Science and the Law, 14,* 180–183.

Gondolf, E. W. (1993). Treating the batterer. In M. Hansen & M. Harway (Eds.), *Battering and family therapy: A feminist perspective* (pp. 105–118). Newbury Park, CA: Sage.

Hamberger, L.K., & Hastings, J.E. (1988). Characteristics of male spouse abusers consistent with personality disorders. *Hospital Community Psychiatry, 39,* 763–770.

Hamberger, L.K., & Hastings, J.E. (1991). Personality correlates of men who batter and nonviolent men: Some continuities and discontinuities. *Journal of Family Violence, 6,* 131–147.

Hamberger, L.K., & Lohr, J.M. (1989). Proximal causes of spouse abuse: Cognitive and behavioral factors. In P.L. Caesar & L.K. Hamberger (Eds.) *Treating men who batter: Theory, practice and programs* (pp. 53–76). New York: Springer.

Harway, M., & Segal–Evans, K. (in press). Working in groups with men who batter. In M. Andronico (Ed.), *Working with men in groups*. Washington, DC: APA Books.

Hotaling, G. T., & Sugarman, D. B. (1986). An analysis of risk markers in husband to wife violence: The current state of knowledge. *Violence and Victims, 1,* 101–124.

Island, D., & Letellier, P. (1991). *Men who beat the men who love them.* Binghamton, NY: Harrington Park Press.

Jacobsen, N. (1993, October). *Domestic violence: What the couples look like.* Paper presented at the Annual Meeting of the American Association for Marriage and Family Therapy, San Diego.

Kraska, P. B. (1989). The sophistication of Hans Jurgen Eysenck: An analysis and critique of contemporary biological criminology. *Criminal Justice Research Bulletin, 4* (5), 2–10.

Kuhl, A. (1984). Personality traits of abused women: Masochism myth refuted. *Victimology: An International Journal, 9,* 450–463.

Macoby, E.E., & Jacklin, A.N. (1974). *The psychology of sex differences.* California: Stanford University Press.

Margolies, L., & Leeder, E. (1995). Violence at the door: Treatment of lesbian-batterers. *Violence Against Women, 1,* 139–157.

O'Leary, K. D. (1993). Through a psychological lens: Personality traits, personality disorders, and levels of violence. In R. J. Gelles & D. R. Loseke (Eds.), *Current controversies on family violence* (pp. 7–30). Newbury Park, CA: Sage.

Rosenbaum, A. (1991, August). *Spouse-abusive men: Current research and future directions.* Paper presented at the meeting of the American Psychological Association, San Francisco, CA.

Rosenbaum, A., & Hoge, S.K. (1989). Head injury and marital aggression. *American Journal of Psychiatry, 146,* 1048–1051.

Rosewater, L.B. (1987). The clinical and courtroom applications of battered women's personality assessments. In D.J. Sonkin (Ed.), *Domestic violence on trial: Psychological and legal dimensions of family violence* (pp. 86–94). New York: Springer.

Saunders, D.G. (1994). Posttraumatic stress symptom profiles of battered women: A comparison of survivors in two settings. *Violence and Victims, 9,* 31–44.

Snell, J.E., Rosenwald, R.J., & Robey, A. (1964). The wifebeater's wife. *Archives of General Psychiatry, 11,* 107–112.

Stets, J.E., & Straus, M.A. (1989). The marriage license as a hitting license: A comparison of assaults in dating, cohabiting and married couples. *Journal of Family Violence, 4,* 161–180.

Straus, M.A., & Gelles, R.J. (1986). Societal change and change in family violence from 1975 to 1985 as revealed by two national surveys. *Journal of Marriage and the Family, 48,* 465–479.

U.S. Department of Justice (1994). *Violence against women.* Washington, DC: Author.

Walker, L. E. (1984). *The battered woman syndrome.* New York: Springer.

1

Gay and Bisexual Male Domestic Violence Victimization

Challenges to Feminist Theory and Responses to Violence

Patrick Letellier

This article demonstrates how same-sex male battering challenges contemporary feminist domestic violence theory. The author shows current theory to be heterosexist and therefore insufficient to explain the phenomenon of battering among gay/bisexual men. Domestic violence theories that integrate a sociopolitical and a psychological analysis of battering are presented as more inclusive of same-sex domestic violence. Differences between battered gay/bisexual men and battered women are illustrated, focusing on how these men conceptualize and respond to violence against them. The author also examines the social context of homophobia in which same-sex battering occurs; the impact of AIDS on gay/bisexual men as it pertains to battering; the misconception of "mutual combat"; and the difficulty of seeking help. The article highlights the need for empirical research on same-sex male battering.

Through the influence of the feminist movement of the mid-1970s, domestic violence came to be understood primarily as a heterosexual, sociopolitical phenomenon with its basis in sexism, that is, gender (Schecter, 1982). As a result, the domestic violence movement historically has focused almost exclusively on the battering of heterosexual women. The feminist political view of the male-female dyad has been the basis of the movement's core philosophies, shaping everything from batterer treatment policies (Frank & Houghton, 1987; Sonkin & Durphy, 1989) to victimization theory (Browne, 1987; Dobash & Dobash, 1979; Martin, 1976; Schecter, 1982; Walker, 1979), to current domestic violence law (Sonkin, 1987). The feminist analysis of gender socialization and its role in domestic violence has been tremendously effective in illuminating the relationship between discrimination and violence against women in society at large and the at-home version of that "gender oppression": battering (Pharr, 1988).

Unfortunately, feminist theory, with its doctrine of male victimizers and female victims, has also contributed to the invisibility of gay and lesbian domestic violence because it precludes the possibility of such violence occurring. Indeed, the movement to stop domestic violence has been extremely reluctant to address and work to prevent same-sex battering (Lobel, 1986), in large part because of the fundamental challenge to domestic violence theory that gay and lesbian battering represents (Island & Letellier, 1991a). The existence of female batterers and male victims defies the strict gender categorizations of victims and perpetrators that are central to a feminist analysis of domestic violence (Schneider, 1992). The dearth of knowledge about same-sex battering, particularly concerning gay and bisexual men, allows much of the current work in the field, both in theory and in practice, to remain heterosexist. Without a wider dissemination of information about same-sex domestic violence, there is little hope for a more inclusive approach to the topic of battering in general.

The purpose of this chapter is to demonstrate how gay and bisexual male battering (and, though not directly addressed, lesbian battering) challenges the current ideologies about victimization. While acknowledging the importance, and drawing on certain aspects, of the feminist analysis of gender socialization as it pertains to domestic violence, it will be shown that such an analysis is fundamentally heterosexist and is furthermore insufficient to explain the phenomenon of same-sex battering. This chapter begins with a brief examination of the current gender-based theory of domestic violence and an overview of more inclusive theories. These latter theories integrate an analysis of the sociopolitical perspective with an examination of the role that individual psychological factors play in the dynamics of domestic violence. The author then illustrates several ways in which battered gay and bisexual men differ from battered women and shows how current theory fails to account for male victimization. The role of homophobia in same-sex male battering as well as the difficulties battered gay and bisexual men have accessing help will also be discussed. The article ends with a call for a more integrated domestic violence theory based on an understanding and inclusion of same-sex battering.

It is important to emphasize from the outset that no empirical research has been published about gay and bisexual male victims of domestic violence. Hence, many of the ideas and examples described in this article are based on the author's clinical experience with this population as well as his own experience as a victim of gay men's domestic violence.

Gender-Based Theory

Documenting the central role of sexism in domestic violence, Dobash and Dobash (1979) assert that, "The use of physical violence against women in their position as wives is not the only means by which they are controlled and oppressed but it is one of the most brutal and explicit expressions of patriarchical domination" (p. ix). According to these researchers, and virtually all feminist-identified writers and experts to follow, men who assault their partners are following cultural prescriptions that dictate male dominance and female subordination. Being a victim of domestic violence is equated with, or seen as the natural consequence of, being a wife. As Pharr (1988) points out, battered women are "victims of sexism at its worst" (p. 9).

A more specific analysis of the role of gender in domestic violence victimization is put forth by Walker (1979), who writes that the battered woman is a "traditionalist about the home," who has strong convictions about family unity and the socially prescribed feminine sex-role stereotype (p. 35) . As children, battered women "were expected to be pretty and ladylike and grow up to marry nice young men who would care for them as their fathers had" (p. 35). As adults, they believed that a woman's place is in the home. According to this doctrine, relationships in which violence occurs are extreme examples of the traditional marriage that is characterized by male supremacy.

Throughout most of the 1980s, battering was regarded almost exclusively as a political phenomenon. Succinctly expressing this view, Graham, Rawlings, and Rimini (1988) contend that, like hostages, "battered women are political prisoners. Battering ... is a political act since it reinforces the existing structure of male dominance" (p. 228). Like other theoreticians in the field, Graham and colleagues rely exclusively on heterosexuality as a fundamental assumption in their work.

Almost without exception, domestic violence theory has been established solely on an analysis of heterosexual relationships where batterers are viewed as "oversocialized males who rigidly adhere to sexist patriarchal values" (Hamberger & Hastings, 1988, p. 763), and victims have one singular uniting characteristic: They are female (Browne, 1987). These gender-based theories inherently exclude same-sex relationships where both perpetrators and victims of battering can be either male or female. As a result, same-sex domestic violence has been rendered almost completely invisible in the mainstream domestic violence literature, receiving only token mention in several books and articles. When gay and lesbian battering is mentioned, the challenges it presents to heterosexual domestic violence theories are simply not addressed. Instead, same-sex domestic violence has been tailored by theoreticians to fit the dominant paradigm of male/female sex role socialization and sexism, or it is referred to as a so-called "exception to the rule" (Geffner, 1992).

Martin (1976, p. 67), for example, claims that battering occurs in same-sex relationships when lesbians and gay men act out masculine and feminine (butch/femme) roles, but is less likely to occur in couples who do not imitate these "Mom and Dad"-type relationships. Although Martin made this assertion 18 years ago, little has changed. As late as 1991, experts were still trying to conform lesbian and gay male experiences of domestic violence into theories developed about heterosexuals. Walker asserts that "most lesbians and gay men were raised in heterosexual homes where power differences between men and women fueled the sex-role socialization patterns that they model in their own relationships" (Island & Letellier, 1991a, p. xix). She, too, defines same-sex relationships as imitations of heterosexual relationships and implies that lesbians or gay men affected by domestic violence are actually acting out heterosexual male or female sex roles. This attitude persists despite widespread evidence that the vast majority of lesbians and gay men actively reject heterosexual sex roles as models for their own relationships (Peplau, 1991).

Integration of Sociopolitical and Psychological Theories

Recent exceptions to this pervasive heterosexism, however, reveal an integration of social and psychological domestic violence theory that challenges gender-based assumptions and allows for the inclusion of same-sex relationships. For example, in an article on cross-cultural aspects of battering, Campbell (1991) points out that there is not, as most feminist theory would contend, a linear correlation between female status in society and rates of wife abuse. Campbell proposes that "individual psychological factors within a context of cultural tolerance" predict individual incidents of domestic abuse, while cultural, political, and economic factors may lead to increases in its frequency and severity (p. 19) . Thus, the individual is examined psychologically and in the context of the social milieu, regardless of gender.

In an article on the social-psychological model of battering, Merrill (in press) also argues that feminist theory that sees cultural misogyny as the root cause of domestic violence contributes to the denial of same-sex battering. Merrill asserts that domestic violence must be understood as both a psychological and social phenomenon in order to satisfactorily explain the occurrence of same-sex battering. He writes, "Feminist theory and psychological theory are not necessarily mutually exclusive; one does not have to negate the other, and in fact, if synthesized and placed together, they can enhance our vision" (p. 5).

Hamberger and Hastings (1988) also integrate sociopolitical and psychological theory in their work, stating that "psychopathology must be considered part of the picture for a majority of identified batterers" (p. 769) . These researchers point out that although sociopolitical theory helps to focus attention on societal factors in spouse abuse, such as legislation and public policy, the psychological characteristics of individual batterers must also be taken into account.

Obviously, battered gay and bisexual men do not have that single quality that has been the focus of the domestic violence movement: They are not female. By definition, they cannot adhere to the profile of the passive or submissive woman who is in a powerless position in relation to men in society. Sexism and misogyny cannot be the root cause of violence against these men. Their sexual orientation and gender may influence their reaction to the violence and their ability to escape from it, but they are not battered because they are men, nor because they are fulfilling a feminine sex-role stereotype.

The integrated theories of battering that combine an analysis of the social context in which domestic violence occurs with the psychological characteristics of the individual perpetrator are inclusive of same-sex battering. Such theories account for victims and batterers of either gender and they allow for the inclusion of the social context of homophobia and heterosexism in which same-sex battering occurs. Although there are similarities between battered men and women, under this more inclusive theoretical model, battered gay and bisexual men do not have to be examined as mere versions of battered women. Instead, they can be understood as men who have a similar experience of being battered, but who conceptualize and respond to violence against them differently from battered women. Battered gay and bisexual men also face an array of different problems in their attempts to escape from their violent partners.

Men As Victims

One of the major distinctions between battered gay and bisexual men and all battered women is that gay and bisexual men are often unable to see themselves as victims simply because they are men. Many of the battered gay and bisexual men with whom the author has worked view battering as something that happens only to women, and they are extremely uncomfortable identifying themselves as "battered." Illuminating this point, and drawing on a feminist analysis of sex roles, Lew (1988) reminds us that "our culture provides no room for a man as a victim. Men are simply not supposed to be victimized. A 'real man' is expected to be able to protect himself in any situation. He is supposed to be able to solve any problem and recover from any setback" (p. 41). As is the case with male incest survivors (Hunter, 1990), many battered gay and bisexual men do not conceptualize their experiences as abuse and see victimization as inconsistent with their male identity. As a result, many gay and bisexual men who have experienced considerable violence by their partners do not assign a "victim" label to their own experience because they cannot see themselves as men *and* as victims.

Studies of male sexual assault survivors show that high levels of physical harm or injury to their bodies must be present in order for men to feel self-approval for their emotional or psychic reaction to trauma (Evans, 1990). In other words, men's internal reaction to trauma is often validated through their physical symptomatology. Shifting this feminist analysis of gender socialization into the realm of domestic violence, we see the battered gay or bisexual male who may need to be physically injured in order to see himself as victimized. The common psychological reactions to violence, such as fear, vulnerability, shock, and depression, in the absence of a black eye, a fractured rib, or a stab wound, may not be sufficient for the man to associate his experience with the concept of victimization. In many cases, even physical symptomatology is not enough. A recent article on same-sex battering described a gay man who had been physically battered by his partner for more than a decade. A clinical social worker working with him reported, "After being assaulted with a lead pipe and almost killed … this man was still able to seriously ask the question, 'Well, do you really think that was domestic violence?' " (Snow, 1992, p. 61).

It is likely that many, if not most, gay and bisexual men lack the awareness and language to describe their own victimization, and therefore fail to take the steps necessary to leave their violent partners, particularly early in the relationships when the violence is just starting. Given the virtual silence about same-sex battering by the domestic violence movement (Tuller, 1994) and the gay community (Szymanski, 1991), these men may never have heard of gay domestic violence per se. As the cultural "problem solvers" described above, they are less likely than battered women to tell anyone about the abuse and less likely to seek help. Instead, they stay to "take it like a man" or to "stand their ground," putting themselves at risk for more severe and frequent violence. It is, in part, their inability to see themselves as victims that may contribute to their staying in a relationship in which they are likely to be further victimized.

Adverse Effects Of Homophobia and AIDS

To understand how battered gay and bisexual men code their experience of victimization, it is necessary to examine the context in which that violence occurs by looking at the role that homophobia plays in the lives of these men. In the United States, lesbians, gays, and bisexuals are continually bombarded by homophobia (Blumenfeld, 1992; Herek & Berrill, 1992; Pharr, 1988). Despite the progress of the gay and lesbian civil rights movement of the last 20 years, mainstream society still views most lesbians and gay men as sexual perverts, criminals, a danger to children, and pathologically disturbed (Margolies, Becker, & Jackson-Brewer, 1987). The hatred and denigration of lesbians and gay men in American society take many forms: skyrocketing rates of antigay violence and harassment (Berrill, 1990); legal, sanctioned discrimination against gays in housing and employment (Harvard Law Review, 1990); laws against same-gender sexual conduct in 24 states (Rivera, 1991); policies that prohibit gays from many of the life activities that heterosexuals take for granted, such as serving in the U.S. military (Shilts, 1993); securing the custody of their own children (Herek, 1990); or simply holding hands in public. Indeed, the refusal of the government to prevent or even oppose the violence, discrimination, and prejudice directed at lesbians and gay men makes them among the most threatened of American minorities (Arriola, 1992).

Given the extreme levels of animosity that gay and bisexual men experience in their everyday lives, it is not surprising that it takes a tremendous effort for many to maintain feelings of self-worth and dignity (Isay, 1989). Nonetheless, research indicates that the majority of lesbians and gay men in this country are as healthy and well adjusted as their heterosexual counterparts (Isay, 1989), and that they experience the same rate of relationship satisfaction

(Peplau, 1991). Despite this healthy majority, significant mental health problems plague large numbers of lesbians, gay men, and bisexuals. For example, suicide rates among gays and lesbians, particularly gay and lesbian teens, are estimated to be three times the national average (Gibson, 1989). Alcoholism or other substance abuse is believed to be a problem for as many as one third of all homosexuals in this country (Kus, 1990). The poor self-esteem and sense of inadequacy many gay and bisexual men feel contribute to the difficulty they may have in developing committed and trusting relationships. As Isay (1989) points out, many gay men describe the differentness they feel as homosexuals in terms of "being defective" (p. 25), as if there is something fundamentally wrong with them.

For gay and bisexual men, the AIDS epidemic is adding another dimension to the problem of low self-esteem because "some healthy young adults now perceive themselves as potential carriers of death" (Isay, 1989). Odets (1990) elaborates on this point in his assertion that "the homosexual man, often considered psychologically 'sick' for his sexuality, and who homophobically concurs with this conclusion, is now sick with AIDS, an apparent physical validation of the moral and psychological judgments against homosexuals" (p. 1). Odets's research revealed that so pervasive was "internalized homophobia" that many gay men he studied were more comfortable with their identity as people with AIDS than with their identity as homosexuals (p. 2).

Although not empirically validated, the correlation between the homophobia described above and the phenomenon of gay and bisexual male battering seems clear. Compound the insidious effects of homophobia with the virtual absence of healthy gay relationship role models, and the stage has been set for a group of men who tolerate violence from their own partners. For example, the author recalls a battered gay male whose partner would shout, after a violent attack, "You might as well get used to it. This is how gay relationships are." The victim in this case had no frame of reference other than his abusive partner: This was his first relationship, and like other victims of gay domestic violence, he was extremely isolated from the local gay community. The impact of homophobia is also made clear in the words of a battered lesbian: "I basically accepted my relationship as common to the 'gay experience' ... it seemed to be normal. Although I didn't like it, I saw no acceptable alternatives" (Breeze, 1986, pp. 51-52).

As is the case with victims of antigay violence (Garnets, Herek, & Levy, 1992), battered gay and bisexual men may actually associate their victimization, and the pain and confusion that accompany it, with their homosexuality. The battering may lead to feelings that they are being rightfully punished for being gay—feelings all too often reinforced by homophobic family members. They may feel defective on some fundamental level and are often told by their partners that it is something about them (the way they talk, how they behave, who they are, etc.) that causes them to be hit. Battering may simply reinforce their feeling that as homosexuals they are acceptable targets for abuse and violence (Herek, 1990).

"Mutual Combat"

Although many battered gay and bisexual men may feel that they deserve to be abused because of their sexual orientation, this does not necessarily mean that they stand by passively while their partners assault them. Quite to the contrary, it is often assumed that in same-sex relationships both partners are equally violent and abusive, perhaps because both partners are the same gender and may be approximately the same size and weight. This idea of mutual combat, or reciprocal violence, maintains that both partners are equally capable and willing to commit violence, that each partner is both a victim and a batterer, and, consequently, that both partners are equally accountable for the violence.

Many of the battered gay and bisexual men with whom the author has worked employ the concept of mutual combat to initially describe their own experience of domestic violence. That is, they say, "I hit him, too. We both batter." Mutual combat is also how the police and criminal justice system in California tend to view same-sex domestic violence. The author has seen the words "mutual combat" written directly on police reports by responding officers, further reinforcing for the victim, the batterer, and the rest of society the misconception that same-sex battering is mutual.

Research shows that up to 71% of heterosexual battered women use violence against their partners at least once (Saunders, 1988), most often in self-defense. It is not unreasonable, therefore, to assume that battered gay and bisexual men, who are certainly socialized more than women to use physical force against an attacker, are at least as likely, if not more so, to respond to violence against them with violence of their own.

Supporting this contention in a feminist analysis of sex-role behavior, Browne (1987) points out that when confronted with violence in their relationships, heterosexual women are most likely to respond with attempts at peacemaking and resolution because, culturally, these responses are the most deeply ingrained. Conversely, Browne asserts that, "When threatened with a perceived loss of control in an adult relationship [such as a violent attack], men raised in violent homes may follow the early models by resorting to violence themselves, in an attempt to maintain control and prevent the potential of further victimization and pain" (p. 34). Although Browne is describing men who witnessed or experienced violence in their family of origin, her hypothesis about how some men respond to violence can be more generalized. I hypothesize that battered gay or bisexual men are more likely than battered women, including lesbians or bisexual women, to respond to battering with violence of their own, either in self-defense or in retaliation for prior abuse. As Renzetti (1992) makes clear, however, this does not mean that same-sex battering is mutual.

Based on her research on lesbian battering, Renzetti (1992) challenges what she calls the "myth of mutual battering" (p. 107). Renzetti writes that, "A major weakness in the mutual battering perspective is the underlying assumption that all violence is the same, when, in fact, there are important differences between initiating violence, using violence in self-defense, and retaliating against a violent partner" (pp. 107-108). Renzetti's point here is crucial: Motivation for the violence must be examined within the context of the relationship in order to understand who has the power in the relationship. It is not enough to know who strikes first because a battered person may resort to violence in an attempt to prevent another attack against him or her. With gay and bisexual male battering it is also not enough to know which partner sustained the more severe injuries because both men in the couple may have the physical capacity to injure the other.

For victims of domestic violence, striking back can have debilitating effects on their understanding of the violence and on their motivation to seek help for themselves. Hart (1986) explains that a significant number of battered lesbians question whether or not they are actually battered if they responded even *once* to violence against them with violence of their own: "... especially if it worked in the immediate situation to stop the batterer, they are compelled to see themselves as equally culpable—as batterers" (p. 184). For many battered lesbians then, and, it is hypothesized, for battered gay and bisexual men, there is no perceived distinction between self-defense and battering. Victims identify as perpetrators regardless of the motivation for their violence. This may be particularly true for battered men, given that being a perpetrator of violence is a more socially acceptable role for a male than being a victim.

Battered gay and bisexual men who strike back against their partners may believe they have stooped to the level of physical violence. Having been victimized in the past, they feel they should have known better. They are also vulnerable to the perpetrators' insistence that the violence is really a "relationship problem," or "our problem." Consequently, they may feel they do not have the right to seek help for themselves because now they have become part of the problem.

Help Seeking

Another difference between battered heterosexual women and battered gay and bisexual men involves help seeking. Those battered gay and bisexual men who decide to seek help are likely to encounter a severe problem: the utter lack of resources available to them. One conservative estimate is that in the United States, half a million gay men are battered every year (Island & Letellier, 1991), yet there are only approximately six agencies or organizations in the entire country that exist specifically to help them. With no shelters for battered gay or bisexual men in the United States, there are literally hundreds of thousands of battered men remaining with their male partners because they have nowhere to go to escape their violent attacks.

There are numerous reasons for this void in available services. First, as stated earlier, the domestic violence movement has focused virtually exclusively on the development of services for heterosexual women. Second, domestic violence is still not acknowledged as a serious problem in the gay community itself (Island & Letellier, 1991a; King, 1993; Lobel, 1986; Renzetti, 1992). This community denial will continue as long as gay leaders continue to believe and publicly state that gays and lesbians are "a very non-violent group of people" (Epstein, 1993, p. 1), despite an abundance of evidence to the contrary. The community-wide denial only contributes to the violence because so little is done to stop the battering and hold perpetrators accountable.

In addition to the lack of services, the police are perceived as off limits to many, if not most, gay and bisexual men because of the institutionalized homophobia and heterosexism of most police departments. According to studies on antigay violence, the median number of gay men and lesbians who experienced antigay victimization committed *by the police* was 20% (Herek, 1990). This victimization includes verbal and physical abuse, entrapment, blackmail, and the deliberate mishandling of antigay violence cases. Distrust of the police, and of the criminal justice system in general, may be high among lesbians and gay men, with good reason. Gay and bisexual male victims of domestic violence have reported to the author a variety of dehumanizing and illegal responses by the police to their calls for help. Victims have been harassed and ridiculed as "fags" and "queers who should learn to beat each other up." Responding officers rarely arrest the batterer, or conversely, they arrest the victim, although he may be physically injured. In other cases, both victim and batterer have been arrested and held in the same jail cell where the victim was reassaulted. One battered gay man who called the police for help reported that an officer told him that they "only arrest in these gay things if it gets bloody."

Many domestic violence laws are also discriminatory against gays and lesbians in that they contain opposite-sex language that requires same-sex victims of domestic violence to sustain greater injuries than their heterosexual counterparts in order for an arrest to be made (Island & Letellier, 1991b). For example, in California the domestic violence criminal statute (273.5 Spouse Abuse) specifically excludes same-sex partners by dictating that it applies only to opposite-sex couples (West's California Codes, 1993). The following example from case law highlights this heterosexist discrimination. In an analysis of the 273.5 charge in the case *People v. Cameron,* the presiding judge states, "Some other offenses (besides the 273.5 charge) do require higher degrees of harm to be inflicted before the crime denounced by them is committed . . . *But the legislature has clothed persons of the opposite sex in intimate relationships with greater protection by requiring less harm to be inflicted before the offense is committed"* [emphasis added] (California Appellate Reports, 1985, p. 952) . Thus, according to California law, a battered gay man or lesbian must sustain greater injuries than a heterosexual woman or man in order to have their partners arrested and charged with spouse abuse.

A battered gay or bisexual man interacting with the criminal justice system also faces negative consequences that are unrelated to the violence he experienced. For example, discrimination against people with HIV by employers, insurance companies, and the criminal justice system is well documented (Schulman, 1991) and is widely discussed in the gay male community. Many battered gay men understand that reporting a violent attack by a same-sex partner will almost certainly require them to reveal their sexual orientation, thereby risking unwanted publicity, job loss, and terminated health insurance: a calamity for anyone, particularly someone living with HIV. Thus, homophobia in the criminal justice system forces many gay and bisexual men to choose between the negative and potentially sweeping consequences of revealing their sexual orientation and the help and safety that same system is supposed to provide (Wertheimer, 1992). Hence, calling the police may not even be seen as an option for most gay men.

Conclusion

Battered gay and bisexual men differ from battered women in how they respond to and conceptualize domestic violence, despite the similarity of the abuse they experience. As this article demonstrates, it is perhaps best to understand battered males by examining the literature, albeit scant, on how men respond to violence and trauma in general, such as sexual assault, rather than assuming that gay and bisexual men are male versions of battered women. This article also clearly highlights the need for empirical research on the topic of same-sex male battering.

Men most often cannot see themselves as victims, even if they have experienced considerable violence against them committed by their partners. Their perception that only women can be battered may cloud their abilities to evaluate their own experience and assess the danger they may be in. It is hypothesized that gay and bisexual men are more likely than their female counterparts to fight back against their abusive partners, either in self-defense or in retaliation for past abuse. Their violence may further decrease their ability to acknowledge their own victimization, which, in turn, decreases their help-seeking behavior. Those who do seek help are likely not to find it. The gay community and the domestic violence movement have done remarkably little to help battered gay and bisexual men. Additionally, the homophobia and heterosexism of society's institutions, such as the criminal justice system, rule out many of the sources of help to which heterosexual women have access.

The differences between battered men and women have implications for current, mainstream domestic violence theory. The feminist sociopolitical analysis of domestic violence may be helpful in understanding heterosexual battering, where, given the stark inequalities between men and women in society, gender *is* power, and men have explicit power over their female partners. As made clear throughout this article, there are many aspects of the feminist analysis that are useful in explaining how and why men and women respond the way they do to violence, regardless of sexual orientation. This model, however, is fundamentally heterosexist and cannot be used to explain the phenomenon of same-sex battering. It is an insufficient framework through which to understand gay and lesbian domestic violence. Rather than gender, the use of violence to maintain power and control over one's intimate partner, regardless of sexual orientation, must become the focal point of discussion and analysis for all forms of battering.

More integrated theories incorporate the gender-neutral experience of same-sex battering, focusing instead on power imbalances, both on the societal and interpersonal levels, and on the psychological characteristics of individual perpetrators. Although it is important not to disregard the benefits of feminist scholarship in the understanding and analysis of domestic violence, domestic violence must be regarded as both a social *and* an individual psychological problem requiring social and psychological interventions. Only then will domestic violence theory be applicable to the wide variety of relationships that compose modern society.

Acknowledgments.
The author is grateful to Amy Huber and Greg Merrill for their ideas, feedback, and critical comments on earlier drafts of this chapter.

REFERENCES

Arriola, E. R. (1992). Sexual identity and the constitution: Homosexual persons as a discrete and insular minority. *Women's Rights Law Reporter, 14,* 263–296.

Berrill, K. (1990). Anti-gay violence and victimization in the United States. *Journal of Interpersonal Violence, 5,* 274–294.

Blumenfeld, W. J. (1992). *Homophobia: How we all pay the price.* Boston: Beacon Press.

Breeze. (1986). For better or worse. In K. Lobel (Ed.), *Naming the violence: Speaking out about lesbian battering* (pp. 48–55). Seattle: Seal Press.

Browne, A. (1987). *When battered women kill.* New York: The Free Press.

California Appellate Reports, 3rd Series. (1985). Vol. 171, pp. 947-953. San Francisco: Bancroft-Whitney.

Campbell, J. (1991). Preventing wife abuse: Insights from cultural analysis. *Response, 80,* 18–24.

Dobash, R. E., & Dobash, R. (1979). *Violence against wives: A case against the patriarchy.* New York: The Free Press.

Epstein, E. (1993, January 14). Lesbian's ordeal brings domestic violence in same-sex relationships into focus. *Bay Windows,* pp. 1, 5.

Evans, P. (1990). The needs of a blue eyed Arab: Crisis intervention with male sexual assault survivors. In M. Hunter (Ed.), *The sexually abused male: Prevalence, impact, and treatment* (pp. 193–225). Toronto: Lexington Books.

Frank, P. B., & Houghton, B. O. (1987). *Confronting the batterer.* New City, NY: Volunteer Counseling Services of Rockland County, Inc.

Garnets, L., Herek, G. M., & Levy, B. (1992). Violence and victimization of lesbians and gay men: Mental health consequences. In G. M. Herek & K. Berrill (Eds.), *Hate crimes: Confronting violence against lesbians and gay men* (pp. 207–226). Newbury Park, CA: Sage Publications.

Geffner, B. (1992). Extremist views concerning family violence and sexual assault. *Family Violence and Sexual Assault Bulletin* (Vol. 8, p. 1). Tyler, TX: Family Violence and Sexual Assault Institute.

Gibson, P. (1989). *Gay and lesbian youth suicide.* U.S. Department of Health and Human Services' Report of the Secretary's Task Force on Youth Suicide.

Graham, D. L. R., Rawlings, E., & Rimini, N. (1988). Survivors of terror: Battered women, hostages, and the Stockholm syndrome. In K. Yllo & M. Bograd (Eds.), *Feminist perspectives on wife abuse* (pp. 217–232). Newbury Park, CA: Sage Publications.

Hamberger, L. K., & Hastings, J. E. (1988). Characteristics of male spouse abusers consistent with personality disorders. *Hospital and Community Psychiatry, 39,* 763–770.

Hart, B. (1986). Lesbian battering: An examination. In K. Lobel (Ed.), *Naming the violence: Speaking out about lesbian battering* (pp. 173–189). Seattle: Seal Press.

Harvard Law Review. (Eds.). (1990). *Sexual orientation and the law.* Cambridge: Harvard University Press.

Herek, G. M. (1990). The context of anti-gay violence: Notes on cultural and psychological heterosexism. *Journal of Interpersonal Violence, 5,* 315–333.

Herek, G. M., & Berrill, K. T. (1992). *Hate crimes: Confronting violence against lesbians and gay men.* Newbury Park, CA: Sage Publications.

Hunter, M. (1990). *Abused boys: The neglected victims of sexual abuse.* New York: Fawcett Columbine.

Isay, R. A. (1989). *Being homosexual: Gay men and their development.* New York: Avon Books.

Island, D., & Letellier, P. (1991a). *Men who beat the men who love them: Battered gay men and domestic violence.* Binghamton, NY: Haworth Press.

Island, D., & Letellier, P. (1991b, Fall). Heterosexist domestic violence laws deny many gays and lesbians full civil rights. *Gay and Lesbian Domestic Violence Network Newsletter,* p. 3.

King, P. (1993, October 4). Not so different after all: The trials of gay domestic violence. *Newsweek,* p. 75.

Kus, R. J. (1990). Alcoholism in the gay and lesbian communities. In R. J. Kus (Ed.), *Keys to caring: Assisting your gay and lesbian clients* (pp. 66–81). Boston: Alyson Publications.

Lew, M. (1988). *Victims no longer: Men recovering from incest and other child abuse.* New York: Harper & Row.

Lobel, K. (Ed.). (1986). *Naming the violence: Speaking out about lesbian battering.* Seattle: Seal Press.

Margolies, L., Becker, M., & Jackson-Brewer, K. (1987). Internalized homophobia: Identifying and treating the oppressor within. In The Boston Lesbian Psychologies Collective (Eds.), *Lesbian psychologies* (pp. 229–241). Chicago: University of Illinois Press.

Martin, D. (1976). *Battered wives.* New York: Simon & Schuster.

Merrill, G. (in press). Integrating theories about domestic violence: Arguments for a social-psychological model. *Journal of Lesbian and Gay Social Services.*

Odets, W. (1990). The homosexualization of AIDS. *Focus: A Guide to AIDS Research and Counseling, 5,* 1–2.

Peplau, L. A. (1991). Lesbian and gay relationships. In J. C. Gonsiorek & J. D. Weinrich (Eds.), *Homosexuality: Implications for public policy* (pp. 177–196). Newbury Park, CA: Sage Publications.

Pharr, S. (1988). *Homophobia: A weapon of sexism.* Little Rock: Chardon Press.

Renzetti, C. (1992).*Violent betrayal: Partner abuse in lesbian relationships.* Newbury Park, CA: Sage Publications.

Rivera, R. R. (1991). Sexual orientation and the law. In J. C. Gonsiorek & J. D. Weinrich (Eds.), *Homosexuality: Implications for public policy* (pp. 81–100). Newbury Park, CA: Sage Publications.

Saunders, D. (1988). Wife abuse, husband abuse or mutual combat? A feminist perspective in empirical findings. In K. Yllo & M. Bograd (Eds.), *Feminist perspectives on wife abuse* (pp. 90–113). Newbury Park, CA: Sage Publications.

Schecter, S. (1982). *Women and male violence: The visions and struggles of the battered women's movement.* Boston: South End Press.

Schneider, E. M. (1992). Particularity and generality: Challenges of feminist theory and practice in work on woman-abuse. *New York University Law Review, 67,* 520–568.

Schulman, D. (1991). AIDS discrimination: Its nature, meaning, and function. In N. McKenzie (Ed.), *The AIDS reader: Social, political, and ethical issues* (pp. 463–490). New York: Meridian Books.

Shilts, R. (1993). *Conduct unbecoming: Gays and lesbians in the U.S. military.* New York: St. Martin's Press.

Snow, K. (1992, June 2). The violence at home. *The Advocate,* p. 604.

Sonkin, D. J. (1987). *Domestic violence on trial: Psychological and legal dimensions of family violence.* New York: Springer Publishing Company.

Sonkin, D. J., & Durphy, M. (1989). *Learning to live without violence.* Volcano, CA: Volcano Press.

Szymanski, M. (1991, Fall). Battered husbands: Domestic violence in gay relationships. *Genre,* pp. 32–73.

Tuller, D. (1994, January 3). When gays batter their partners. *San Francisco Chronicle,* pp. 1, 8.

Walker, L. E. (1979). *The battered woman.* New York: Harper & Row.

Wertheimer, D. M. (1992). Treatment and service interventions for lesbian and gay male crime victims. In G. M. Herek & K. Berrill (Eds.), *Hate crimes: Confronting violence against lesbians and gay men* (pp. 227–240). Newbury Park, CA: Sage Publications.

West's California Codes. (1993). *Penal code* (Compact Ed.). St. Paul: West Publishing.

2

Are Bi-Directionally Violent Couples Mutually Victimized?

A Gender-Sensitive Comparison

Dina Vivian and
Jennifer Langhinrichsen-Rohling

Researchers have consistently reported that physical aggression occurs with surprising frequency in both nondiscordant and discordant marriages. For example, in a nationally representative sample, 12% of men and women reported having been aggressive toward their spouses during the prior 12 months, and as many as 28% reported some aggression during the duration of the marriage (Straus, Gelles, & Steinmetz, 1980). In a community dating sample, O'Leary and colleagues (1989) found that 44% of the women and 31% of the men had been physically aggressive toward their partners in the prior year. With respect to spouses seeking marital therapy, Cascardi, Langhinrichsen, and Vivian (1992) found that as many as 71% of the couples reported physical aggression in their marriage during the prior year. Furthermore, 85% of the "aggressive" couples reported bi-directional aggression

(Cascardi et al., 1992). These prevalence rates were determined primarily with use of the Conflict Tactics Scale (CTS; Straus, 1979), a self-report inventory that measures the presence and frequency of aggressive behaviors. A summary of these studies might suggest that (1) physical aggression is a relatively frequent phenomenon, particularly in unhappy marriages; (2) both sexes are likely to self-report being victims and perpetrators of physical aggression; and (3) physical aggression in marriage appears to be a dyadic and interactive phenomenon (Steinmetz, 1981, 1987; Steinmetz & Lucca, 1988).

The view that marital aggression is a bi-directional and an interactive phenomenon may be supported further by research documenting that marital conflict/mutual verbal aggression is one of the strongest correlates of physical abuse. In fact, of the 2,143 spouses surveyed by Straus and colleagues (1980), those reporting low levels of verbal conflict were 16 times less likely to report physical aggression than spouses reporting high verbal conflict. Moreover, high levels of verbal/psychological aggression in both spouses have been shown to predict the onset of physical aggression in couples during the first 3 years of marriage (Murphy & O'Leary, 1989). Observational studies have also shown that physically aggressive couples are characterized by mutual negativity and reciprocal negative escalations (Burman, Margolin, & John, 1993; Vivian & O'Leary, 1987; Vivian, Smith, Mayer, Sandeen, & O'Leary, 1987). In addition, mutual verbal hostility appears to be a stable conflict style of physically aggressive couples during the first year of marriage (Vivian, Mayer, Sandeen, & O'Leary, 1988). Supporting the researchers' impression that dyadic communication problems may be of primary importance in explaining marital aggression, clinic couples themselves, even those endorsing severe husband-to-wife aggression on the CTS, do not present the aggression as a primary concern; rather, they view mutual communication problems as their main marital complaint (Masters, Vivian, & O'Leary, 1989; O'Leary, Vivian, & Malone, 1992). In parallel with these research findings, some have argued that couples, rather than husbands, should be considered verbally and physically aggressive and both spouses need to develop better anger control and communication skills (Deschner, 1984; Neidig & Friedman, 1984).

The view that bi-directional communication problems are critically associated with physical aggression in marriage, however, is not consistently supported by the observational literature. Some studies, in fact, suggest that aggressive husbands' negativity during marital conflict is more directly correlated with physical aggression in marriage than mutual hostility (Margolin, Burman, & John, 1989; Margolin, John, & Gleberman, 1988; Roberts, Leonard, & Levy, 1992). Methodological differences among observational studies in this area, as well as differences in the populations evaluated (e.g., clinic aggressive couples vs. discordant aggressive but not clinic couples), preclude, at this time, firm conclusions about the role of husbands' and wives' communication styles in marital aggression.

From a theoretical perspective, feminist analyses of domestic violence challenge interactive models that see both spouses contributing to the marital violence (Bograd, 1990; Dobash, Dobash, Wilson, & Daly, 1992). Criticisms have primarily focused on the fact that assessment of physical aggression in marriage has been frequently conducted with scales such as the CTS (Straus, 1979) that evaluate the phenomenon only "topographically," or through a description of the form of the behavior (i.e., event presence), without considering the context and impact of aggression. Therefore, two dissimilar acts (e.g., a push that is barely felt vs. one that breaks the victim's arm) may be unfairly equated. The CTS clearly fails to assess who initiated the violence and for what purpose (i.e., self-defense vs. control) and with what results (i.e., psychological impact or injury).

Researchers who have considered these issues have found that husbands' and wives' violence in marriage is far from equal. For example, when injuries resulting from marital aggression have been assessed, wives report more negative consequences than do husbands (Cantos, Neidig, & O'Leary, 1994; Cascardi et al., 1992; Stets & Straus, 1990). Second, the presence and frequency of aggression are not always directly related to the severity of impact or injury. In fact, in the study of Cascardi and colleagues (1992), as many as 15% of the wives who reported being "mildly" victimized according to the CTS (items 11–13) and 11% of wives who were "severely" victimized (CTS items 14–18) reported significant injuries (e.g., broken bones, broken teeth, and injuries to sensory organs) compared to 2% and 0% of the husbands, respectively, suggesting that for wives any victimization may have serious consequences. Third, wives typically report that their aggression is due to self-defense or for retaliatory reasons (Saunders, 1986). Violent husbands, on the other hand, attribute their aggression to external causes and situational factors (Holtzworth-Munroe, 1988; Holtzworth-Munroe, Jacobson, Fehrenbach, & Fruzetti, 1990; Shields & Hanneke, 1983) or to coercive and controlling reasons (Cascardi & Vivian, 1993).

Overall, context-based, gender-sensitive research and theory suggest that even in marriages where the aggression is bi-directional it may not be symmetrical, as wives are affected more negatively by the aggression than husbands. In order to capture gender differences in marital aggression, a multidimensional assessment is clearly necessary (e.g., including information about severity, psychological impact, injury, function, consequences, and precipitating events). Furthermore, it seems important to avoid holding a monolithic model of marital aggression (e.g., dyadic/interactionist or sociopolitical), as this phenomenon may present different individual/marital dynamics for different subgroups of couples. Existing research in marital aggression has not fully addressed these issues.

Accordingly, the main purpose of the present study was to advance our understanding of gender differences in marital aggression by adopting a multidimensional approach to the identification of subgroups of aggressive couples. Only couples reporting mutual physical victimization were included in the present study because prior research indicated that the vast majority of clinic couples fall into this group (Cascardi et al., 1992). It was hypothesized that, as a feminist analysis would suggest, mutually victimized husbands' and wives' experience of aggression would be differentiated if the marital violence is assessed "in context" (rather than unidimensionally or "topographically" only). Moreover, whereas any dimension of physical victimization could be used to classify unidirectionally victimized spouses (e.g., a spouse reports experiencing a particular aggressive act with particular impact or injury), multiple dimensions are necessary when comparing a wife's and husband's victimization in the *same* marriage (e.g., which spouse is receiving more severe aggression, with greater impact and greater likelihood of injury). Consistent with prior findings (O'Leary et al., 1989), husbands and wives were expected to report experiencing equivalent frequencies of a range of violent acts. However, we also expected wives to report greater negative impact and injury than husbands (Cascardi et al., 1992). Moreover, in the current study, we were primarily interested in using multiple dimensions to identify subgroups of heretofore "mutually" victimized couples.

Originally, we predicted that two clear subgroups would emerge. We expected the largest subgroup to include "mutually" victimized couples according to information about the topography of physical aggression (event presence and frequency) but predominant wife victimization according to other dimensions of aggression (e.g., greater negative impact and injury for wives than for husbands) (a "highly victimized wife" group). Consistent with the possibility that interactional models of marital aggression may indeed describe the experience of a limited proportion of clinic couples and on the basis of clinical observation, we expected a second subgroup of couples to report mutual and low (or nonsevere) levels of victimization on all dimensions (e.g., low frequency, low impact, no injuries for either spouse, etc.) (a "mutual low" group). In addition, based on the clinical observation that a small proportion of couples seeking marital therapy present with either mutually severe levels of physical victimization or greater victimization on the part of the husband, we planned to conduct exploratory analyses to identify other relevant subgroups of mutually victimized spouses. In particular, we thought that we may identify a third (heterogeneous) subgroup including couples characterized by mutual and severe levels of aggression (e.g., mutual high frequency, severity, and injury) and couples with predominant husband victimization on some but not all dimensions of aggression (e.g., mutual high frequency, sole husband injury) (a "mutual high"/"highly victimized husband group").

Finally, we expected the subgroups of "mutually victimized" couples to differ from each other and from a clinic nonaggressive control group on marital and individual functioning. Specifically, wives in the "highly victimized wife" group, as compared to their husbands and spouses in all other groups, were expected to show the greatest level of marital distress as measured by several indices of dyadic functioning (e.g., high partner verbal hostility, more frequent and more negative psychological victimization, reduced marital adjustment, and greater negative impact as a result of marital conflicts). We also expected these wives to report more negative affective states (e.g., depressive symptomatology) as a result of the victimization. Spouses in the "mutual low" group were expected to treat the violence as inconsequential. Accordingly, we expected the "mutual low" and clinic nonaggressive groups to report similar and higher levels of marital and individual adjustment than the other aggressive groups. Expectations about the "mutual high"/"highly victimized husband" group were purely tentative, because the nature of such a group was predicted least clearly. However, in keeping with a gender-sensitive approach to marital aggression, we expected husbands and wives in the "mutual high"/"highly victimized husband" subgroup to show comparable levels of marital distress even though some of the husbands may be reporting greater levels of physical victimization. In addition, we believed that wives in this subgroup may exhibit greater distress than their husbands in some particular indices of relationship and personal functioning (e.g., partner psychological abuse, depressive symptomatology). Lastly, both spouses in this third group were expected to show greater levels of distress than spouses in the "mutual low" and clinic nonaggressive subgroups.

Method

Subjects

The participants for this study were selected from a pool of 145 couples who had sought marital therapy at the University Marital Therapy Clinic (UMTC) at Stony Brook, New York. First, on the basis of spouses' reports about self and/or partner physical aggression on a modified version of the CTS, the Adapted Conflict Tactics Scale (ACTS; Vivian, 1990), 111 couples were identified as experiencing marital aggression (76.5% of the clinic sample). From that group, a subgroup of 57 couples was selected (39% of the clinic sample and 51% of the aggressive group, respectively) where *both* spouses reported *partner aggression* (i.e., a mutually victimized subgroup). Both spouses in this mutually victimized group (MV) received at least one act of physical aggression from their partners within the year *and* provided information about other dimensions of victimization assessed with the ACTS (i.e., psychological impact and injury).[1] Second, a nonaggressive, comparison subgroup of clinic couples (NA) who reported *no* physical aggression and victimization in the marriage was identified (N = 34, 23.4% of the clinic sample). The remaining 54 clinic couples (48.6% of the aggressive group) were not included in the study because they reported unilateral victimization (approximately 15% of the sample), they disagreed about mutual victimization, or they had missing data.

Clinic Nonaggressive (NA) Versus Clinic Mutually Victimized Couples (MV). A 2 (Group) × 2 (Sex) mixed design multivariate analysis of variance (MANOVA), with sex as the repeated measures factor, indicated significant differences between the NA and

MV couples on age and education (group main effect: Rao's R [2,86] = 8.8, $p < .001$; sex main effect: Rao's R [2,86] = 21.7, $p < .0001$, respectively). Follow-up univariate analyses of variance (ANOVAs) indicated that the MV group was younger (mean ages, 33.5 and 40.7, respectively; F [1,87] = 10.97, $p < .001$) and less educated than the NA group (mean years of education, 13.5 and 14.8, respectively; F [1,87], $p < .01$). Furthermore, husbands were older than wives (mean ages, 38.6 and 35.5, respectively; F [1,87] = 43.9; $p < .0001$).

A second one-way MANOVA was conducted to compare the NA and MV groups with regard to the duration of their marriage, number of children, and family income (Rao's R [3,58] = 4.47, $p < .01$). The two groups did not differ significantly on years married (mean for NA = 15 and for MV = 9, respectively) or number of children (mean for NA = 2.3 and for MV = 1.7, respectively). They differed, however, in their yearly family income (mean for NA = $61,263 and MV = $37,039, respectively; F [1,60] = 11.08, $p < .001$).

Measures

Multidimensional Assessment of Physical Victimization

The Adapted Conflict Tactics Scale (ACTS) Vivian, 1990). The ACTS is a 29-item inventory that evaluates marital aggression as a conflict tactic used by spouses during arguments. Participants are asked to rate the frequency (0 = never, 1 = once, 2 = twice, 3 = 3–5 times, 4 = 6–10 times, 5 = 11–20 times, and 6 = more than 20 times) with which they (aggression) and/or their partners (victimization) engaged in a number of specific conflict behaviors during the prior 12 months. As described in the report of Cascardi and colleagues (1992), the ACTS was designed as an extension and modification of both the original CTS (Straus, 1979) and of the modified CTS (Neidig & Friedman, 1984). The primary modifications were to increase the number of positive and negative communication items, to include global assessments of the psychological impact of aggression/victimization on self, partner, and relationship, degree of self and partner blame, and type of injuries sustained. Ratings of impact, blame, and injury for acts of aggression and victimization were made immediately after each of three sections of the ACTS and were obtained for clusters of items. In accord with prior research with the CTS (Straus et al., 1980), Section 1 of the ACTS assessed psychological aggression/victimization (items 11–18), Section 2, mild physical aggression/victimization (items 19–22), and Section 3, severe aggression/victimization (items 23–29).[2] Global impact ratings were obtained on a 7-point scale (i.e., 1 = extremely negative, 7= extremely positive) in response to the following three questions: "What was the effect of these behaviors on you?", "What was the effect of these behaviors on your partner?", and "What was the effect of these behaviors on the relationship?" Assessments of blame were also obtained on a 7-point scale (i.e., 1 = I totally blame myself/my partner, 7 = I don't blame myself/my partner at all) in response to the following two questions: "How much do you blame yourself for these behaviors?", and "How much do you blame your partner for these behaviors?" (blame ratings were not used in the present study). Injuries received from mild and severe physical aggression and victimization were assessed using a Guttman-scaled list of injuries (i.e., 1 = no injuries; 2 = bruises, cuts, or abrasions of a superficial nature; 3 = bruises, cuts, or abrasions, but not of a superficial nature; 4 = broken bones, broken teeth, or injuries to sensory organs [e.g., eyes, nose]; and 5 = internal injuries or concussion) in response to the following questions: "Did your partner receive any of the following injuries as a result of your behavior in any of the situations described above?" (aggression), and "Did you receive any of the following injuries as a result of your partner's behavior in any of the situations described above?" (victimization).

Dimensions of physical victimization derived from the ACTS. Frequency: In keeping with prior research with the CTS (Straus et al., 1980), a frequency-based physical victimization index was created by summing the frequency of each endorsed item (range 0–6) across that section of the scale (i.e., items 19–29, for partner report).

Accordingly, the frequency index ranged from 0 to 66.

Severity of aggressive act(s): Given that the 11 physical aggression/victimization items of the ACTS are essentially Guttman-scaled, they were each assigned a weight from 1–11, respectively, to represent increasing levels of severity. A severity index was derived by assigning each spouse the score that reflected the most severe act of victimization reported.

Psychological impact: Because of the high correlation between impact ratings for mild and severe physical victimization and to reduce problems due to missing data, the ratings of spouses who reported both mild and severe victimization were averaged. In addition, only ratings of negative impact for self were used.

Injury: A severity of injury index was derived by assigning each spouse the score that reflected the most severe injury received by any act of partner aggression (range 1–5).

Measures of Partner, Relationship, and Individual Functioning.

Spouse Verbal Problem Checklist (SVPC) (Haynes, Chavez, & Samuel, 1984). The SVPC is a 27-item inventory that provides an index of how spouses perceive their partners' communication. The SVPC is highly correlated with observers' ratings of negative communication during problem-solving (Haynes et al., 1984). For the purposes of this study, a principal component factor analysis was conducted on the SVPC with data from all the clinic spouses who had completed this scale (N = 235). Two factors were retained; only Factor 1 was used in the current study because it appeared to be the most conceptually relevant measure of perceived partner negative communication (eigenvalue = 7.40; alpha = .91; average interitem correlation =.40). Labeled SVPC-Verbal Hostility, Factor 1 included 15 items (with loadings > .40) that were connotative of negativity and hostility in problem-solving (e.g., expresses views in rigid and dogmatic ways, globally criticizes, brings up the past, etc.).

Partner psychological abuse on the ACTS. As for the physical victimization, *frequency* and *impact* (self and relationship) indices for partner psychological aggression/abuse were derived for each spouse.

Dyadic Adjustment Scale (DAS) (Spanier, 1976). The DAS is a 32-item measure of marital satisfaction that has been widely used in the marital literature to assess couples' perception of their marital satisfaction. Spanier (1976) provided substantial evidence supporting the psychometric properties of this instrument.

Conflict Emotion Checklist (CEC) (Fincham & Bradbury, 1987). The CEC is a 10-item adjective checklist that has typically been administered in conjunction with the Conflict Rating Scale (CRS), a 41-item inventory that is designed to assess spouses' attributional styles regarding conflict in marriage. After spouses complete the CRS they are asked to rate on a 7-point scale (1 = true, 7 = false) the extent to which 10 emotional adjectives are descriptive of their affective state with regard to their marital conflicts. A principal component factor analysis was conducted with the CEC obtained from 228 clinic spouses. Although three factors emerged, only Factor 1 was retained for the present study (eigenvalue = 2.95; five items with loadings > .40). We labeled this factor CEC-Negative Affect. It included the adjectives sad, angry, frustrated, anxious, and afraid. However, the CEC-Negative Affect was only moderately internally consistent (alpha = .75; average interitem correlation =.38) and was used primarily for exploratory purposes in the present study.

Beck Depression Inventory (BDI) (Beck, Steer, & Garbin, 1988; Beck, Ward, Mendelson, Mock, & Erbaugh, 1961). The BDI is a well-known 21-item inventory designed to assess depressive symptomatology in the week prior to administration. It has been found to correlate consistently with clinical ratings of depression, and a score equal to or greater than 14 has been used to indicate the presence of moderate depressive symptomatology or dysphoria.

Intercorrelations were conducted to ascertain that variables we intended to group in MANOVAs on a theoretical basis were also related empirically. As shown in Table 2.1, two measures of partner negative behavior (i.e., SVPC-Hostility, and frequency of partner's psychological abuse on the ACTS) and marital satisfaction (DAS) were moderately associated for both husbands and wives. All other measures were treated as separate measures of individual affective functioning; additionally, reports about impact of psychological abuse on self and relationship were averaged for each spouse.

Procedure

During their first visit at the UMTC prior to the start of therapy, each spouse was interviewed individually. While one spouse was interviewed, the other spouse completed the self-report measures. The information used in the present investigation represents a subset of data from a larger study on the communication styles of physically aggressive couples. Each couple was paid $80.00 for their complete participation.

Results

Overall Gender Differences in Physical Victimization

Gender differences on the four dimensions of physical victimization (i.e., frequency, severity of aggressive act[s], psychological impact–self, and severity of injury) were evaluated in the mutual victimization group $(N = 57)$. Paired t tests for dependent samples with Bonferroni corrections for multiple comparisons were used in these initial analyses. Overall, as predicted, husbands' and wives' reports about the frequency and severity of acts of physical victimization did not differ (see Table 2.2). On the other hand, victimized wives appeared to be more negatively affected by the physical victimization than their husbands. Specifically, wives reported more negative psychological impact and more severe injuries than did husbands. In addition, when prevalence of injury was evaluated on a nominal scale (presence/absence of any injury), 32 of the wives (56% of the MV group) and 25 of the husbands (44% of the

TABLE 2.1 Correlations Among Measures of Partner Behavior, Marital and Individual Functioning (Wives on Top Right, Husbands on Bottom Left)

	SVPC-Hostility	ACTS-Psy/Abuse	ACTS-Impact/S	ACTS-Impact/R	DAS	CEC-Neg/Affect	BDI
SVPC-Hostility		.65**	-.31**	-.38**	-.71**	.45**	.34**
ACTS-Psy/Abuse	.54**		-.34**	-.34**	-.58**	.39**	.32**
ACTS-Impact/S	-.07	-.16		.75**	.19	-.28*	-.07
ACTS-Impact/R	-.27*	-.27*	.69**		.36**	-.24*	-.05
DAS	-.60**	-.62**	.09	.26*		-.48**	-.28**
CEC-Neg/Affect	.27*	.37*	-.30*	-.36**	-.28*		.35**
BDI	.30*	.31**	-.00	-.08	-.41**	.14	

*p < .05   **p < .01

MV group) reported an injury as a result of partner aggression. Overall, wives sustained more injuries than their husbands (chi-square [1] = 6.56, $p < .01$).

Typology of Mutual Victimization in Marriage

In order to identify the predicted subgroups of mutually victimized couples, we conducted cluster analyses by using the standardized scores from the four indices of physical victimization derived from the ACTS for both victimized wives and husbands (i.e., frequency, severity of aggressive act[s], psychological impact, and severity of injury). A k-means clustering algorithm was employed to quantitatively create a set of discrete groups. K-means clustering produces a predetermined number of clusters via an agglomeration technique. Moreover, this technique assigns each case to the nearest cluster center and subsequently updates the center with the addition of each new case. For exploratory purposes, in addition to a three-cluster solution, two- and four-cluster solutions were also examined.

The two-cluster solution yielded one group characterized by high amounts of mutual victimization according to all indices of victimization except husbands' impact ratings ($N = 27$) and a second group reporting low amounts of mutual victimization according to all indices except husbands' impact ratings ($N = 30$). Impact ratings contributed least to the solution, and these clusters did not appear to differentiate clinic subgroups according to our predictions.

Next, a three-cluster solution was examined and the resulting graph is presented in Figure 2.1. As predicted, Cluster 1 consisted of couples who presented moderate to relatively low levels of victimization for the husbands and elevated levels of victimization for the wife, a "highly victimized wife" subgroup (HVW; $N = 15$). As predicted, Cluster 2 was characterized by "mutually low" levels of victimization on all indices (Mut/Low; $N = 32$). Only partially confirming our expectations, however, Cluster 3 included a small group of couples characterized by high levels of victimization on the part of the husband and, with the exception of negative

TABLE 2.2 Mutually Victimized Couples *(N = 57)*: Husbands' and Wives' Comparisons on Multiple Dimensions of Physical Victimization

	Husbands		Wives		
	Mean	*(SD)*	Mean	*(SD)*	t^{ab}
Overall frequency	10.5	(7.1)	12.4	(9.2)	1.9 *ns*
Act Severity	6.2	(2.2)	6.7	(2.3)	1.6 *ns*
Psychological impact/					
self	2.5	(1.2)	1.75	(.84)	14.7**
Severity of injury	1.61	(.75)	2.1	(1.23)	6.7*

[a] (Paired *t*-test; *d.f.* = 56)
[b] The significance of *p* values includes correction for multiple comparisons
*$p < .05$, **$p < .01$

impact (which was rated as highly negative by both husbands and wives), with moderate levels of victimization on the part of the wife, a "highly victimized husband" subgroup (HVH; *N* = 10). A review of the follow-up univariate ANOVAs for the three-factor solution indicated that seven of the eight indices significantly differentiated the couple clusters. Only the wives' impact scores failed to reach significance, *F* = 2.93, *p* > .05. Multivariate group comparisons on age, education, years married, and income indicated that there were no significant group differences among the three MV subgroups (Rao's *R* [12,58] = .79, NS).

Last, a four-cluster solution yielded clusters with unclear patterns of interpretation and/or with very small Ns. After examining the results provided by the three-cluster analyses, the three-group solution was chosen as optimal, since it yielded the clearest interpretative clusters, and sufficient cases in each cluster to conduct further analyses, was most consistent with our predictions.

Mutually Victimized Subgroups Versus Clinic Nonaggressive Couples

Partner Behavior and Marital Satisfaction. A 4 (Group) × 2 (Sex) mixed design MANOVA, with Sex as the repeated measures factor, was conducted to assess group differences in partner behavior and

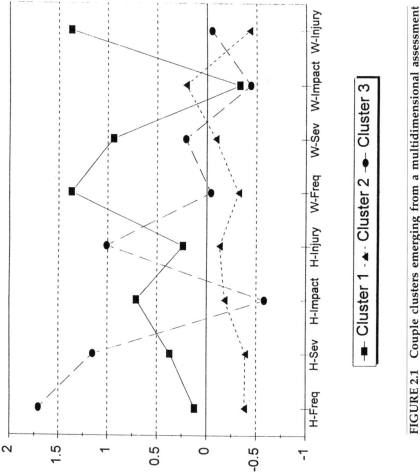

FIGURE 2.1 Couple clusters emerging from a multidimensional assessment of physical victimization: plot of means for each cluster.

■ Cluster 1 ▲ Cluster 2 ● Cluster 3

marital satisfaction[3] (see Table 2.3). A significant main effect for Group, Rao's R (9,141) = 7.74, $p < .0001$, and a significant Group × Sex interaction, Rao's R (12,141) = 2.05, $p < .05$, emerged from this initial analysis. Follow-up univariate ANOVAs for the Group effect indicated that the four groups differed significantly with regard to partner's verbal hostility, F (3,60) = 13.5, $p < .0001$, frequency of partner's psychological abuse, F (3,60) = 30.5, $p < .0001$, and marital satisfaction, F (3,60) = 8.9, $p < .0001$. Univariate ANOVAs for the Group × Sex interaction indicated significant effects for reports of partner psychological abuse, F (3,60) = 4.7, $p < .005$, and partner verbal hostility, F (3,60) = 4.0, $p < .01$, but not for DAS scores, F (3,60) = .62, $p = .59$. Simple effects were examined next with post-hoc comparisons (Fisher's LSD) according to our predictions. This approach to group comparison was adopted for all the subsequent analyses.

Partner's Verbal Hostility. As predicted, HVW wives reported significantly more partner verbal hostility than their own husbands ($p < .01$) and than spouses in the Mut/Low and NA groups (p's ranging from $< .05$ to $< .0001$). They did not differ, however, from either spouse in the HVH group. Consistent with prediction, husbands and wives in the HVH group reported equivalent levels of partner verbal hostility. Additionally, they reported more verbal hostility than the Mut/Low and NA groups (p's ranging from .06 to $< .001$). Surprisingly, spouses in the Mut/Low group viewed their partners more negatively than NA spouses (p's $< .01$ and $< .0001$, respectively).

Partner's Psychological Abuse. A similar pattern was obtained for partner's psychological abuse. As expected, HVW wives reported more psychological victimization than their husbands did ($p < .01$) and than spouses in the Mut/Low and NA groups (p's ranging from $< .01$ to $< .0001$). Contrary to expectations, however, they did not report more frequent psychological victimization than husbands and wives in the HVH group. Unexpectedly, HVH husbands reported more psychological victimization than their wives ($p < .05$) and, as predicted, more frequent victimization than NA spouses (all p's < .0001). Husbands and wives in the Mut/Low group reported equivalent levels of psychological victimization, while reporting more frequent psychological victimization than NA spouses (p's < .0001 and < .0001, respectively).

Marital Satisfaction. Unexpectedly, there were few differences among the three MV subgroups with regard to marital satisfaction as measured by the DAS. In fact, with the exception of couples in the HVH group, who showed a trend toward reporting lower levels of marital satisfaction than couples in the Mut/Low group (*p* = .058), there were no other group differences among the three victimized subgroups. As predicted, however, NA couples were significantly more satisfied than all other clinic groups (all *p*'s <.0001).

Impact of Psychological Victimization. A 4 (Group) × 2 (Sex) mixed design ANOVA revealed a significant main effect for Sex, *F* (1, 76) = 6.0, *p* <.05, and a significant Sex × Group interaction, *F* (3, 76) = 4.6, *p* <.01. The main effect for Group only approached significance (*F* [3,76] = 2.5, *p* =.06).

An examination of the simple effects of the Sex × Group interaction indicated that the differences were mostly due to wives in the HVW group. As predicted, wives in the HVW group rated the impact of their psychological victimization more negatively than did their husbands (*p* <.0001). Surprisingly, however, the HVW wives' ratings were comparable to those of husbands and wives in the Mut/Low and HVH groups. In addition, husbands' and wives' ratings in the HVH group did not differ. Second, although these effects were not predicted, it is interesting to note that husbands in the HVW group gave the least negative impact ratings in comparison to all other spouses in the MV groups (*p*'s ranging from < .001 to < .0001). In fact, HVW husbands'ratings were similar to those of NA spouses. As expected, however, all other spouses in aggressive marriages rated the psychological victimization more negatively than nonaggressive spouses (all *p*'s < .001).

TABLE 2.3 Clinic Couples Subgroups: Husbands' and Wives' Ratings of Partner, Relationship, and Individual Functioning

	HVW (N = 15) Mean	(SD)	MUT/LOW (N = 32) Mean	(SD)	HVH (N = 10) Mean	(SD)	NA (N = 34) Mean	(SD)
SVPC-Hostility								
H	31.1	(11.2)	35.0	(9.0)	44.9	(8.1)	25.4	(9.0)
W	43.5	(7.2)	32.6	(14.2)	39.3	(9.3)	25.0	(8.2)
ACTS-Psychological abuse								
H	22.4	(10.2)	21.8	(6.5)	31.0	(6.7)	8.7	(5.4)
W	29.2	(8.9)	18.6	(9.43)	24.1	(9.09)	9.3	(5.8)
DAS								
H	78.8	(21.8)	83.5	(18.7)	65.5	(23.0)	104.0	(12.0)
W	69.0	(19.9)	78.2	(31.8)	67.0	(26.8)	94.7	(19.9)
ACTS-Impact of psychological abuse								
H	3.0	(1.5)	2.1	(.82)	1.8	(.78)	2.6	(.90)
W	1.7	(1.07)	2.1	(1.03)	1.8	(.79)	2.6	(1.13)
CEC-Negative affect								
H	22.3	(7.05)	25.4	(5.37)	25.1	(6.36)	23.0	(8.12)
W	29.7	(5.08)	27.2	(6.9)	32.43	(2.57)	25.48	(6.7)
BDI								
H	12.9	(10.7)	11.9	(8.1)	15.7	(10.2)	9.4	(7.0)
W	16.6	(10.4)	15.1	(10.7)	15.0	(7.8)	10.1	(8.8)

Emotional Reactions to Marital Conflicts. A 4 (Group) × 2 (Sex) mixed design ANOVA with spouses' ratings on the CEC-Negative Affect revealed only a significant main effect for Sex, F (1,65) = 18.9, $p < .0001$. As shown in Table 2.3, wives across all clinic groups consistently rated their emotional reaction to marital conflicts as being more negative than their husbands did. However, as exemplified by their mean ratings, wives in the two highly victimized subgroups appeared to report the strongest negative emotions.

Depression. Contrary to predictions, a 4 (Group) × 2 (Sex) mixed design ANOVA with spouses' ratings on the BDI indicated only a significant main effect for Group, F (3,70) = 2.8, p = .05. Unexpectedly, as shown in Table 2.3, HVW, Mut/Low, and HVH couples reported similar and elevated levels of depressive symptomatology, which were significantly higher than those of couples in the nonaggressive group *(p's* ranging from $< .04$ to $< .03$). With the exception of husbands in the HVW and Mut/Low group, in fact, the mean depression score for all victimized groups indicated moderate depression (Beck et al., 1961). These group differences, however, became statistically insignificant when demographic differences among MV and NA spouses were covaried *(F* [3, 62] = 1.65, p = .18).

Discussion

The current study was undertaken to demonstrate that experiencing physical aggression in marriage, even when it occurs bi-directionally, is not an equivalent phenomenon for most husbands and wives. On the basis of prior empirical evidence about impact and function of marital aggression, we believed that wives were more at risk for experiencing profound physical victimization in marriage than husbands and that this gender difference was best assessed using multiple dimensions of victimization. We proposed that a multidimensional assessment would allow us to identify subgroups of couples characterized by different configurations of mutual victimization. We expected the subgroup of highly victimized wives to be the largest. Moreover, wives in this group were expected to be more negatively affected by their physical victimization, as reflected by their reports in measures of relationship and individual functioning, than their own husbands and husbands in other victimized subgroups.

Confirming our predictions, clinic wives were more negatively affected by their physical victimization than their husbands. As found in prior work (Cascardi et al., 1992), the greatest gender differences were related to dimensions of aggression other than event presence and frequency. Specifically, the victimized wives reported more negative impact and more frequent and severe injuries than their husbands.

As we had hypothesized, multiple indices of victimization, such as frequency, severity of aggressive acts, psychological impact, and physical injury, successfully identified three conceptually meaningful and distinct subgroups of mutually victimized couples. Moreover, husbands' and wives' experience of aggression in these three groups could be differentiated. In fact, the first subgroup (26.3% of the sample) included couples in whom the wives were more severely victimized than their husbands; the second subgroup (56.1% of the sample) included couples characterized by reports of low levels of victimization for both spouses. Only partially confirming our predictions, however, a third and small subgroup (17.5% of the sample) reporting preponderant husband victimization was also differentiated. We had expected this group to include both couples presenting with mutual/high victimization and preponderant husband victimization.

Although highly victimized spouses in the two asymmetrically victimized subgroups appeared to report similar experiences of physical victimization, some interesting differences were obtained. In fact, whereas *both* spouses in the highly victimized husband's group rated the impact of the physical victimization as being significantly negative, husbands of highly victimized wives rated the impact of their own physical victimization less negatively than all other spouses. Additionally, injury level emerged as a very strong discriminator for the wives in the highly victimized wife group only. Thus, consistent with predictions, the group typology emerging from the cluster analysis suggested that wives appeared to be more at risk for severe and asymmetrical marital victimization than their husbands.

However, a greater proportion of clinic couples than we had anticipated, in fact, as much as half of those couples reporting mutual physical victimization, were likely to be characterized by low levels of mild bi-directional aggression. This result suggests that some couples seeking conjoint marital therapy may indeed present with mutual physical victimization, but only when such aggression is "mild" for both spouses (e.g., low frequency, mildly negative impact, low severity of acts, and infrequent/nonserious injury). Serious physical victimization, as assessed through multiple dimensions, tends to be preponderantly unilateral in this population. We believe that these findings underscore the importance of using a multidimensional approach to the evaluation of physical victimization in marriage in order to capture gender differences and couple differences with regard to this marital problem.

The second major goal of the present study was to validate the group typology we obtained by evaluating group differences on additional measures of perceived partner behavior and marital/individual adjustment. Initially, we had predicted that highly victimized wives would report greater distress, as assessed by measures of relationship and individual functioning, than their husbands and spouses in other types of mutually victimized marriages. Second, couples characterized by mutual/low intensity victimization were expected to exhibit similar functioning as would nonaggressive couples. Finally, couples in the highly victimized husband group (which we had predicted to be more heterogeneous in nature) were expected to show intermediate levels of distress when compared to highly victimized wives and spouses in the mutual/low victimization group. Wives in this third group, however, were expected to show greater psychological victimization and depressive symptomatology than their husbands.

Partially confirming our predictions, highly victimized wives did report greater partner verbal hostility and higher frequency of and more negative impact from the psychological victimization than did their husbands and couples in the mutual/low victimization and nonaggressive groups. However, contrary to our predictions, their reports did not differ substantially from those of spouses in the highly victimized husband group. It appears that highly victimized spouses, regardless of gender, are negatively affected by the marital violence. On the other hand, the marriages of the two highly victimized subgroups did differ in conceptually relevant ways. Specifically, while highly victimized husbands reported experiencing more frequent psychological abuse than their wives, *both* spouses in this group reported equivalent levels of partner verbal hostility and similar negative impact from the psychological victimization. This pattern suggests that highly victimized wives tend to be more "unilaterally" victimized than highly victimized husbands.

Our final hypothesis was that husbands and wives reporting mutual/low victimization confirms the relative "nonseriousness" of the aggression by reporting similar levels of marital and individual distress as would nonaggressive clinic spouses. Although, as expected, no gender differences were observed in the mutual/low group, these spouses reported greater marital and individual distress than spouses in the clinic nonaggressive group. With the exception of their reports about partner behavior, in fact, mutual/low victimization couples were more similar in their levels of marital satisfaction, impact of partner psychological abuse, and dysphoria to spouses in the highly victimized subgroups than to the nonaggressive clinic spouses.

Overall, the present study confirms our view that a monolithic etiological model of marital aggression is inadequate to capture the diversity of relationship and individual dynamics in physically aggressive marriages (cf. O'Leary & Vivian, 1990). The group typology emerging from the current study is only a first step in this direction; it suggests, however, the need to adopt multiple models of marital aggression when evaluating this clinic population. Ganley (1989) has pioneered this effort by proposing an integration of social learning and feminist views. We believe that the current findings support a theoretical integration of interactive/dyadic views of marital aggression and feminist analyses to best understand the dynamics of such marriages.

The interactive/dyadic perspective, in fact, appeared to characterize mild (or non-mutually-severe) forms of aggression. Specifically, when physical victimization was mild in impact, frequency, and injury for both spouses, wife-to-husband and husband-to-wife aggression appeared to be similar phenomena as measured by their correlates. In addition, these results suggested that even mutual and low levels of aggression in marriage are significant risk factors for both spouses in terms of their marital and individual functioning. This conclusion is made cautiously, however, in the absence of alternative or additional measures of victimization and individual functioning. Alternative measures (e.g., psychological abuse, states of anxiety, fear, perception of psychological and marital powerlessness) could be more "sensitive" to gender differences in mild/mutual marital aggression than the current measures.

On the other hand, feminist analyses of marital aggression did provide a heuristically valid framework to interpret our findings about more severe reports of victimization. Severe forms of aggression, although less frequent in this clinic population than mutual/low forms of aggression, appeared to be primarily asymmetrical with regard to victim/perpetrator roles. Second, the present study confirmed that, in discordant marriages, preponderant wife victimization is a phenomenon more likely to occur than preponderant husband victimization. Furthermore, whereas both highly victimized wives and highly victimized husbands reported more distress than spouses reporting mutual/nonsevere victimization, the marriages characterized by greater husband victimization exhibited more mutual negativity and "shared" marital distress than marriages of highly victimized wives. One could speculate that perhaps the functions of marital aggression may differ across "perpetrator" gender (e.g., husbands' violence may be primarily coercive in the highly victimized wife group; conversely, wives' violence may be primarily expressive or in self-defense in the highly victimized husband group). These results may also result from "perpetrating wives" taking more responsibility for their behavior than "perpetrating husbands." Assessment of additional dimensions of aggression (e.g., function, attribution of responsibility) in these asymmetrical groups, as well as replication with alternative measures of individual emotional functioning, may further differentiate the experience of highly victimized wives and highly victimized husbands.

Overall, our conclusions are tempered by conceptual and methodological considerations. First, using a subgroup of couples who agree that there is mutual victimization may introduce significant measurement error because of low interspousal reliability (Langhinrichsen-Rohling & Vivian, 1994; O'Leary et al., 1992). Couples who disagree about the occurrence of violence, in fact, may differ significantly from couples who agree (Langhinrichsen-Rohling & Vivian, 1994). Second, the relative small sample size of the two highly victimized groups may have limited the power of our analyses; replications with larger samples may highlight better differences in these groups. Third, pending replication, caution should also be used in interpreting results derived from cluster analyses. Different cluster solutions, variables, and algorithms may, in fact, generate different groupings (Hartigan, 1975). Last, the generalizability of these findings to other populations of discordant and physically aggressive spouses may be limited. Spouses in this study are seeking conjoint therapy and most of them do *not* spontaneously identify the physical aggression as a marital problem. Wives seeking individual therapy for marital aggression may report more marital distress and depressive symptomatology than wives in the current study. Further, women seeking services in a domestic violence agency, although expected to be most similar to the wives in the highly victimized wife group, are likely to experience greater levels of physical victimization, psychological abuse, and powerlessness in their marriage than most clinic wives who participated in our study. Again, replications with different samples are needed.

Methodological issues notwithstanding, the current study demonstrates that a multidimensional assessment of mutual aggression in marriage reveals distinct subgroups of couples for whom the experiences of aggression differ in significant ways. Unidimensional evaluations of aggression may have obscured such differences. Furthermore, the current findings bear some important clinical implications. Specifically, when couples present with "truly" mutual and mild victimization according to a multidimensional assessment, dyadic interventions may best address the marital and individual issues related to such aggression. In addition, it is clear that the marital aggression should be addressed explicitly in the treatment of these couples, as even mild forms of physical victimization are linked to more dyadic and individual distress than the absence of aggression, and spouses do not spontaneously report this marital problem (O'Leary et al., 1992). Conversely, treatments that consider the gender of the primary perpetrator (i.e., gender-specific) may be more appropriate for couples presenting with asymmetrical yet mutual victimization. These gender-specific programs, however, should particularly address contextual differences (e.g., function, partner/relationship characteristics) in wives' and husbands' aggression. In fact, the current study confirms that, even when appearing to be the primary perpetrators of physical aggression, wives experience more negativity in marriage than husbands who are primary perpetrators. Finally, we believe that efforts to generalize treatments across settings (e.g., from a battered women's shelter to a marital clinic) must proceed with great caution and attention to the specific patterns of aggression experienced.

Notes

[1]The rate of mutual victimization in this clinic sample was lower than prior research would have indicated (Cascardi et al., 1992) because both spouses had to agree that mutual victimization had occurred; inter-spousal agreement regarding marital aggression, in fact, tends to be only moderate (O'Leary et al., 1992).

[2]The Adapted Conflict Tactics Scale (ACTS) includes three items assessing *negative* tactics used by self or received from the spouse (items 8–10; insulting/swearing; saying something to spite partner; criticizing in an unhelpful way), and eight items assessing *psychological abuse* (items 11–18; threatening to leave the marriage; threatening to withhold money, having an affair, etc.; refusing to give affection/sex; sulking/refusing to talk; stomping out of the room/house/yard; threatening to hit/throw something at partner; throwing, smashing, kicking something; driving recklessly to frighten partner). Items 19–29 of the ACTS assess *physical aggression* (trying to control partner physically, holding down, etc.; throwing something at partner; pushing, grabbing, or shoving; slapping; kicking/biting/hitting with a fist; hitting or trying to hit with something; choking/strangling partner; physically forcing partner to have sex against her/his will; beating up; threatening with knife/gun; using knife/gun on partner).

[3]Differences in age and education between the nonaggressive and mutually victimized couples (combined across the three subgroups) were not statistically equated in this multivariate comparison or in any of the analyses to follow because these two demographic variables were not highly correlated with the dependent measures (wives: r's .27 - .03, mean r = .10; and husbands: r's .32 - .00, mean r = 11, respectively). Additionally, with the exception of the results regarding group differences in depressive symptomatology (BDI), exploratory analyses of covariance (controlling for age and education) did not alter significant findings. Results pertaining to the analysis of covariance with the BDI are reported directly in the text.

Acknowledgments.
The authors would like to express their deep appreciation for the helpful editorial and theoretical comments provided by Drs. Richard Heyman and Christopher Murphy. We are also thankful for the dedicated assistance provided by Mary Samios in subject recruitment. This study was supported by Grant MH 44665 to D. Vivian and Training Grant MH19107 to K. D. O'Leary.

REFERENCES

Beck, A. T., Steer, R. A., & Garbin, M. G. (1988). Psychometric properties of the Beck Depression Inventory: Twenty-five years of evaluation. *Clinical Psychological Review, 8,* 77–100.

Beck, A. T., Ward, C., Mendelson, M., Mock, J., & Erbaugh, J. (1961). An inventory for measuring depression. *Archives of General Psychiatry, 4,* 561–571.

Bograd, M. (1990). Why we need gender to understand human violence. *Journal of Interpersonal Violence, 5,* 132–135.

Burman, B., Margolin, G., & John, R. S. (1993). America's angriest home videos: Behavioral contingencies observed in home reenactments of marital conflicts. *Journal of Consulting and Clinical Psychology, 61,* 28–39.

Cantos, A., Neidig, O., & O'Leary, K. D. (1994). Injuries of women and men in a treatment program for domestic violence. *Journal of Family Violence, 9*(2), 113–124.

Cascardi, M., Langhinrichsen, J., & Vivian, D. (1992). Marital aggression: Impact, injury and correlates for husbands and wives. *Archives of Internal Medicine, 152,* 1178–1184.

Cascardi, M., & Vivian, D. (1993, June). *Themes and context for specific episodes of marital aggression.* Paper presented at the Hartman Conference on Family Violence, "Violence: Issues in Children's and Families' Lives," New London, CT.

Deschner, J. P. (1984). *The hitting habit: Anger control for battering couples.* New York: The Free Press.

Dobash, R. P., Dobash, R. E., Wilson, M., & Daly, M. (1992). The myth of sexual symmetry in marital violence. *Social Problems, 39,* 71–91.

Fincham, F. D., & Bradbury, T. N. (1987). The impact of attributions in marriage: A longitudinal analysis. *Journal of Personality and Social Psychology, 53,* 510–517.

Ganley, A. L. (1989). Integrating feminist and social learning analyses of aggression: Creating multiple models for intervention with men who batter. In P. L. Caesar & L. K. Hamberger (Eds.), *Treating men who batter* (pp. 196–235). New York: Springer Publishing Company.

Hartigan, J. A. (1975). *Clustering algorithms.* New York: Wiley.

Haynes, S. N., Chavez, R. E., & Samuel, V. (1984). Assessment of marital communication and distress. *Behavioral Assessment, 6,* 315–322.

Holtzworth-Munroe, A. (1988). Causal attributions in marital violence: Theoretical and methodological issues. *Clinical Psychology Review, 8,* 331–344.

Holtzworth-Munroe, A., Jacobson, N. S., Fehrenbach, P. A., & Fruzetti, A. (1990). *Causal attributions offered by violent married couples for relationship behaviors.* Unpublished manuscript.

Langhinrichsen-Rohling, J., & Vivian, D. (1994). The correlates of spouses' incongruent reports of marital aggression. *Journal of Family Violence, 9*(3), 265–284.

Margolin, G., Burman, B., & John, R. S. (1989). Home observation of married couples reenacting naturalistic conflicts. *Behavioral Assessment, 11,* 101–118.

Margolin, G., John, R. S., & Gleberman, L. (1988). Affective responses to conflictual discussions in violent and nonviolent couples. *Journal of Consulting and Clinical Psychology, 49,* 554–567.

Masters, C. M., Vivian, D., & O'Leary, K. D. (1989). *Presenting problems in marital therapy: What has changed in the past 12 years?* Poster presented at the 23rd Annual Convention of the Association for the Advancement of Behavior Therapy, Washington, DC.

Murphy, C. M., & O'Leary, K. D. (1989). Psychological aggression predicts physical aggression in early marriage. *Journal of Consulting and Clinical Psychology, 57,* 579–582.

Neidig, P. H., & Friedman, D. H. (1984). Spouse abuse: A treatment program for couples. Champaign, IL: Research Press.

O'Leary, K. D., Barling, J., Arias, I., Rosenbaum, A., Malone, J., & Tyree, A. (1989). Prevalence and stability of physical aggression between spouses: A longitudinal analysis. *Journal of Consulting and Clinical Psychology, 57,* 263–268.

O'Leary, K. D., & Vivian, D. (1990). Physical aggression in marriage. In F. Fincham & T. Bradbury (Eds.), *The psychology of marriage: Basic issues and applications* (pp. 323–348). New York: The Guilford Press.

O'Leary, K. D., Vivian, D., & Malone, J. (1992). Assessment of physical aggression against women in marriage: The need for multimodal assessment. *Behavioral Assessment, 14,* 5–14.

Roberts, L. J., Leonard, K. E., & Levy, R. (1992, November). *Marital communication in conflictual interactions: Differences related to a history of husband-to-wife physical aggression.* Poster presented at the 26th Annual Convention of the Association for the Advancement of Behavior Therapy, Boston, MA.

Saunders, D. G. (1986). When battered women use violence: Husband abuse or self-defense. *Violence and Victims, 1,* 47–60.

Shields, N. M., & Hanneke, C. R. (1983). Attribution processes in violent relationships: Perceptions of violent husbands and their wives. *Journal of Applied Social Psychology, 13,* 515–527.

Spanier, G. B. (1976). Measuring dyadic adjustment: New scales for assessing the quality of marriage and similar dyads. *Journal of Marriage and the Family, 38,* 15–28.

Steinmetz, S. K. (1981). Across-cultural comparison of marital abuse. *Journal of Sociology and Social Welfare, 8,* 404–414.

Steinmetz, S. K. (1987). Family violence: Past, present and future. In M. B. Sussman & S. K. Steinmetz (Eds.), *Handbook of marriage and the family* (pp. 725–765). New York: Plenum Press.

Steinmetz, S. K., & Lucca, J. (1988). Husband battering. In V. B. Van Hasselt, R. L. Morrison, A. S. Bellack, & M. Hensen (Eds.), *Handbook of family violence* (pp. 233–246). New York: Plenum Press.

Stets, J., & Straus, M. A. (1990). Gender differences in reporting marital violence and its medical and psychological consequences. In M. A. Straus & R. J. Gelles (Eds.), *Physical violence in American families: Risk factors adaptations in 8,145 American families* (pp. 151–166). New Brunswick, NJ: Transaction Books.

Straus, M. (1979). Measuring intrafamily conflict and violence: The Conflict Tactics Scale. *Journal of the Marriage and the Family, 41,* 75–88.

Straus, M. A., Gelles, R. J., & Steinmetz, S. K. (1980). *Behind closed doors: Violence in the American family.* New York: Anchor Books.

Vivian, D. (1990). *The Adapted Conflict Tactics Scale.* Stony Brook, NY: Department of Psychology, SUNY at Stony Brook.

Vivian, D., Mayer, F., Sandeen, E., & O'Leary, K. D. (1988, September). *Longitudinal assessment of the role of communication skills in interspousal aggression.* Paper presented at the World Congress in Behavior Therapy, Edinburgh, Scotland.

Vivian, D., & O'Leary, K. D. (1987, July). *Communication patterns in physically aggressive engaged couples.* Paper presented at the Third National Family Violence Research Conference, University of New Hampshire, Durham, NH.

Vivian, D., Smith, D., Mayer, F., Sandeen, E., & O'Leary, K. D. (1987, November). *Problem-solving skills and emotional styles of aggressive and nonaggressive maritally discordant couples.* Poster presented at the 21st Annual AABT Convention, Boston, MA.

3

Counseling Heterosexual Women Arrested for Domestic Violence

Implications for Theory and Practice

L. Kevin Hamberger and
Theresa Potente

Historically, discussions about treatment of partner assault perpetrators have focused on men who have been violent with their female partners. There has been virtually no discussion about treating domestically violent women in heterosexual relationships, except in passing. There are several reasons why discussion of domestically violent women in heterosexual relationships has lagged behind that of treating their male counterparts. First, as noted by Pagelow (1984, 1992), the actual rates at which women batter their male partners are very low compared to

This chapter is based on a paper presented at the meeting of the American Psychological Association, Washington, DC, August 17, 1992.

rates of woman battering by men, approximately 5% versus 95%, respectively. Furthermore, Straus and Gelles (1986) demonstrated that female-to-male assaults tend to be much less physically injurious than male-to-female. This is probably due to male-female differences in size, strength, and socialization to fight (Pagelow, 1984). Hence, the low rates of female-perpetrated violence, as well as the generally lower intensity of women's physical violence compared to that of men, constitute one set of reasons why treatment services for domestically violent women have not proliferated.

Another reason for this lack of information has been the historical focus of the battered women's movement, emphasizing the protection of large numbers of battered women from the violence of their male partners. Men, for the reasons noted above, have historically been viewed as the physically violent gender in need of change. Furthermore, the battered women's movement has largely understood male-to-female violence as part and parcel of the very fabric of the sexist, hierarchal power structures that characterize the United States and other Western societies (Dobash & Dobash, 1979; Martin, 1985).

A counterpoint to the well-accepted notions described and discussed above are findings from two national surveys and other studies that have shown women to physically assault their male partners at rates nearly equal to or slightly higher than rates of male-to-female violence (Steinmetz, 1977-1978; Straus & Gelles, 1986; Straus, Gelles, & Steinmetz, 1980). Such research has led some analysts to conclude that traditional, sociopolitical views of domestic violence are inaccurate and falsely framed and have led to social and legal policies that have left men socially and legally defenseless, while ignoring the problem of husband abuse (McNeely & Robinson-Simpson, 1987).

Indeed, a cursory look at national survey rates suggests that women are just as violent as men and that domestic violence is a "two-way street" (McNeely & Robinson-Simpson, 1987). Furthermore, data from the Kenosha Domestic Abuse Intervention Project (Hamberger, 1990) indicate that after institution of a domestic violence mandatory arrest law, women exhibited a 12-fold increase in arrests relative to premandatory arrest. In contrast, men exhibited a twofold increase during the same time period. Again, a cursory interpretation of the findings would be that the law was finally catching up with all those women who had been battering their male partners. The subsequent controversy generated over varying interpretations of the meaning and context of women's violence compared to that of men will be discussed later, particularly in terms of how it was resolved for purposes of intervening with domestically violent women.

For the present, however, suffice it to say that following the onset of mandatory arrest, the large number of women arrested and adjudicated led to increased pressure from the court system to develop specific services for women. The high arrest and referral rates for women mandated to perpetrator counseling services led to serious questioning about whether partner violence is truly a social problem with roots in gender inequality, or whether it constitutes a "two-way street" (McNeely & Robinson-Simpson, 1987), the solution to which goes "… beyond … how to control assaulting husbands" (Straus et al., 1980, p. 44).

From the court perspective, perpetrators of partner violence, regardless of gender, should be provided the opportunity to receive some type of intervention to reduce the use of violence in their lives. From the perspective of battered women's advocates, any such intervention must address issues unique to women, acknowledging that their powerlessness and victimization make partner violence by women a very different entity from partner violence by men.

The manner in which this conflict is resolved is no mere academic exercise. Rather, the assumptions made about women's violence toward their partners will guide the development of intervention strategies and public policy. Indeed, resolution of the conflict can even have implications for how we label women's violence, as well as the perpetrators themselves. For example, are these violent women "husband abusers" or "husband batterers" and their treatment "abuser/batterer" treatment? Conversely, are they battered women who have acted violently and assaultively out of self-defense or in retaliation for previous physical assaults upon them?

With respect to intervention conceptualization, if women use violence to dominate and control, that is, batter, their partners, then regardless of issues of severity and impact (i.e., injury), it would be expected that issues of power and control, long the hallmark of sociopolitically based male offender treatment, would also apply to the treatment of female offenders. On the other hand, if women use violence for reasons such as self-protection, then sociopolitical conceptualizations of violence based on oppression of women can be maintained. In such cases, women's violence may be more than a simple reaction to their partner's violence. Instead, such violence constitutes active efforts to resist the oppressive coercion of their battering partners. Interventions with domestically violent women in the latter circumstance would have to be tailored to take their own victimization issues into account, as well as build on their extant strengths, to achieve autonomy and freedom from violence.

To address the question of how properly to conceptualize women's violence, one must carefully examine the research. Having done so, we believe that male and female partner violence is essentially different, and that close scrutiny of the research corrects mistaken attributions that the two are equivalent.

Let us now return to consideration of research of men's and women's violence to determine whether there are any empirical and/or conceptual clues to assist in resolving how to think about women's violence and its treatment. Such information comes from a variety of sources.

Browne (1993) has critiqued claims that women are as violent as men and has offered several insights. In particular, Browne points out that national surveys conducted by Straus and colleagues (1980, 1986) have observed different patterns of violence perpetration in men and women. Men are violent more *frequently* than women. Men are also more likely to injure their partners than are assaultive women. Furthermore, women are more likely to be killed by a male partner than vice versa. These observations are consistent with other research on gender differences in homicide patterns. For example, Jurik and Winn (1990) found homicides committed by women to have occurred primarily against intimate partners, typically in self-defense, or at least in response to violence initiated by the male partner/victim. When the man killed, he was also more likely to have initiated the physical aggression.

Saunders (1989), as well as Straus (1989), have criticized the national survey data for only assessing whether or not a male or female respondent had initiated violence in the past year. The question about who started the physical fight, however, has been criticized as open to misunderstanding by the respondent. Specifically, it could be interpreted to mean who started the argument that led to the physical assault, not who initiated the actual physical assault. Second, even among female respondents who reported initiating violence, the survey did not account for whether they had been physically battered and subsequently initiated violence because they felt in imminent danger of an attack. Further, as pointed out by Saunders (1989), the index question was framed in terms of mutual combat, which may have led to underreporting by male respondents of self-generated attacks. Saunders (1989) reported analysis of the 1975 National Survey Data (Straus et al., 1980) to determine the reported sequence of events for men and women in marital aggression. He concluded that men were "more likely to be the first and last to use violence when couples report the details of their behavior in a sequential fashion" (p. 14). Despite these findings, the survey data are not helpful in determining the reasons women and men initiate violence.

A number of studies have investigated the motives and context for assault among domestically violent men and women. Saunders (1986) found that among women in a battered women's shelter, 71% who used severe violence did so in self-defense. Hamberger (1991a, 1991b) reported on the motives given by men and women who had been arrested for domestic violence. The modal response given by women involved self-defense, retaliation, or violence in response to cues perceived as suggesting imminent violence against them. Furthermore, examining their histories disclosed that over two thirds of the women had been previously battered by the partner they assaulted.

Barnett and Thelen (unpublished manuscript) compared the motivations of male batterers and battered women who had also used violence. Motivations were assessed for each of a range of acts from grabbing to using weapons. Results showed that women were more likely to identify self-defense as their primary motivation for violence. Men identified control and punishment as their primary motivations. Cascardi, Vivian, and Meyer (1991) reported qualitative data from structured interviews with 36 couples (seen separately) who were maritally violent. Their findings were similar to those reviewed above. Namely, women who committed severe violence reported their aggression as self-defensive, and that assaults against them were related to bids for autonomy. Men who used severe violence, in contrast, reported their aggression as functioning to control their partners.

A study by Follingstad, Wright, Lloyd, and Sebastian (1991) revealed that female college students were more likely than males to report using violence to control, show anger, or retaliate for emotional hurt. Males, in contrast, reported using violence to retaliate for being hit first and to assault their partners out of jealousy. In general, these findings are different from those reported above. However, participants in the study of Follingstad and colleagues tended to be younger, dating students. Participants in the studies reviewed previously were recruited from clinical settings. There may be dynamics unique to nonclinical dating couples experiencing violence that do not apply to people involved in clinical treatment or intervention settings.

In summary, when considering how to develop and conceptualize counseling intervention for domestically violent women, our clinical experience, together with a number of completed studies, has provided several important insights. First, although women are domestically violent, often at levels of severity similar to that of men (Hamberger, 1991a, 1991b), the impact of their violence is typically less than men's violence. Second, women tend to commit violence less frequently than do men, and for different reasons. Specifically, women tend to initiate physical assault motivated by a need for self-protection or retaliation of a previous assault by their partner (Marshall & Rose, 1990). Men, in contrast, tend to identify control or punishment as the primary motivations for assaults on their partners. For these reasons, it is appropriate to view domestically violent women, as a group, as battered women who have gotten caught up in a pattern of violence that, most often, they did not initiate and do not control. A caveat remains: At the individual case level, a careful assessment must be conducted to determine whether the situation at hand fits the generalization or not. The elements of such an assessment include determination of the sequencing pattern of violence, the history of the initiation and pattern of violence, and the situation in which the violence was perpetrated. We believe that it is never right to blame the victim, whatever the victim's sex. We also believe, with the exception of those with diminished capacities, all individuals hold some level of responsibility for their actions, and that violence in retribution is not identical to violence in self-defense.

Implications for Terminology

The language used to describe women's violence should be different from that used for men's violence; accordingly, different labels have been developed for female offenders and their actions. To merely substitute gender in terms from male violence, changing "wife beating" or "woman batterer" to "husband beating" or "male batterer," would be inappropriate. First, terms developed to describe male violence and male offenders are both political (Straus et al., 1980, p. 38) and imbued with emotional connotations that would not fit many woman perpetrators' experience (Hamberger,

1991a, 1991b). "Battering" and "woman abuse" connote not only physical abuse but also abuse of gender-based power by men over women. Moreover, men's violence reinforces differences between male and female power bases. Since women do not have access to the levels of physical, economic, or political power afforded men, it does not make sense to view their use of violence as abuse of power. Women and men would appear to have equal access to emotional power and emotional abuse, such as name-calling and the use of threats. However, in the context of a relationship in which physical power is abused by men, female-initiated emotional abuse does not have the same potential to terrorize and control (Ganley, 1989). As reviewed above, the primary motivation offered by women for their violence tends to be self-defense or protection, not abuse of power. As men's motivations do suggest intentional abuse of power, the politically valenced terms used to describe their violence are appropriately restricted to men and should not be transposed to women who assault their partners.

The terms "batterer" and "abuser" are highly connotative, evoking responses that include revulsion and disgust at the idea that someone could harm, maim, or kill his partner for no other reason than to dominate. Although women, too, kill their partners (Browne, 1987) or assault them (Pagelow, 1984), the *context* of violence in the vast majority of cases is self-defense or escape from a violent partner (Hamberger, 1991a, 1991b). More neutral terminology seems justified in women's violence. Hamberger (1991a, 1991b) has proposed using a context-descriptive term such as "domestically violent" to describe and label women who assault their partners. Such a term does not describe an abuse of power, nor does it conjure images of intentional, systematic harm to an intimate; however, it does identify the intimate context of the violence perpetrated by the women. "Domestic violence" may also be flawed, focusing as it does on the state of domesticity, rather than on the individuals involved. People outside the field of family violence may misinterpret this term to include child and elder abuse. Other suggestions are to name or describe the specific actions and their context, substituting objective descriptors for labeling.

Should Women be Ordered Into Intervention? The Kenosha Experience

Because the majority of arrested domestically violent women have themselves been battered, the question of whether they should be provided counseling under the auspices of a court mandate is often raised. As a community task force, the Kenosha Domestic Abuse Intervention Project struggled with this issue. On the one hand, people argued that in creating a treatment program, the community was delivering the message that women were no different from their male counterparts. This group argued that, instead, the task force should invest its energy in (a) advocating in the courts for battered women who were arrested; and (b) changing police and prosecutory policies for arresting and charging battered women in such situations. Such advocacy and educational efforts have been described in detail by Hamberger (in press). These include collecting and presenting data on men's and women's use of violence to police and prosecution groups, providing educational programs to police, prosecutors, and judges on the dynamics of battered women's use of violence, and providing expert testimony on behalf of battered women who have used violence in self-defense.

Despite such efforts, on the other hand, policy and criminal justice representatives pointed out that many battered women who assaulted their partners did so outside the legal bounds of self-defense and were therefore culpable. Identifying the primary perpetrator was very difficult in many cases; this task was often left to the clinical assessment process. Furthermore, male batterers were often ordered to counseling with the added incentive of reduced fines or dropped or reduced charges. By not providing intervention alternatives and incentives to domestically violent women, the system was operating unfairly and sending a very negative message: Women could expect to be dealt with *more* harshly than men. Furthermore, most of the battered women arrested for violence had not previously used battered women's advocacy services. Providing court-ordered services appeared to be an opportunity to expose battered women to services available through the local shelter, to decrease their isolation, and to provide them with an opportunity to receive support in coping with a difficult life situation (Nurius, Furrey, & Berliner, 1992).

The decision was made to order women to treatment. Although it is reasonable to assume that a woman arrested for violence toward an abusive partner would resist ordered intervention, the majority of women who entered such a program expressed a desire to learn techniques for preventing a recurrence of the situation that led to their arrest. Almost without exception, the women noted that they had become clearly focused on their own goals of self-protection. The arrest freed many women to express their anger and helplessness, which in turn helped them to establish their own goals during the women's treatment program.

The program was structured to avoid any implication that domestically violent women were no different from male batterers. First, the violence and the women were clearly identified and labeled as being different from male batterers. Second, the program format and philosophy were developed in collaboration with the women's shelter, highlighting issues of empowerment. (In the early history of the program, the shelter actually housed and provided staffing for the group sessions.) Third, domestic violence task force members agreed to continue discussion, advocacy, and review of police and prosecution policies regarding arrest of domestically violent women. The goal of this advocacy is to (a) seek changes in the law to reduce inappropriate arrest and adjudication of victims; and (b) train police and prosecutors in the dynamics of victimization and victim use of violence. Such training is aimed at enhancing officer and prosecutor investigation skills to better identify battered women—a skill that should reduce rates of arrest or criminal charges in situations where the act arose from fear of endangerment or the need to defend oneself.

Philosophic Orientation of the Program

The primary philosophical orientation of the women's violence intervention program is that women commit acts of violence in response to having been victimized, either in the current relationship or a previous one. Data support this contention: 49% of women in the program reported prior relationship abuse, 35% reported sexual abuse or assault, 54% had witnessed their mothers being abused, and 48% had been abused as children. Nevertheless, although violence in this context is viewed as an understandable response to having been battered or abused and having found no effective solutions, except in cases of documented diminished capacity, a woman is responsible for her behavior and capable of continuing to seek nonviolent options for ensuring her safety and the safety of her children. The notion of "responsibility" used here refers to behavioral choice and does not imply blameworthiness. As noted previously, most domestically violent women are caught up in a system of control, terror, and violence brought about by their male partners. One might argue that these women never would have chosen violence in any other situation. Nevertheless, their use of violence, although understandable, has brought them more untoward negative consequences: often, more battering from their partners plus arrest and adjudication, along with the attendant feelings of humiliation, futility, and loss of energy to continue the struggle.

Goals of Intervention

As with men's treatment, the primary goal of intervention with domestically violent women is to stop the violence and protect the women and children. However, methods for accomplishing these goals are different. Men are challenged to stop abusing power and to learn to share power equally with their partners. Women, however, are empowered to (a) break through their isolation, develop trust, and make use of advocacy systems; (b) identify resources; and (c) assess family and community blocks to achieving safety in their lives, including assessing immediate safety and developing a plan. Underlying issues include developing assertiveness and self-esteem, accessing formal and informal social supports, and resolving family-of-origin issues (such as physical or sexual abuse) underpinning personal helplessness and victimhood.

Content of Treatment

The actual treatment program consists of 12 two-hour small group sessions. Many of the content areas appear similar to those of many men's treatment programs. As noted previously, however, the philosophical orientation is quite different, altering both the presentation and the process.

Defining Violence and Abuse. The initial sessions consist of discussing and defining domestic violence, primarily using Pence's (1989) model, which emphasizes power, control, and domination of women. Through analysis of this model, women come to understand how their use of violence stems from the abuse of power and control to which they have been subjected by their partners. The consequences of the woman's violence are also discussed, often echoing practical themes such as increased danger to the woman for physically challenging her abuser.

Safety Planning. Safety planning is the next step. We have been particularly influenced by the work of Hart and Stuehling (1992) in the presentation of safety-planning strategies. This involves developing a number of strategies to increase the probability of avoiding violence altogether, or of escaping an attack and thus minimizing damage to the woman and her children. Examples include development of preplanned escape routes and identifying safe-house locations, including the homes of friends or relatives or women's shelters. Where feasible, women are encouraged to enlist the aid of trusted neighbors to call police when they hear sounds of fighting. Guns should be removed from the house. Important papers should be gathered and stored in one location so that they can be readily retrieved. Attempts should be made to accumulate a supply of money to pay for food, transportation, or temporary housing.

In situations where the woman does not perceive the need to actually leave for a period of time, strategies for monitoring her partner's anger arousal and behavior patterns and for managing her own behaviors are discussed. Identifying personal reactions to tension and threat and developing strategies to keep herself in control of her own responses are worked on weekly. One technique is taking timeouts, not to control the man's behavior or arousal, but to enable the woman to funnel her own arousal into problem solving and coping. She is also encouraged to avoid pursuing or obstructing her partner if he decides to leave or stop a discussion. This strategy is not viewed as approving of the man's manipulation and control through these actions, but rather is construed as a practical maneuver to temporarily deescalate the situation and, in the interim, engage in other problem-solving behaviors. Name calling and other inflammatory behaviors are discouraged. Women are also encouraged to remain near the phone, doorway, or other previously identified escape routes during arguments.

Although it is not always possible to predict a partner's violence, many women are able to identify certain situations, argument themes, partner behaviors, and words or states that have frequently led to violence in the past. Such "red flag" situations are discussed as cues to begin implementing safety strategies. The women's internal red flags are also identified and discussed, with a goal of finding short-term alternatives to undesirable responses. Longer-term alternatives leading to different approaches to managing the situation are also examined. For example, one woman consistently became very angry and offered verbal criticisms when her partner arrived home drunk. He then used violence to "shut her up." As a short-term strategy, she gave up her verbal confrontations while he was drunk and often slept in a spare room. As a long-term strategy, she began attending Al-Anon for support in living with an addicted partner. With further work, she expressed willingness to call the police when she felt danger. Very quickly, the violence in such situations diminished.

A woman is encouraged to practice taking charge of her reactions in other difficult, stressful situations such as at work or with her children. The practice helps her identify what she can control and what she cannot. Specifically, she learns that she has control over her actions and bids for safety; however, she does not have control over her partner's violence—nor can she expect always to predict it.

Emphasis in this segment of counseling is personal responsibility for behavior. Thus, safety strategies are not developed to stop the man's violence; she learns that she cannot and must not take responsibility for her partner. Instead, the strategies are designed to empower the women, as much as possible, to (a) initiate positive safety-related behaviors, and (b) remove herself or find alternative behaviors in situations likely to evoke violence by or against her. Her primary responsibility, then, is to maintain her own safety and her children's safety and to take charge of her own reactions. In short, she must decide what she wants to do. The counseling helps her to clarify her options, including the difficult and dangerous choice of leaving her partner.

Anger Management. Because most women attending the program have been victimized many times (including family-of-origin abuse, incest, sexual abuse, and/or abuse in previous relationships), anger is a key issue. Patterns of anger, aggression, and control in the family of origin are analyzed, and the effects of patterns on the women are identified. The woman's continuation of such patterns in her adult relationships is also targeted for change.

Cognitive-behavioral approaches to anger management are used to facilitate such change. One effective method is anger inoculation (Novaco, 1975). Anger is conceptualized as an emotion that can lead to constructive behavior. In particular, women are encouraged to use their anger as a source of energy for problem solving rather than for aggression. Other examples of constructive uses of anger include developing plans to get out of the relationship (if this is what the woman wants to do) or getting involved in battered women's advocacy groups to challenge current police policies that foster arrest of battered women. Facilitative, constructive use of anger can also involve securing her safety should she choose to remain with her abusive partner, including having him arrested for his violence. The concept of anger as a potentially constructive emotion is juxtaposed with the concept of aggression, an act most often done to injure or control and seldom leading to a constructive outcome.

Other Cognitive-Behavioral Strategies. Many domestically violent women believe they are responsible for their partner's feelings and actions. They believe that (a) they *can* change their partner, (b) it is their *job* to change their partner, and (c) their partner hits them because *they have failed* their male partners. In addition, because many women have been trapped for long periods of time in violent, abusive relationships, they may also hold beliefs that they are not entitled to their own autonomy or cannot survive separately from their batterer. These beliefs are challenged as ultimately self-defeating. Issues of responsibility, again, are emphasized. These include recognizing limits of responsibility, such as viewing the partner as solely responsible for his own happiness, misery, and violence. She, in turn, is responsible for her own feelings and behaviors. Seeing herself as a separate person frees her to focus strictly on her issues, rather than trying in vain to manage his problems. As other group members identify common patterns of women's reactions, the woman becomes aware of her own patterns. All cognitive-behavioral strategies used in the group minimize judgment and blame while offering encouragement at each step, however small.

Children's Issues. Because many of the women attending counseling have children, the effects of parental violence on child emotional and social welfare are discussed. Community resources for assisting children in violent families are identified and ways to access such programs are explored.

Alcohol and Drug Abuse. Alcohol and drug use generally is construed as a factor that increases the probability of violence in these women's lives. Accordingly, the role of alcohol and drug abuse in partner violence is also considered in the women's intervention program. Although alcohol and other drugs are acknowledged to numb the pain and stress, as many domestically violent women report, substance use is viewed as self-defeating in the long term, facilitating the women's entrapment. Women with substance-abusing partners are encouraged to join appropriate support groups, such as Al-Anon. Women who themselves are substance abusers are assessed further and may be referred for alcohol and drug counseling before they complete the program.

Assertiveness. With this treatment population, the issue of responsible assertive behavior has important implications. Women who have themselves been battered, often for years, exhibit high levels of compliant, submissive, and startle behavior, as measured both by self-report and by psychometric evaluation. Using the Millon Clinical Multiaxial Inventory (MCMI; Millon, 1983), we have observed modal elevations on personality subscales measuring passive-submissive and compulsive characteristics. As one battered, domestically violent woman explained, "When you've been beaten for 12 years, you become compliant if it's in your best interest."

Viewed superficially, domestically violent women are aggressive and need to "tone down" their assertiveness. However, although these women become verbally aggressive at times, such aggression appears to be more a reaction to aggression against them (Marshall & Rose, 1990) and a self-defensive strategy (Barnett, Keyson, & Thelen, 1992). Tempered with this understanding, assertiveness interventions targeting aggressive interpersonal interactions must provide women with other, less inflammatory verbal responses to their partner's verbal attacks. Women practice avoiding name-calling and dirty fighting tactics, "agreeing to disagree," and knowing when to quit. These tactics are not intended to change the partner's behavior; although they may have the desirable side effect of deescalating his responses, their primary intent is to help her remain clear and problem focused during difficult interactions.

Assertiveness training with this population involves decreasing situational aggressive behaviors and increasing assertion of personal rights, expectations, plans, and desires. However, it must be remembered that, although the battered women are in treatment for their aggression, most of their partners are not. Women, therefore, are also warned of the potential risks that accompany asserting rights to a person who has habitually resorted to violence in response to past bids for autonomy (O'Leary, Curley, Rosenbaum, & Clarke, 1985). Responsible assertive training with this population emphasizes not only respecting the rights of others, but understanding, in a self-interested way, that certain forms of assertiveness may pose a hazard to the woman's immediate safety.

We also believe that assertiveness skills should be taught within a conceptual framework extending beyond immediate relationship issues. For example, women in the Kenosha program are almost universally court ordered to attend, and thus are involved with the criminal justice system. Many are also involved with the social welfare system, job training programs, child protective or mediation services, and a host of other social service, bureaucratic institutions. Interactions with such agencies can be frustrating, dehumanizing, and disempowering. Often assertiveness training targets effective—or at least, less exasperating—navigation through these systems. Assertiveness training also involves reducing discomfort in developing informal social support networks, such as getting to know a neighbor well enough to set up a safety support system (calling the police or providing safe housing in the event of a future assault). Done this way, assertiveness training functions as training in self-advocacy skills.

Meeting With the Partner. Finally, the therapist attempts to meet with the client and her partner. The goal of these sessions is to present nonviolence as a constructive form of a relationship and abuse of power and control as destructive forms. The effect of violence on the health and well-being of children is also discussed. Other issues covered with the woman's partner include the responsibility of each partner to stay in control and make appropriate use of resources. For women who have partners in the program for male batterers, there is ongoing coordination between respective therapists. Such coordination facilitates provision of accurate information and feedback about progress, problems, and levels of danger.

Summary

As the above discussion illustrates, any interventions with domestically violent women are not as straightforward as a cursory look might suggest. In retrospect, our very early conceptualizations of domestically violent women as essentially similar to male batterers challenged our traditional, sociopolitical models of intimate violence as a manifestation of male oppression of females. However, as we gained experience with this population through careful questioning and exploration, we have consistently observed that feminist sociopolitical models provide a closer fit with the data. Most women who resort to violence against their partners do so as a direct outgrowth of violence and oppression perpetrated against them in a context that has permitted or encouraged violence to be used as a problem-solving strategy. Of the 67 women treated to date, only 3 clearly exhibited primary perpetrator characteristics and battered their male partners. Each of these three came from severely dysfunctional and multiabusive families-of-origin.

Future Directions

The program described in this chapter is an initial effort to develop a program of counseling for domestically violent women. As such, much work remains to refine conceptual, clinical, and empirical issues.

Although the association between our conceptualization of domestically violent women and the treatment approach has been described, it must be acknowledged that the association is somewhat preliminary, particularly with respect to specific techniques. That battered women benefit from safety planning seems quite obvious. It is presently less certain, however, whether women, such as those in the present program, exhibit assertiveness deficits requiring intervention. The utilization of anger management techniques may be controversial and needs to be studied further. Such research must include study of how anger may inhibit effective coping in this population, as well as whether specific techniques are necessary in achieving treatment outcome goals. Since many of the women reported numerous and severe assault victimizations, interventions that focus on resolving traumatic stress responses may be appropriate for some domestically violent women. Although there are many questions about specific therapeutic approaches with this population, work by other researchers (Gleason, 1993; Nurius et al., 1992) does suggest that various cognitive-behavioral skills approaches are appropriate.

It must also be determined to what degree the counseling intervention affects the lives of these women. Since the primary goal of such counseling is safety and empowerment, outcome studies must measure these concepts. These could include subjective ratings of safety; increased willingness to utilize police and shelter services; and planning and following through on leaving an abusive relationship.

Our work to date has also revealed a small number of domestically violent women who appear to be primary perpetrators. To date, they have been placed in the same program with women viewed as victims. It needs to be determined whether primary perpetrators need other treatment or can benefit from a program designed primarily for victims.

Another important issue involves the role of other community agencies that have contact with domestically violent women— especially the police and prosecution offices. In the Kenosha Domestic Abuse Intervention Program, information related to the self-defensive/retaliatory nature of most women's violence has helped in the training of police and prosecutors, as well as counselors. The goal of such training is lower rates of arrest and prosecution of domestic violence victims. The impact of such training, however, is not yet known and must be assessed.

To answer the question put forth at the outset of this chapter, we have come to believe that women who commit acts of domestic violence should be referred to counseling. The benefits of increasing opportunities for social and personal support and of learning techniques and information that add to a woman's personal safety and sense of personal efficacy can be accomplished without victim blaming or labeling the woman as a batterer. Compliance in the Kenosha program is extremely high, indicating that the program has perceived value to the clients. However, this does not mean that we believe the women were all appropriately arrested under the mandatory arrest law. Neither does it mean that treatment for domestically violent women should be the same as treatment for men who batter. To intervene effectively with this population requires that we not assume universal mutuality. Women are not "just as violent" as men. Although surveys indicate that women report comparable rates of violence, the context, meaning, and function of women's violence appears very different from that of men. Treatment approaches must reflect those differences. When carefully designed, treatment programs for domestically violent women can be a useful adjunct to other social and criminal justice system approaches aiming to secure the safety of women and their children.

REFERENCES

Barnett, O. W., Keyson, M., & Thelen, R. E. (1992, August). *Women's violence as a response to male abuse.* Paper presented at the meeting of the American Psychological Association, Washington, DC

Barnett, O. W., & Thelen, R. E. (1992).*Gender differences in forms, outcomes and motivations for marital violence.* Unpublished manuscript.

Browne, A., (1987). *When battered women kill.* New York: Free Press.

Browne, A. (1993). Violence against women by male parnters: Prevalence, outcomes and policy implications. *American Psychologist, 48,* 1077–1087.

Cascardi, M., Vivian, D., & Meyer, S. L. (1991, November). *Context and attributions for marital violence in discordant couples.* Paper presented at the meeting of the Association for the Advancement of Behavior Therapy, New York, NY.

Dobash, R., & Dobash, R. (1979). *Violence against wives.* New York: Free Press.

Follingstad, D. R., Wright, S., Lloyd, S., & Sebastian, J. A. (1991). Sex differences in motivations and effects of dating violence. *Family Relations, 40,* 51–57.

Ganley, A. (1989). Integrating feminist and social learning analyses of aggression: Creating multiple models for intervention with men who batter. In P. L. Caesar & L. K. Hamberger (Eds.), *Treating men who batter: Theory, practice, and programs* (pp. 196–235). New York: Springer.

Gleason, W. J. (1993). Mental disorders in battered women: An empirical study. *Violence and Victims, 8,* 53–68.

Hamberger, L. K. (1990, January). *Effects of the mandatory arrest law on domestic violence perpetrator counseling.* Invited testimony before the Wisconsin Equal Justice Task Force, Kenosha, WI.

Hamberger, L. K. (1991a, May). *Characteristics and context of women arrested for domestic violence: Context and implications.* Marital violence: Theoretical and empirical perspectives, Indiana University Conference on Research and Clinical Problems, Bloomington, IN.

Hamberger, L. K. (1991b, August). Research concerning wife abuse: Implications for training police and physicians. In R. Geffner (Chair), *State-of-the-art research in family violence: Practical applications.* Symposium presented at the meeting of the American Psychological Association, San Francisco, CA.

Hamberger, L. K. (in press). Female offenders in domestic violence: A look at actions in their context. *Abuse, Aggression and Assault.*

Hart, B., & Stuehling, J. (1992). *Personalized safety plan.* Pennsylvania Coalition Against Domestic Violence. Reading, PA.

Jurik, N. C., & Winn, R. (1990). Gender and homicide: A comparison of men and women who kill. *Violence and Victims, 5,* 1990, 227–242.

McNeely, R. L., & Robinson-Simpson, G. (1987). The truth about domestic violence: A falsely framed issue. *Social Work, 32,* 485–490.

Marshall, L. L., & Rose, P. (1990). Premarital violence: The impact of family of origin violence, stress, and reciprocity. *Journal of Family Violence, 5,* 1990.

Martin, D. (1985). Domestic violence: A sociological perspective. In D. J. Sonkin, D. Martin, & L. E. A. Walker, *The male batterer: A treatment approach* (pp. 1–32). New York: Springer.

Millon, T. (1983). *Millon Clinical Multiaxial Inventory Manual.* Minneapolis: National Computer Scoring.

Novaco, R. (1975). *Anger control.* Lexington, MA: Lexington Books.

Nurius, P., Furrey, T., & Berliner, L. (1992). Coping capacity among women with abusive partners. *Violence and Victims, 7,* 229–244.

O'Leary, K. D., Curley, A., Rosenbaum, A., & Clarke, C. (1985). Assertion training for abused wives: A potentially hazardous treatment. *Journal of Marital and Family Therapy, 11,* 319–322.

Pagelow, M. D. (1984). *Family violence* (pp. 267–277). New York: Praeger.

Pagelow, M. D. (1992). Adult victims of domestic violence: Battered women. *Journal of Interpersonal Violence, 7,* 87–120.

Pence, E. (1989). Batterer programs: Shifting from community collusion to community confrontation. In P. L. Caesar & L. K. Hamberger (Eds.), *Treating men who batter: Theory, practice, and programs* (pp. 24–50). New York: Springer.

Saunders, D. G. (1986). When battered women use violence: Husband abuse or self defense. *Violence and Victims, 1,* 47–60.

Saunders, D. G. (1989, November). *Who hits first and who hits most? Evidence for the greater victimization of women in intimate relationships.* Paper presented at the meeting of the American Society of Criminology, Reno, NV.

Steinmetz, S. K. (1977–1978). The battered husband syndrome. *Victimology: An International Journal, 2,* 499–509.

Straus, M. A. (1989, November). *Assaults by wives on husbands: Implications for primary prevention of marital violence.* Paper presented at the meeting of the American Society of Criminology, Reno, NV.

Straus, M. A., & Gelles, R. J. (1986). Societal change and change in family violence from 1975 to 1985 as revealed by two national surveys. *Journal of Marriage and the Family, 48,* 465–479.

Straus, M. A., Gelles, R. J., & Steinmetz, S. K. (1980). *Behind closed doors: Violence in the American family.* New York: Anchor.

4

Lesbian Battering

The Relationship Between Personality and the Perpetration of Violence

Vallerie E. Coleman

Traditionally, the battered women's movement and domestic violence theory have focused on heterosexual battering and the perpetration of violence by men. Only within recent years has violence in lesbian relationships begun to be acknowledged and addressed. The reality of women battering other women challenges societal stereotypes of women and dismantles the structure of gender-based, sociopolitical domestic violence theory. In addition, for lesbians to acknowledge battering in their relationships stands in opposition to the lesbian myth of healthy, violence-free, egalitarian relationships. Consequently, the reluctance

This chapter was based, in part, on the paper *Breaking silence about lesbian battering: New directions in domestic violence theory,* presented at the American Psychological Convention, Washington, DC, August 17, 1992.

to acknowledge lesbian battering has been significant, both within mainstream society as well as in the lesbian community. This chapter will propose that a multidimensional theory of partner abuse, which incorporates an emphasis on individual personality dynamics, is necessary in order to more fully understand the heterogeneity of batterers. After an overview of battering in lesbian relationships, various theoretical perspectives on domestic violence will be highlighted. This will be followed by an examination of batterers' personality traits and the relationship between psychopathology and battering in lesbian relationships. Although this chapter is primarily concerned with the relationship between personality and domestic violence in lesbian relationships, this is not meant to infer that lesbians have higher levels of psychopathology than any other group.

Violence in Lesbian Relationships

Although limited, the available literature suggests that the prevalence and severity of lesbian battering are comparable to that of heterosexual relationships. Researchers examining the prevalence of battering in heterosexual couples have found rates of violence ranging from approximately 28% (Straus & Gelles, 1986; Straus, Gelles, & Steinmetz, 1980) to 55% (Gelles, 1974; Gelles & Straus, 1979). Similarly, studies on lesbian battering have demonstrated rates of violence in committed lesbian relationships ranging from 25% (Brand & Kidd, 1986) to 48% (Gardner, 1989).

In a study examining the frequency of violence in heterosexual and lesbian couples, Brand and Kidd (1986) found that 27% of the heterosexual women and 25% of the lesbians had been physically abused by their partners while in a committed relationship. In contrast, 5% of the lesbian women were victims of physical violence while in dating relationships compared to 19% of the heterosexual women. There were no significant differences in age, race, education, or socioeconomic status between the two groups.

Kelly and Warshafsky (1987) conducted an exploratory, nation-wide survey examining factors associated with gay and lesbian partner abuse. The respondents, 48 women and 50 men, were pre-dominantly white, professional, middle-class individuals. The majority of the participants were open about their sexuality and active in the gay and lesbian community. Using a modified version of the Conflict Tactics Scale (CTS) (Straus, 1979), Kelly and Warshafsky found that assertive tactics and verbal abuse tactics were used most often, 100% and 95 % of the time, respectively. The participants reported that physical aggression was used 47% of the time and violent tactics 3% of the time.

Gardner (1989) examined correlates of domestic violence in a comparison study of 43 heterosexual, 43 lesbian, and 39 gay male couples. Gardner used the CTS to assess physical aggression, and couples were categorized as violent if either one or both partners endorsed any act of physical aggression as occurring within the past year. Gardner found no significant differences in prevalence of partner abuse among the couple types. Heterosexual couples evidenced the lowest rate of abuse (28%), whereas lesbian couples had the highest rate (48%). Gay men had a prevalence rate of 38%. A similar rate of violence was demonstrated by Coleman (1991) in a study examining the prevalence and severity of lesbian battering in a sample of 90 predominantly white, lower- and middle-class lesbian couples. Using scores obtained through a modified version of the CTS completed by both partners, Coleman found that 42 of the 90 couples (46.6%) reported repeated acts of physical abuse in their current relationship.

In a study of 100 self-identified battered lesbians, Renzetti (1988, 1992) demonstrated that violence in lesbian relationships increased in frequency and severity over time. She found that 77% of the women had experienced at least one incident of violence within the first 6 months of the relationship, and 71 % reported that the battering increased in both frequency and severity over time. This finding, in addition to clinical discussions in the litera-

ture, indicates that the cycle of violence (Walker, 1979, 1984) identified in heterosexual couples also applies to lesbian battering.

In summary, research has demonstrated that violence in lesbian
relationships is a significant problem that can no longer be overlooked. Although many of the dynamics involved in lesbian battering are similar to those of heterosexual battering, there are also
some significant differences. In order to better understand the phenomenon of women battering other women, we must reexamine
domestic violence theory and consider some of the similarities and
differences that exist between heterosexual male violence and lesbian battering.

Domestic Violence Theory

As exemplified by the occurrence of lesbian battering, domestic
violence is a complex phenomenon that in my opinion, is best
understood through the use of a multidimensional theory. These
dimensions include sociopolitical factors, social learning theory,
family dynamics, physiological factors, and individual personality
dynamics.

Sociopolitical Factors

A sociopolitical analysis of domestic violence contributes an
understanding of how social systems, cultural beliefs, and political factors facilitate and perpetuate the occurrence of battering.
For example, social stress, social isolation, low socioeconomic
status, and rigid sex roles have been identified as factors that
tend to increase the incidence of violence in couples and families
(Weidman, 1986). As a result of riving in a patriarchal society that
condones male domination, subordination, and control of
women (Dobash & Dobash, 1978), social relationships tend to be
hierarchical. Moreover, violence is often viewed as a socially
acceptable means for both groups and individuals to exert power
and maintain dominance over others (Gamache, 1991). The wide-

spread institutionalization of such oppression is evident in the social tenets of sexism, heterosexism, racism, and classism. Since we live within a cultural atmosphere of hierarchical structures and patriarchal values, the predominant model for intimate relationships is one of domination and subordination. These values and relationship norms are internalized by women, as well as by men. Consequently, even in lesbian relationships there is a heightened potential for one partner to seek domination and control over the other.

The internalization of these values plays a major role in the perpetration of violence by all individuals regardless of their gender or sexual orientation. For instance, as a result of homophobia and heterosexism, lesbians are faced with discrimination, social isolation, and a general lack of available resources and social support. Individuals living under such conditions may develop low self-esteem, internalized homophobia, and feelings of powerlessness or helplessness. As noted by Gamache (1991), batterers tend to believe that they have the fight to control or punish their partners for perceived wrongdoings. As a result, dominance and control over one's partner may be used as a means to cope with feelings of powerlessness and inferiority. The existence of these dynamics in battering aptly illustrates how the widespread influence of sociopolitical factors perpetuates and maintains a cultural environment conducive to domestic violence.

Social Learning Theory and Family Dynamics

Social learning theory suggests that violence is a way of coping one learns through observation and experience. In our society, violence is a common phenomenon that penetrates almost every aspect of daily life. One of the most fundamental arenas for learning is one's family. The intergenerational transmission of domestic violence is one component of social learning theory. An intergenerational model of battering purports that children who grow up in families where they experience violence, either by witnessing violence between their caretakers or by being the victim of violent acts, are more likely to incorporate violent behavior as a coping mechanism. As adults, these individuals may then pass on a legacy of violence in their own families.

Several studies have shown a high level of correlation between violence in an individual's family of origin, either by witnessing or being a victim of violence, and the use of violence as a coping mechanism in later relationships (Ceaser, 1988; Dutton, 1988; Edleson, Eisikovits, & Guttmann, 1985; Rosenbaum & O'Leary, 1981). Thus, families, as well as society in general, often serve as an environment in which one learns that violence is a viable and effective means of solving problems.

Individual Variables and Partner Abuse

Although theories examining the roles of sociopolitical factors, social learning, and family dynamics in battering have contributed a great deal to our understanding of domestic violence, there are numerous individual differences among batterers that they do not address. For instance, these theories cannot explain why some men who are abused or witness abuse go on to abuse their partners and others do not nor do they adequately explain the phenomenon of lesbian battering. In order to more fully understand the occurrence of domestic violence, we must also examine individual differences among batterers. Researchers have generated numerous characteristics of men who batter women but have been unable to develop consistent typologies of batterers (Dutton, 1988; Edleson et al., 1985; Rosenbaum & O'Leary, 1981). Although there are many factors that contribute to an individual's need to dominate and control others, several studies have found that male batterers frequently have personality traits that are consistent with various levels of psychopathology. Researchers have also demonstrated that physiological and neuropsychological factors can play a role in violent behavior (Dilalla & Gottesman, 1991; B. Geffner, personal communication, August 17, 1992; Mungas, 1988; Weller, 1986).

Historically, many theorists and persons working in the field of domestic violence have been hesitant to acknowledge individual variables as a significant component in battering, for fear that such a perspective would detract from important sociopolitical factors and serve as an excuse for violent behavior. Rather than negating the importance of social influences, the consideration of individual factors as mediating variables in domestic violence can complement sociological and sociopolitical perspectives. For instance, continued research in the area of biological and neuropsychological factors in partner abuse may provide us with important insights relevant to the advancement of treatment interventions tailored to meet the specific needs of individual batterers. By integrating these various factors, we can design more effective interventions for batterers' treatment programs, while at the same time furthering the development and implementation of effective legal and social policies (Hamberger & Hastings, 1988).

Personality Characteristics of Batterers

Characteristics of Heterosexual Male Batterers

Hamberger and Hastings (1986), in a study examining personality profiles of male batterers using the Millon Clinical Multiaxial Inventory (MCMI), identified three primary personality traits: asocial/borderline, narcissistic/antisocial, and dependent/compulsive. In a later study, Hastings and Hamberger (1988) compared non-alcohol-abusing batterers and alcohol-abusing batterers with a control group of nonbatterers using the MCMI and several other scales. They found that overall, batterers evidenced higher levels of anxiety, depression, somatic complaints, unemployment separation and divorce, problems with substance abuse, and less education. In addition, the batterers demonstrated significantly higher levels of pathology than nonbatterers on the MCMI. Specifically, alcohol-abusing batterers were found to have higher levels of asocial, avoidant, and aggressive traits and to be less socially conforming than nonbatterers. They also scored higher on scales measuring poor reality testing and distorted thought processes. As a group, batterers scored significantly higher than nonbatterers on measures of borderline personality traits and negativistic, passive-aggressive tendencies. As noted by Hastings and Hamberger (1988),

> the picture of the batterer that emerges from these data is one of a psychologically rigid and unstable individual who, while capable of forming highly intense relationships, is self-absorbed to such an extent that true empathy and reciprocity in relationships is impossible. (p. 44)

Gondolf (1988) developed a behavioral typology of male batterers using self-report inventories from 525 battered women. He identified three general typologies: the sociopathic batterer, the antisocial batterer, and the typical batterer. The first two types were classified as extremely physically and verbally abusive individuals, with the sociopathic batterer having a higher number of arrests. The typical batterer was classified as committing less severe physical and verbal abuse and as demonstrating fewer antisocial characteristics.

Additional evidence for high rates of antisocial or sociopathic traits in male batterers was demonstrated by Flournoy and Wilson (199 1) using the Minnesota Multiphasic Personality Inventory (MMPI). Similar to the findings of other studies, batterers in Flournoy and Wilson's sample demonstrated high levels of antisocial traits, depression, passive-dependence, and a tendency to externalize blame (4-2 profile). The researchers suggest that the 4-2 profile is consistent with clinical evidence that indicates that battering and depression are both related to feelings of helplessness and a profound fear of loss and abandonment.

In an attempt to move away from a pathology-based model of personality, Barnett and Hamberger (1992) compared male batterers with maritally satisfied and maritally distressed nonbatterers on the California Psychological Inventory (CPI), which measures nonpathological aspects of personality. They found that overall, batterers evidenced poorer levels of adjustment, as well as greater rigidity and a lack of resourcefulness in problem solving. As a group, batterers demonstrated more anxiety, defensiveness, and impulsivity. They also tended to be moody, self-centered, demanding, and aloof. In addition, batterers reported higher levels of violence in their families of origin, both as victims and as witnesses.

Characteristics of Lesbian Batterers

Although there are no studies that have specifically examined personality correlates of lesbian batterers, the available literature suggests that abusive lesbians demonstrate personality traits similar to those of heterosexual men who batter. Clinical and anecdotal reports have shown that lesbian batterers frequently abuse alcohol or drugs, feel powerless, have low self-esteem, and tend to be overly dependent and jealous (Leeder, 1988; Lobel, 1986; Schilit & Lie, 1990). These findings are supported by Renzetti's (1988, 1992) research, which demonstrated correlations between batterers' levels of dependency, jealousy, substance abuse, and the use of violence. According to Leeder (1988), many lesbian batterers fear abandonment, have poor communication skills, tend to be self-absorbed, and are unable to empathically relate to their partners.

Studies examining the relationship between violence in one's family of origin and lesbian battering have provided inconsistent results. Lie, Schilit, Bush, Montagne, and Reyes (1991) found that experiencing or witnessing domestic violence as a child was correlated with becoming either an adult victim of violence, a perpetrator, or both. However, other researchers have not found statistically significant correlations between abuse in an individual's family of origin and lesbian battering (Coleman, 1991; Kelly & Warshafsky, 1987; Renzetti, 1992). Clearly, further research is needed to discern and clarify the role psychopathology plays in an individual's choice to batter.

Personality Disorders

As shown above, there are many identifiable differences in personality characteristics between individuals who batter and those who do not. However, it is beyond the scope of this chapter to discuss each of these characteristics in depth. In my clinical experience, many batterers have personality structures indicative of the borderline, narcissistic, or antisocial disorders; and certainly, in some instances they exhibit more than one disorder. In addition, they may have a personality disorder, such as borderline personality disorder, and also exhibit traits of other disorders, such as dependent passive-aggressive, or compulsive traits. It is important to keep in mind that an individual may have personality traits characteristic of a disorder without having a diagnosable disorder. It is when personality traits are inflexible and maladaptive, resulting in significantly impaired functioning, internal distress, and interpersonal difficulties, that they form a personality disorder (American Psychiatric Association, 1987, p. 335). Although the identification of personality disorders is a critical component in understanding and treating an individual, one must also keep in mind the dangers of objectification and dehumanization inherent in labeling. However, for the sake of simplicity and clarity the term *disorder* will be used throughout this article. Following a brief overview of personality development and the etiology of psychopathology, a discussion of batterers with narcissistic and borderline character structures will be provided.

Personality Development and Psychopathology

According to psychodynamic theory, personality disorders result from early childhood traumas and disruptions in interpersonal relations. Two psychoanalytic perspectives that are useful in conceptualizing personality development and psychopathology are object-relations theory and self psychology. In general object-relations theorists focus on how one's intrapsychic structure and personality are shaped through the incorporation of external objects into the psyche. Goldstein (1990) notes that the term *object-relations*

> encompasses the nature of a person's internal images or representations of the self and the object world, the relationship among these self- and object-representations, and the impact of these internalized object relations on the development of intrapsychic structure and interpersonal relationships. (P. 54)

Although self psychology also emphasizes interpersonal relationships and the role of the environment in individual development, the primary focus is on the structure of the self and the organizations of the self-object system (Goldstein, 1990; Kohut, 1977; Wolf, 1988). As noted by Wolf (1988), a self-object is "neither a self or object' but the intrapsychic experience of one's relationship to another, "...who by their presence or activity evoke and maintain the self and the experience of selfhood" (p. 184).

The Borderline and Narcissistic Disorders

According to psychodynamic theory, the borderline and narcissistic disorders both involve basic deficits in the self resulting from early trauma and a failure to negotiate the separation-individuation process of normal development (Goldstein, 1990; Masterson, 1981). Although individuals may have traits common to both disorders, they differ in their specific defensive structure and the resulting symptomatology.

Batterers With Borderline Personality Disorder

Typically, object-relations theorists conceptualize borderline personality disorder (BPO) as originating in early childhood because of a failure in the negotiation of the rapprochement subphase during the process of separation-individuation (Goldstein, 1990;

Mahler, Pine, & Bergman, 1975). Such a failure can occur, for instance, if a child's attempts at gradually separating and developing an independent self are thwarted by an emotionally unavailable or overly enmeshed primary caretaker. If the child does not fully negotiate separation-individuation, he or she does not develop object constancy and there is a buildup of frustration and aggression. In order to protect and maintain the experience of good and soothing objects, self and object representations are split into good and bad aspects. In other words, there is a good and bad self representation, rather than an integration of good and bad aspects, to create a whole self (Freed, 1984; Goldstein, 1990; Kemberg, 1984).

Self psychologists view individuals with borderline personality disorder as lacking a cohesive sense of self. This chaotic self is covered by complex defenses, and under stressful conditions there is a heightened potential for fragmentation. According to self psychology, because persons with BPO lack the capacity to self-soothe, feelings such as anxiety and fear result in extreme rage reactions (Wastell, 1992; Wolf, 1988). Thus, rage is seen as a defense against fragmentation.

Although psychoanalytic theorists have hypothesized that the fundamentals of personality are formed during the first few years of life, some theorists have gone beyond a focus on infant-caretaker relationships to look at the role of family functioning in the development of BPO. Theorists such as Wolberg (1982) have postulated that the triangulation of children by their parents and the projection of parents' split-off aspects onto the child can lead to the development of borderline personality structures. Another area of study has been the relationship between BPO and post-traumatic stress disorder (PTSD). Studies have shown that individuals with BPO and PTSD share similar symptomatology and that there is a significant relationship between childhood abuse and the development of BPO (Herman, Perry, & van der Kolk, 1989; Landecker, 1992).

For individuals with BPO, the following characteristics are common:

- fear of abandonment
- poor boundaries and a lack of a clear sense of self
- poor impulse control
- poor reality testing under stress
- lack of frustration tolerance
- need for immediate gratification
- lack of ability to self-soothe
- fragile self-cohesion
- super-ego deficits
- problems in self-esteem regulation
- poor affect regulation (Goldstein, 1990)

Many of these characteristics are easily identifiable in individuals who batter. For batterers with a borderline personality structure, abandonment fear tends to be a central issue. In an attempt to avoid real or perceived abandonment, the individual seeks merger with others. Since self-cohesion is extremely fragile for individuals with BPO, seemingly minor disruptions or psychic injuries in relation to their partner can lead to fragmentation. Using self psychology theory, one can conceptualize individuals with borderline personality disorder as "merger hungry personalities" who merge with their partners in lieu of maintaining their own self-structure (Wolf, 1988, p. 74). Thus, any attempt at separation or independence by the battered partner results in rage against the self-object and the use of violence in an attempt to control her. In addition to acting aggressively toward their partners, batterers with BPO often engage in manipulative, self-destructive behaviors in an attempt to control their partners and ward off fragmentation.

For lesbians, the struggle of intimacy versus autonomy may be enhanced as a result of sex-role socialization. From a very young age, little girls learn to define themselves in relation to others (Chodorow, 1978); consequently, women tend to have less rigid ego boundaries and a greater capacity for identification with others (Burch, 1986). As noted by Elise (1986), "the lesser degree of differentiation of the female ego may result in a greater capacity for the lesbian couple to relate infinitely, but also leads to a tendency for the couple to become more intrapsychically merged" (p. 309). This tendency toward merger in lesbian relationships is heightened by a tendency for the lesbian community, as a function of its small size and minority status, to become a closed system. As a result, the potential for dependency and the loss of individual identity is increased. Although the individual with BPO longs for merger, closeness intensifies feelings of need and the fear of abandonment, resulting in periodic episodes of withdrawal (Goldstein, 1990). Some authors have suggested that in an attempt to create distance and avoid the stimulation of abandonment fear, an individual may resort to the use of arguments and/or physical fights (Krestan & Bepko, 1980).

This dynamic is exemplified by the relationship of Judy and Mary. Judy, an individual with BPO, had a great need for closeness and felt that she and Mary should do nearly all of their activities together. Judy would often comment that lovers had to "stick together" for a relationship to last in the lesbian community. She was always planning activities for the two of them and was extremely sensitive to any perceived reluctance on Mary's part to participate. When Mary indicated an interest in spending time separate from Judy, Judy became sullen and withdrawn or openly angry and argumentative. This was often followed by the initiation of a verbal, and at times physical, fight. For Judy, any movement by Mary toward independence was felt as a threat and stimulated her extreme fear of abandonment. Judy would withdraw or argue in an attempt to protect herself from the perceived threat by distancing and controlling Mary.

Object-relations theory provides a useful perspective in under-standing how splitting is used as a defense to prevent the destruc-tion of good self and object representations. Other common bor-derline defenses, such as omnipotent control, idealization, devalu-ation, and projection (Goldstein, 1990; Ogdon, 1979), are often used by individuals who batter. The following is one way to con-ceptualize how these dynamics may emerge in partner abuse. For example, if we consider the cycle of violence, the beginning of the relationship is usually marked by idealization of the love object and pressure from the batterer for increased closeness or merger. This is frequently followed by a threat to the individual's self-cohesion, often related to abandonment, which stimulates the internal representation of the bad object. In an attempt to protect and maintain the good internal object the bad object representation may be projected onto the battered partner.

For lesbians, internalized homophobia and misogyny can lead to feelings of shame, powerlessness, and self-hatred, which may be projected onto one's lover. When the bad object is projected onto the partner, she is perceived as threatening or attacking and thus must be destroyed or controlled. Through devaluation and attack of the now external bad object the batterer can once again reunite with the good object representation. The reunion with the battered partner completes the cycle with a return to the honeymoon phase. For example, when Mary attempts to separate from Judy, this feels extremely threatening for Judy and stimulates an internalized bad object. In order to protect and maintain internal good object repre-sentations, Judy projects the bad object onto Mary. Judy then expe-riences Mary as a threatening and abandoning object instead of as a person whom she loves. By attacking and controlling Mary, Judy inhibits the stimulation of the internal bad object representation. She can then reunite with her internal good objects and return to a more stable sense of self. In this later state, she is able to once again merge with Mary during the honeymoon phase.

Batterers With Narcissistic Personality Disorder

In contrast to the individual with BPO, for narcissistic individuals, the self and object representations are fused, forming an omnipotent, grandiose unit (Freed, 1984; Masterson, 1981). This is hypothesized as occurring as a result of fixation during the symbiotic phase of development. During this phase, the infant is in a narcissistic, omnipotent state of oneness with the mother and perceives himself or herself as magically controlling the environment (Mahler, Pine, & Bergman, 1975). If there are serious traumas or disappointments during this time, there is a failure to move beyond this state into the development of healthy, adaptive narcissism. As a consequence, the individual remains narcissistically invested in himself or herself and unable to tolerate the real world and the needs of others. In an attempt to defend against reality and remain linked with the omnipotent object, the person remains stuck in a state of infantile narcissism and grandiosity (Masterson, 1981).

Freed (1984) describes how as a result of narcissistic or perfectionistic demands being placed on the child by the parents, the child experiences extreme frustration, and there is a fusion between the self and object representations. She notes:

> The child reassumes the special, perfect grandiose stance expected of it; underneath however, there is a pool of aggression, emptiness, punitiveness, harshness, humiliation, shame, depression, and victimization. The self must be denied and becomes fragmented as it fears abandonment by the parents unless it conforms. Aggression is, therefore, directed toward the pursuit of perfection, power, acceptance, beauty, and the avoidance of depression. Reality gets distorted to serve and protect the self. Aggression is further used to force others to justify their goals, and if they fail to do so they are devalued and not tolerated. (Freed, 1984, p. 398)

Self psychology postulates that there are two poles of development, the grandiose self and the idealized parent image, that are critical components in the development of healthy versus pathological narcissism. During development, infantile omnipotence and grandiosity are transformed into initiative, independence, self-confidence, pride, worthiness, and goal directedness. At the same time, through the incorporation of and identification with the idealized parental image, the child develops a capacity for self-soothing and internalizes a feeling of safety, as well as ideals and values. As a consequence of traumatic experiences or disappointments along either pole, there may be a failure of development, resulting in a defective self-structure rather than a coherent stable self (Freed, 1984; Wastell, 1992).

The primary characteristics of narcissistic personality disorder include

- grandiose self-importance
- hypersensitivity to criticism
- lack of empathy
- blame of others interpersonal exploitation need for power and success
- feelings of envy
- fragile self-esteem
- sense of entitlement (American Psychiatric Association, 1987; Rosen, 1991)

For individuals with a narcissistic personality disorder, maintenance of self-esteem is dependent on the admiration of others or merger with an idealized self-object (Rosen, 1991). In self psychology terms, narcissistic individuals seek out mirroring and idealizing self-objects in order to maintain their self-esteem and self-cohesion. According to Kohut (1972), any loss of control over the mirroring self-object or unavailability of the omnipotent self-object results in intense narcissistic rage. Narcissistic rage differs from normal aggression in that the individual will use any means to right a wrong, undo a hurt, or obtain revenge (Kohut, 1972). Thus, for individuals predisposed towards battering, the experience of a narcissistic wound may lead to the use of violence in an attempt to raise their self-esteem (Rosen, 1991). For example, if when Sue comes home her partner is on the phone and does not shift her attention to Sue, this lack of attention may be experienced as a failure in the self-object function. This failure threatens Sue's grandiose, omnipotent self-structure and reactivates the original trauma. The inability to control the mirroring function of her partner results in feelings of powerlessness and worthlessness. Sue then attempts to replace her feelings of impotence with omnipotence and grandiosity through the use of violence as a means to exert power and control over the self-object her partner.

For lesbians the mirroring or idealizing function of the self-object may be heightened as a result of being in a relationship with a partner of the same sex. In addition, feelings of jealousy and envy, which are common in battering, may also be intensified in lesbian couples. In the relatively closed system of the lesbian community, friends are not implicitly distinct from potential lovers. Consequently, a woman may feel jealous if she perceives that another woman is becoming close with her lover. Moreover, she may be envious because of potential competition with her partner for the sexual attentions of others (Berzon, 1988). Although conflicts regarding jealousy and envy are common in lesbian relationships, for the lesbian batterer with a narcissistic disorder these issues can result in increased threats to her self-esteem. In contrast for batterers with a borderline character structure, fear of abandonment may be intensified.

Treatment Implications

Although individuals with BPO and narcissistic personality disorder may both use violence as a way to restore their sense of self, the underlying dynamics differ. There is a vast body of literature on the treatment of borderline and narcissistic personality disorders. Different theorists have proposed different clinical models for both BPO and narcissistic personality disorder on the basis of their own particular theoretical orientation and developmental perspective. For instance, in the treatment of BPO, self psychologists emphasize empathic, supportive therapy in which the therapist provides a soothing and containing self-object function for the client (Waster, 1992). In contrast, object-relations theorists tend to emphasize the importance of a clear and consistent treatment frame and the use of interpretation and confrontation.

A thorough discussion of these various treatment approaches is beyond the scope of this chapter. However, it is important to note that although there may be some overlap, individuals with narcissistic character structures differ in significant ways from those with BPO. For instance, for batterers with BPO, salient areas of treatment include limited tolerance of affect, lack of impulse control, the use of defenses such as splitting and projection, and fear of abandonment. In contrast, treatment goals for batterers with narcissistic personality disorder include increasing capacity for empathy, decreasing hypersensitivity to criticism, and increasing tolerance for, and the ability to cope with, feelings of powerlessness and envy. In addition, the defensive use of omnipotence and entitlement must be gently confronted and gradually replaced by the development of self-worth and self-confidence that is independent of others. For those batterers who were victims of childhood abuse, the trauma they experienced must be internally integrated for them to develop an integrated self-identity and the capacity for appropriate relationships with others (Herman et al., 1989).

For lesbians with BPO, the development of a cohesive sense of self may be facilitated by addressing issues related to internalized homophobia and misogyny. In addition, clinicians working with lesbians should be knowledgeable of and sensitive to dynamics in lesbian relationships that may compound some of the difficulties (i.e., merger/autonomy)that are inherent in BPO.

When working with any lesbian batterer, the interrelationship between factors specific to the lesbian community and feelings of envy, powerlessness, and worthlessness must be assessed and addressed. For example, the clinician must be knowledgeable about the impact of both internal and external homophobia, as well as misogyny. In addition, he or she must be aware of how feelings of envy and jealousy may be heightened for lesbian batterers with narcissistic personality traits.

Although the above are some general treatment considerations, one must keep in mind that there are numerous individual differences among batterers who may share a common diagnosis. Although diagnostic categories can provide clinicians with a useful framework for organizing developmental differences and various symptomatology, an individual is *not* merely a diagnosis. Consequently, therapeutic interventions must be tailored to address each batterer's unique internal structure and interpersonal dynamics.

Furthermore, the impact of sociocultural factors must be considered. For instance, stress often results from a lack of social, psychological, and economic resources—leading to feelings of inadequacy and powerlessness. It is important to note that although such stressors do not cause violence, violent behavior is often used as an attempt to regain a sense of power and control. These issues are particularly salient for lesbians and gays, who as a result of homophobia are faced with discrimination, social isolation, and a general lack of available and accessible resources.

Traditionally, group therapy programs, which often include cognitive-behavioral strategies and psychoeducational techniques, have been the predominant form of treatment for batterers. For group treatment to be effective with lesbian batterers, groups must be designed to address cultural issues, such as the impact of homophobia, that are specific to lesbians (Zemsky, 1989). Regardless of the batterer's gender or sexual orientation, therapeutic interventions that address his or her internal deficits and accompanying defensive structure are essential. For some batterers, individual treatment may be most effective in conjunction with group treatment whereas for others individual therapy may follow group treatment. Although not every batterer will be able to benefit from such a treatment format for those that do, recidivism rates may be greatly reduced.

Conclusion

To acknowledge lesbian battering challenges optional ways of conceptualizing and addressing domestic violence. There has been a tendency within the domestic violence movement to focus on patriarchal values and sociocultural institutions while excluding the importance of personality variables. Although women, as well as men, internalize an ideology of domination and subordination, gender-based sociopolitical theories of domestic violence cannot adequately explain why lesbian battering occurs at rates comparable to that of heterosexual battering.

Studies have shown that regardless of sexual orientation, personality characteristics play a significant role in the perpetration of domestic violence. Although battering by both men and women has been linked to feelings of powerlessness, low self-esteem, and fear of abandonment, men and women tend to internally experience and deal with these struggles in different ways. Further research is needed to determine the extent to which factors such as child abuse, misogyny, and internalized homophobia influence lesbian battering.

For the lesbian community, lesbian battering is a painful reality that shatters a utopian vision of relationships and community. However, it is an issue that cannot be ignored at the expense of women's physical and emotional well-being. Furthermore, only by addressing violence in all relationships can we move toward the creation of a violence-free, egalitarian society.

This chapter has identified and hopefully illuminated some of the dynamics and treatment issues involved in lesbian battering. In order to improve our understanding of domestic violence and provide effective treatment, we must continue to pursue critical thinking and research regarding the role of personality dynamics, and the relationship between these dynamics and other variables.

REFERENCES

American Psychiatric Association. (1987). *Diagnostic and statistical manual of mental disorders* (3rd ed.-rev.). Washington, DC: Author.

Barnett, 0. W., & Hamberger, L. K. (1992). The assessment of maritally violent men on the California Psychological Inventory. *Violence and Victims, 7,* 15–28.

Berzon, B. (1988). *Permanent partners: Building gay and lesbian relationships that last.* New York: Plume.

Brand, P. A., & Kidd, A. H. (1986). Frequency of physical aggression in heterosexual and female homosexual dyads. *Psychological Reports, 59,* 1307–1313.

Burch, B. (1986). Psychotherapy and the dynamics of merger in lesbian couples. In T. S. Stein & C. J. Cohen (Eds.), *Contemporary perspectives on psychotherapy with lesbians and gay men* (pp. 57–72). New York: Plenum Medical Book.

Ceaser, P. L. (1988). Exposure to violence in the families of origin among wife-abusers and maritally non-violent men. *Violence and Victims, 3,* 49–63.

Chodorow, N. (1978). *The reproduction of mothering: Psychoanalysis and the sociology of gender* Berkeley: University of California Press.

Coleman, V. E. (1991). Violence in lesbian couples: A between groups comparison. (Doctoral dissertation, California School of Professional Psychology—Los Angeles, 1990). *Dissertation Abstracts International, 51,* 5634B.

Dilalla, L.F., & Gottesman, I. I. (1991). Biological and genetic contributors to violence—Widom's untold tale. *Psychological Bulletin, 109,* 125–129.

Dobash, R. E., & Dobash, R. P. (1978). Wives: The "appropriate" victims of marital violence. *Victimology: An International Journal, 2,* 426–442.

Dutton, D. G. (1988). Profiling of wife assaulters: Preliminary evidence for a trimodal analysis. *Violence and Victims, 3,* 5–30.

Eagle, M. N. (1984). *Recent developments in psychoanalysis.* New York: McGraw-Hill.

Edleson, J., Eisikovits, Z., & Gut E.(1985).Men who batter women: A critical review of the evidence. *Journal of Family Issues, 6,* 229–247.

Elise, D. (1986). Lesbian couples: The implications of sex differences in separation and individuation. *Psychotherapy, 23,* 305–3 1 0.

Flournoy, P. S., & Wilson, G. L. (1991). Assessment of MMPI profiles of male batterers. *Violence and Victims, 6,* 309–320.

Freed, A. 0. (1984). Differentiating between borderline and narcissistic personalities. *Social Casework, 65,* 395–404.

Gamache, E. (1991). Domination and control: The social context of dating violence. In B. Levy (Ed.), *Dating violence: Young women in danger* (pp. 69–83). Seattle: The Seal Press.

Gardner, R. (1989). Method of conflict resolution and characteristics of abuse and victimization in heterosexual, lesbian, and gay male couples (Doctoral dissertation, University of Georgia, 1988). *Dissertation Abstracts International, 50,* 746B.

Gelles, R. J. (1974). *The violent home: A study of physical aggression between husbands and wives.* Beverly Hills: Sage Publications.

Gelles, R. J., & Straus, M. A. (1979). Determinants of violence in the family: Toward a theory of integration. In W. R. Burr, R. Hill, F. I. Nye, & K. Reiss (Eds.), *Contemporary theories about the family (Vol.* 1, pp. 549–581). New York: The Free Press.

Goldstein, E. G. (I 990). *Borderline disorders: Clinical models and techniques.* New York: The Guilford Press.

Gondolf, E. W. (1988). Who are those guys? Toward a behavioral typology of batterers. *Violence and Victims, 3,* 187–203.

Hamberger, L. K., & Hastings, J. E. (1986). Personality correlates of men who abuse their partners: A cross-validation study. *Journal of Family Violence, 1,* 323–341.

Hamberger, L. K., & Hastings, J. E. (1988). Characteristics of male spouse abusers consistent with personality disorders. *Hospital and Community Psychiatry, 39,* 763–770.

Hastings, J. E., & Hamberger, L. K. (1988). Personality characteristics of spouse abusers: A controlled comparison. *Violence and Victims, 3,* 31–48.

Herman, J. L. (1992). *Trauma and recovery: The aftermath of violence—from domestic abuse to political terror.* New York: Basic Books.

Herman, J. L., Perry, J. C., & van der Kolk, B. A. (1989). Childhood trauma in borderline personality disorder. *American Journal of Psychiatry, 146,* 490–495.

Kelly, C. E., & Warshafsky, L. (1987). *Partner abuse in gay male and lesbian couples.* Unpublished manuscript.

Kemberg, 0. F. (1984). *Severe personality disorders: Psychotherapeutic strategies.* New Haven: Yale University Press.

Kohut H. (1972). Thoughts on narcissism and narcissistic rage. *The Psychoanalytic Study of the Child, 2 7,* 360–400.

Kohut H. (1977). *The restoration of the self.* New York: International Universities Press.

Krestan, J., & Bepko, C. (1980). The problem of fusion in the lesbian relationship. *Family Process, 19,* 277–289.

Landecker, H. (1992). The role of childhood sexual trauma in the etiology of borderline personality disorder: Considerations for diagnosis and treatment. *Psychotherapy, 29,* 234–242.

Leeder, E. (1988). Enmeshed in pain: Counseling the lesbian battering couple. *Women and Therapy, 7,* 81–99.

Lie, G., Schilit, R., Bush, J., Montagne, M., & Reyes, L. (1991). Lesbians in currently aggressive relationships: How frequently do they report aggressive past relationships? *Violence and Victims, 6,* 121–135.

Lobel, K. (1986). *Naming the violence: Speaking out about lesbian battering.* Seattle, WA: Seal Press.

Mahler, M., Pine, F., & Bergman, A., (1975). *The psychological birth of the human infant: Symbiosis and individuation.* New York: Basic Books.

Masterson, J. F. (1981). *The narcissistic and borderline disorders.* New York: Brunner/Mazel.

Mungas, D. (1988). Psychometric correlates of episodic violent behavior: A multidimensional neuropsychological approach. *British Journal of Psychiatry, 152,* 180–197.

Ogdon, T. H. (1979). On projective identification. *International Journal of psychoanalysis, 60,* 357–373.

Renzetti, C. M. (1988). Violence in lesbian relationships: A preliminary analysis of causal factors. *Journal of Interpersonal Violence, 3,* 381–399.

Renzetti, C. M. (1992). *Violent betrayal: Partner abuse in lesbian relationships.* Newbury Park, CA: Sage Publications.

Rosen, I. (1991). Self-esteem as a factor in social and domestic violence. *British Journal of Psychiatry, 158,* 18–23.

Rosenbaum, A., & O'Leary, D. K. (1981). Marital violence: Characteristics of abusive couples. *Journal of Consulting and Clinical Psychology, 49,* 63–71.

Schilit, R., & Lie, G. (1990). Substance use as a correlate of violence in intimate lesbian relationships. *Journal of Homosexuality, 19,* 51–65.

Straus, M. A. (1979). Measuring intrafamily conflict and violence: The Conflict Tactics (CT) *Scales. Journal of Marriage and the Family, 41,* 75–88.

Straus, M. A., & Gelles, R. J. (1986). Societal change and change in family violence from 1975–1985: As revealed by two national surveys. *Journal of Marriage and the Family, 48,* 465–479.

Straus, M. A., Gelles, R. J., & Steinmetz, S. K. (1980). *Behind closed doors: Violence in the American family.* New York: Anchor Books.

Walker, L. E. (1979). *The battered woman.* New York: Harper and Row.

Walker, L. E. (1984). *The battered woman syndrome.* New York: Springer.

Wastell, C. A. (1992). Self psychology and the etiology of borderline personality disorder. *Psychotherapy, 29,* 225–233.

Weidman, A. (1986). Family therapy with violent couples. *Social Casework, 67,* 211–218.

Weller, M. P. (1986). Medical concepts in psychopathy and violence. *Medicine, Science, and the Law, 26,* 131–143.

Wolberg, A. R. (1982). *Psychoanalytic psychotherapy of borderline patient.* New York: Thieme-Stratton.

Wolf, E. S. (1 988). *Treating the self: Elements of clinical self psychology.* New York: Guilford Press.

Zemsky, B. (1989). Lesbian battering: Considerations for intervention. In P. Elliott (Ed.) *Confronting lesbian battering: A manual for the battered women's movement.* Minnesota Coalition for Battered Women.

5

Head-Injured Males

A Population at Risk for Relationship Aggression?

William J. Warnken
Alan Rosenbaum
Kenneth E. Fletcher
Steven K. Hoge
Steven A. Adelman

Relationship aggression continues to affect large segments of the married and dating populations. Increased awareness of the magnitude of the problem has led to increased efforts to understand its etiology. Numerous paradigms have been invoked to explain male-to-female relationship aggression. Indeed, such aggression has been attributed to marital dysfunction, defective self-esteem, exposure to aggressive models in the family of origin, poor impulse control, alcohol and drug use, stress, low frustration tolerance, lack of assertiveness, and dependency. In addition to these intrapersonal and interpersonal variables, it has become clear that sociocultural and political factors must also be included in any comprehensive explanatory model (Adams, 1984).

Unlike some areas of psychological inquiry, research in relationship aggression, or battering, has political and legal ramifications. The issue of court-mandated batterer treatment offers a case in point. How the court conceptualizes battering often determines the decision regarding the type of treatment ordered. Research studies examining the contributions of the intracouple dynamics, alcohol and drugs, psychopathology, and physiology are rightfully viewed with concern because of their potential use in a "diminished capacity" defense. Legal issues aside, such factors readily lend themselves to efforts by batterers to disavow responsibility for their aggression and to efforts by victims to justify remaining in abusive relationships. Unfortunately, these legitimate concerns have served to constrict empirical and theoretical inquiry into multivariate models regarding the etiology of battering, which may include physiological factors.

Biological variables, especially the neurological and neuroendocrine, are increasingly viewed as important factors in aggression. The association between neurological dysfunction, head injury, and aggression in other domains has been documented (Detre, Kupfer, & Taub, 1975; Lewis et al., 1988; Lewis, Pincus, Feldman, Jackson, & Bard, 1986) and the possibility that it is also a factor in relationship aggression merits attention. In this article, we will examine existing research and present some new data that suggest that there is an association between head injury and relationship aggression. We also will propose a mechanism whereby these factors might be integrated into an etiological model.

Just as marital aggression affects large segments of the population, so too does traumatic head injury. Bond (1986) has estimated that annually there are more than 7 million occurrences of head injury in the United States, and that at least half a million of these injuries are serious enough to require hospital attention. Like relationship aggression, head injury is most likely to occur in men who are in their 20s and 30s. It is often related to alcohol use, divorce, and lower socioeconomic status (Levin, Benton, & Grossman, 1982; Rimel & Jane, 1983).

These commonalties may be more than coincidental. Since the brain is the organ responsible for cognition, emotion, behavior, and memory, it stands to reason that damage to the brain profoundly affects interpersonal relationships and functioning.

Remarkably, our knowledge of brain function and the mechanisms by which damage to the brain translates to behavioral changes is rudimentary. This may be attributed in large part to its complexity. As Coen (1985) has stated: "The brain is quite simply the most complicated object known" (p. IX). Consider, for example, that the brain is thought to consist of about 100 billion individual neurons. Each of these neurons in turn may synapse with large numbers of other neurons. According to Thompson (1985), "the number of possible different synaptic connections among neurons in a single human brain is larger than the total number of atomic particles that make up the known universe" (p. 3). Although we do not yet know how much, or how little, injury is necessary to alter behavior, or which injury sites produce specific behavioral or emotional changes, it is clear that head injuries produce behavioral change and that reduced impulse control and aggression are two of those most commonly reported.

Numerous studies have assessed the relationship between brain injury and aggression in both animals and humans. They generally have concluded that there is an association between neurological impairment and violent behavior (Detre et al., 1975). Lewis and colleagues (1986, 1988) have assessed traumatic brain injury in two samples of violent criminals and reported that almost 80% had a positive history for head injury. Episodic dyscontrol syndrome, characterized by recurrent outbursts of rage and violence, is known to occur subsequent to a traumatic brain insult (Elliott, 1982). In fact, both verbal aggression and physical aggression are among the most frequently mentioned sequelae of traumatic head injury (Lundholm, Jepsen, & Thornval, 1975; Panting & Merry, 1972; Shukla, Cook, Mukherjee, Godwin, & Miller, 1987; Wood, 1984).

Several mechanisms have been proposed to explain the association between head injury and aggression. Lishman (1978) proposed that aggression resulted from reduced impulse control consequent to frontal lobe damage. The orbitofrontal cortex exercises control over lower limbic centers. Damage to the orbitofrontal cortex has been associated with aggression (Price, Daffner, Stowe, & Mesulam, 1990). Studies employing electroencephalography and positron emission tomography have identified abnormalities in the frontal and temporal areas of the brains of violent individuals (Bach-y-Rita, Lion, Climent, & Ervin, 1971; Volkow & Tancredi, 1987). Similarly, neuropsychological evaluations of violent offenders yield results that are consistent with frontotemporal dysfunction, especially in the left hemisphere (Yeudall, 1978; Yeudall & Flor-Henry, 1975). Although there is substantial evidence implicating frontotemporal lobe damage in aggression, the evidence is not necessarily conclusive (Raine & Scerbo, 1991). Of concern is the high base rate of frontotemporal injuries in brain-injured populations, because of the location of these brain areas and the types of accidents that typically cause such brain injuries (e.g., auto accidents in which the forehead hits against the windshield, steering wheel, or dashboard) (Adams, Mitchell, Graham, & Doyle, 1977).

Injury to brain centers responsible for self-regulation may directly reduce an individual's ability to control aggressive impulses and modulate aggressive behavior. Alternatively, changes in personality wrought by head injury might impact negatively on intimate relationships and indirectly lead to relationship aggression. Jennett (1972) has identified personality change as the most consistent sequela to a severe head injury. A number of researchers have interviewed the relatives of severely brain-injured patients and have reported changes in temperament and personality to be the most disturbing (Fahy, Irving, & Millac, 1967; Thomsen, 1974) and the most persistent (Miller & Stern, 1965; Panting & Merry, 1972). These changes have included increased irritability, temper, lack of spontaneity, increased restlessness, enhanced dependency, and immaturity. Wives of brain-injured men also note subtle behavioral differences that persist even after the husband has recovered from the injury and made a good social readjustment. In many circumstances, wives see their husbands as changed in some way and avow "that he is not the man she married" (Jennett, 1972, p. 444).

Not surprisingly, such personality changes place a burden on the marital relationship. Rosenbaum and Najenson (1976) studied a sample of severely brain-injured men, many of whom suffered from a penetrating injury. They reported that the wives of these men recounted drastic life changes, including greater reductions in sexual activity, child-care responsibilities, leisure-time activities, and social life, as compared to the reports by wives of paraplegics. Brain-injured husbands also were more likely to be described as self-oriented and dependent.

Penetrating brain injuries of the severity described by Rosenbaum and Najenson (1976) are usually lethal and, therefore, uncommon in a surviving head-injured population. However, it is unclear whether these types and severities of injury are necessary to produce such changes. In fact, there is some indication that the level of stress in the caretaking relatives of head-injured patients may not be related directly to the severity of the disability incurred by the patient (McKinlay, Brooks, Bond, Martinage, & Marshall, 1981). Brooks and McKinlay (1983) reported that the severity of injury did not correlate with the type of personality change, although there was a relationship between severity of injury and the occurrence of personality change.

The foregoing narrative suggests that head-injured males may be at increased risk for both marital difficulties and generalized aggression, and thus at increased risk for marital aggression. There is some research that supports this hypothesis. Elliott (1982) has reported that episodic dyscontrol syndrome was responsible for instances of intrafamilial violence in 17% of the cases studied. Rosenbaum and Hoge (1989) have found that 61% of the male batterers in their sample had histories of significant head injury. Additionally, Rosenbaum and colleagues (1994) have conducted a controlled study in which the assessments of head injury were made by a physician "blind" to group membership and found that a history of significant head injury produced a sixfold increase in the risk of marital aggression. The latter two studies have established that batterers are significantly more likely than nonbatterers to have had a serious head injury. The subsequent issue is whether head-injured males are more likely to be batterers. At present, there is no published research addressing this question.

The present study was designed to examine whether or not head-injured men were more likely to be aggressive in their heterosexual relationships than were other men. To assess this, a group of head-injured men was compared to a group of orthopedically injured men, utilizing standardized measures of relationship aggression. It was expected that because of the association between head trauma and aggressive behavior in other domains, the head-injured men would exhibit more violent behavior (including relationship aggression) after injury than their orthopedic counterparts.

Head injury may directly affect the brain centers responsible for impulse control. Since head injury often produces changes in behavior and emotion that negatively affect interpersonal functioning, it is possible that such personality and behavioral changes may cause a deterioration of an intimate relationship, thereby increasing the probability of aggression. The latter may interact with a reduced ability by the man to control impulses and thus further contribute to the occurrence of aggression. Specifically, it was expected that head-injured men would experience greater changes in behaviors that would adversely affect their relationships. Consequently, head-injured and orthopedically injured men also were compared regarding relationship satisfaction, as well as other factors known to be associated with relationship discord and/or aggression. These variables included: poor self-esteem (Geffner, Jordan, Hicks, & Cook, 1985; Goldstein & Rosenbaum, 1985); poor impulse control (Barnett & Hamberger, 1992); presence of depression (Hastings & Hamberger, 1988); presence of alcohol and substance abuse (Fitch & Papantonio, 1983; Kantor & Straus, 1986); communication deficits (LaViolette, Barnett, & Miller, 1984; Maiuro, Cahn, & Vitaliano, 1986; Rosenbaum & O'Leary, 1981); and status differences between husbands and wives (Hornung, McCullough, & Sugimoto, 1981).

METHOD

Subjects

Names of potential subjects were generated through a computer search of hospital medical records (both emergency room and inpatient) using age (at least 20), sex (male), and primary ICD-9 diagnosis as screening factors. This procedure generated a list of 982 men who had sustained either an orthopedic or head injury between 1985 and 1990.

Once potential subjects were identified by a computer search, each medical record was examined to determine whether an individual had any preexisting or current medical condition that would preclude him from participation in the study. Specifically, exclusion criteria for the orthopedic group included (a) past history of head injury; (b) any secondary diagnosis that included loss of consciousness, hypotensive reaction, or hypoxic reaction; (c) other factors that could affect neurological functioning, including histories of seizure disorders, hyperactivity, and attention deficit disorder (ADD). Similarly, a subject was excluded from the head-injured group if he had a head injury prior to the one identified by the medical record search, or if he had a prior condition that produced a loss of consciousness, hypotensive reaction, or hypoxic reaction. Additionally, individuals with histories of seizure disorders, hyperactivity, or ADD were excluded.

Information packets soliciting participation in the research and containing the questionnaires were mailed to all potential subjects meeting these criteria. A stamped return postcard stating that it should be mailed only if subjects wanted no further contact with the researchers was also included in the packet. A substantial number of potential subjects could not be contacted because of inactive or inaccurate addresses, death, or unresponsiveness (to the mailing and follow-up telephone calls). We were able to contact 235 men (who either responded to our mailing or telephone calls or sent back the refusal card). Of these, 130 (58%) completed the forms and returned them to us.

In addition to meeting the criteria described above, subjects for both groups were required to be involved in a heterosexual relationship and to have had no prior history of marital aggression. Many of the 130 men who completed the questionnaire were excluded on the basis of at least one of these criteria. The final sample included 33 head-injured men and 42 orthopedically injured men.

Although not a prerequisite for the subject's participation, the female partners were also asked to complete questionnaires similar to those of the men. Completed questionnaires were received from 65 women: 27 were partners of head-injured men and 38 were partners of orthopedically injured men.

Measures

The measures that were mailed to men and their current partners were

The Conflict Tactics Scale (CTS; Straus, 1979). This scale has been widely used to assess marital aggression. It lists 18 behaviors ranging from calm discussion to the use of weapons to resolve conflict and asks respondents to indicate how often during the past year this behavior was employed with respect to disagreements with their female partners. Its validity and reliability have been demonstrated (Hornung et al., 1981; Jouriles & O'Leary, 1985). Additionally, the subjects were asked to report the dates of the first occurrence of marital violence, if appropriate.

The Locke-Wallace Short Marital Adjustment Test (SMAT; Locke & Wallace, 1959). This test consists of 15 items that have been shown to discriminate between harmonious and discordant marriages (O'Leary & Turkewitz, 1978). This test asks the respondents to rate their marital satisfaction on a scale ranging from "very unhappy" to "perfectly happy" and to report their degree of agreement with their spouses regarding issues related to marital satisfaction such as sexual relations, friends, ways of dealing with in-laws, expressions of affection, management of finances, and leisure activities, and to indicate whether they would marry the same person again, given the opportunity to do so.

Hollingshead Four Factor Index—Modified (Hollingshead, 1975). This index classifies vocations and assigns them scores based on salaries and skill levels. These scores range from 1–10. Individuals who have lower socioeconomic status jobs receive lower scores than do those who are paid more or are in jobs that require more training. This modification of the original is consistent with other researchers' use of the instrument (C. Edelbrock, personal communication, February 1992).

Each candidate also completed a brief questionnaire regarding demographic information and pre- and post-injury changes in the relationship and in the man's behavior. These questions were selected from a similar questionnaire that assessed changes in behaviors after the head injury (Williams, 1987) and asked the respondents to answer "true" or "false" to a variety of questions concerning changes in behaviors, feelings, and observations about how their lives have changed in other areas since the injury.

The female partners of the men in the study also completed the CTS, the SMAT, and a questionnaire similar to the one filled out by their male partners.

Procedure

Questionnaire packets were mailed to potential subjects identified by the computer search on the basis of diagnosis, sex, and age, and to their female partners. The packet included a letter explaining the study and offering to pay $10 per person ($20 per couple if both participated) for completing the questionnaires. Also included were informed consent forms, a statement explaining the certificate of confidentiality, data questionnaires for both the man and his female partner, and a postcard, which they were instructed to return only if they did not wish any further contact.

All subjects, except those who returned the refusal cards, were contacted by telephone within 3 weeks of the mailing for purposes of encouraging participation and answering any queries. Subjects received payment by mail when the completed forms were returned.

RESULTS

Men in the head-injured group had an average age of 38.9 years compared to 39.3 years for the orthopedically injured men. There were no between-group differences in age $(t = .12, df = 73, ns)$. There were, however, significant differences between groups in education and occupation, with head-injured subjects having less education $(t = -2.48, df = 72, p < .05)$ and lower status jobs $(t = -3.17, df = 67, p < .01)$.

The female partners of the men in the two groups did not differ in educational attainment. The partners of the head-injured men indicated an average of 12.73 years of education, versus 13.50 years for partners of the orthopedically injured men $(t = -1.43, df = 60, ns)$. The two groups of female partners also reported similar levels of employment $(t = .04, df = 63, ns)$.

Consistent with the concept of status incompatibility, which has been proposed as a factor in marital aggression (Hornung et al., 1981), the difference in job status between male subjects and their female partners was significantly greater in the head-injured group than in the orthopedically injured group $(t = 2.21, df = 58, p < .05)$, with the female partners having higher status jobs than the males.

Relationship aggression was assessed using the CTS (Straus, 1979). Subjects were classified as either aggressive or nonaggressive using a cutoff score of 11 (subjects who reported the occurrence of behaviors that were 11 or greater were classified as aggressive). A 2×2 (group by dichotomized CTS score) chi-square test was performed. No significant between-group differences were obtained based on either the men's self-report $(\chi^2 = .64, df = 1, ns)$ or their female partner's report $(\chi^2 = 1.43, df = 1, ns)$.

Although head-injured subjects and their female partners did not report more relationship aggression on the CTS, a number of questions included in the survey did produce responses that indicated increased post-injury generalized aggression and hostility for the head-injured men, as compared to the orthopedically injured men. Specifically, men in the head-injured group were more likely than the men in the orthopedically injured group to report postinjury problems with losing their temper $(p < .01)$, reductions in self-control $(p < .01)$, getting into more trouble $(p < .01)$, arguing more with others $(p < .05)$ and with their female partners $(p < .01)$, and yelling more $(p < .01)$. These findings were corroborated by the female partners, who additionally reported that their head-injured partners were more likely to "smash" things $(p < .05)$ and to get into more fights $(p < .01)$. These data are reported in Table 5.1.

The female partners of the head-injured men reported that their partners were more verbally abusive after the injury, compared with the reports of the partners of the orthopedically injured men $(\chi^2 [1, N = 64] = 10.25, p < .001)$. It should be noted that this finding was not corroborated by the men's self-report of their own verbal aggressiveness after the injury.

The men in the head-injured group experienced other attitude and behavioral changes that negatively impacted the quality of their relationship with their partners. The men in the head-injured group, for example, reported lower self-esteem than did the men in the orthopedically injured group, on the basis of their responses to two "true or false" questions pertaining to post-injury self-esteem levels. The head-injured men were more likely to report that they "felt like less of a man" $(p < .05)$. They also reported feeling more dependent $(p < .01)$ on their female partners since their injury than did the orthopedically injured men.

The partners of the head-injured men were more likely than the partners of the orthopedically injured men to believe that their male partners felt less positive about themselves $(p < .01)$ and were more dependent upon their female partners $(p < .01)$ since the injury. The female partners of the head-injured men also thought that their male partners believed that they (female partners) felt less positively about them since their injury $(p < .01)$ than did the female partners of the orthopedically injured men (See Table 5.2).

Greater communication difficulties were more common among the head-injured men after the injury than among the orthopedically injured men. The head-injured men had more difficulty in

TABLE 5.1   Chi-square Analyses of Behavioral Data

| | | Head Injuries | | Ortho-Injuries | | |
		True	False	True	False	χ^2 (df=1)
Increase loss of temper	(M)	15	18	6	36	7.42**
	(F)	18	9	4	34	19.78***
Increase of loss of control	(M)	13	20	4	38	7.77**
	(F)	12	14	5	33	7.01**
Increase in fights	(M)	3	30	0	42	1.96
	(F)	7	20	0	37	8.27**
Smashed things more	(M)	4	29	2	40	.54
	(F)	5	22	0	37	FET*
Got into trouble more	(M)	7	26	0	42	FET**
	(F)	8	19	0	37	FET***
Argues more (with others)	(M)	11	22	4	38	5.14*
	(F)	15	12	4	34	13.37***
Argues more (with spouse)	(M)	10	22	2	39	7.28**
	(F)	10	17	3	35	6.65**
Yells more	(M)	14	19	4	38	9.23**
	(F)	15	12	3	34	15.12***

M = male responses   F = female responses
FET = Fisher's exact test   *<.05   **<.01   ***<.001

their ability to express themselves verbally ($\chi^2[1, N = 75] = 15.58, p < .001$) and greater difficulty expressing their feelings (Fisher's exact test, $p = .001$). The female partners of the head-injured men agreed that their partners had greater difficulty expressing themselves verbally ($\chi^2[1, N = 65] = 9.19, p < .01$) and expressing their feelings (Fisher's exact test, $p = .002$) after the injury than did the partners of the orthopedically injured men.

Alcohol use frequently is associated with an increased risk for aggressive behavior. The men in the two groups were comparable in their report of current alcohol usage ($\chi^2[3, N = 75] = 4.03, ns$), past use of alcohol ($\chi^2[3, N = 75] = 7.35, ns$), and frequency of intoxication ($\chi^2[3, N = 74] = 3. 97, ns$). However, the head-injured men reported that their drinking had increased more than the men in the orthopedically injured group subsequent to their injuries ($\chi^2[1, N = 75] = 4.17, p < .05$), and that they were more vulnerable ("got drunk on less") to the effects of alcohol since the injury (Fisher's exact test, $p = .018$). The partners of the head-injured men also reported that the head-injured men were more vulnerable to the effects of alcohol (Fisher's exact test, $p = .001$) since the injury, but did not report that their male partners drank more than the orthopedically injured men since the injury.

TABLE 5.2   Chi-square Analyses of Self-Esteem Data

| | | Head Injuries | | Ortho-Injuries | | |
		True	False	True	False	χ^2 (df=1)
Feels less good about self	(F)	12	21	8	34	2.02
	(F)	14	12	6	32	8.71**
Partner feels less	(M)	7	25	3	38	FET
good about men	(F)	11	15	3	35	8.77**
Feels like less of a man	(M)	9	24	2	40	5.79*
	(F)	9	18	4	34	3.81
Feels less desirable	(M)	8	25	3	36	.63
	(F)	6	21	5	33	FET
More dependent on partner	(M)	13	19	4	37	7.94**
	(F)	13	14	6	32	6.50**

M = male responses   F = female responses
FET = Fisher's exact test   *<.05   **<.01   ***<.001

When the men in the two groups were compared regarding changes in temperament and mood since the injury, the head-injured men reported that they were more depressed ($\chi^2[1, N = 75]$ = 4.88, $p < .05$) and angry ($\chi^2[1, N = 75]$ = 12.42, $p < .001$) than the orthopedically injured men. The female partners of the head-injured men also reported the head-injured men to be more depressed ($\chi^2[1, N = 65]$ = 13.37, $p < .001$) and angry ($\chi^2[1, N = 65]$ = 15.38, $p < .001$) than did the female partners of the men in the orthopedically injured group. The men in the two groups could not be differentiated either by self ($\chi^2[1, N = 73]$ = 2.90, *ns*) or partner ($\chi^2[1, N = 64]$ = 1.06, *ns*) report regarding an increase in anxiety since their accidents.

Relationship satisfaction was assessed via the SMAT (Locke & Wallace, 1959). Subjects and their partners were classified as either satisfied or dissatisfied based on a cutoff score of 100. A 2 × 2 (group by dichotomized Locke-Wallace score) chi-square was computed. There were no between-group differences based on the self-report of the men ($\chi^2[1, N = 75]$ = 3.62, *ns*).

The female partners of the head-injured men, on the other hand, reported less relationship satisfaction since the injury than did the partners of the orthopedically injured men ($\chi^2[1, N = 64]$ = 9.23, $p < .01$). In fact, only 48% of the partners of the head-injured men reported marital satisfaction, versus 86% of the female partners of the orthopedically injured men.

When the men in the two groups and their female partners were asked about changes in their relationship after the injury, the head-injured men ($\chi^2[1, N = 72]$ = 4.53, $p < .05$) and their partners (Fisher's exact test, $p = .01$) reported that they had experienced more negative changes in their relationships than the men in the orthopedically injured group and their female partners. Among the head-injured men, 29% stated that their relationship with their partner had changed for the worse, compared to only 7% of the orthopedically injured men. Similarly, 35% of the female partners of the head-injured men reported experiencing negative changes in their relationships, compared to only 5% among the female partners of the orthopedically injured men.

Two of the negative relationship changes that differentiated the head-injured men from the orthopedically injured men after the injury concerned physical and emotional intimacy. Chi-square (group by intimacy) analyses indicated that more of the head-injured men (Fisher's exact test, $p = .001$) and their female partners (Fisher's exact test, $p = .041$) reported not feeling as close to each other. Additionally, more head-injured men reported that their sex lives had deteriorated ("gotten worse") since their accident than did their orthopedically injured counterparts ($\chi^2[1, N = 75] = 6.41$, $p < .05$).

Discussion

Interpersonal aggression is a commonly reported sequela to a traumatic head injury. The most typical causes of closed head injury, for example, motor vehicle accidents, often produce injuries in the areas of the brain responsible for impulse control, thus leaving the victim with reduced capacity for exercising self-control. Other common sequelae of closed head injury include memory deficits and communication and speech problems, all of which may contribute to increased frustration and reduced ability to function autonomously. Head-injury victims frequently suffer vocational difficulties, including performance decrements, increased absences, and sometimes loss of employment. These can contribute to the financial problems of the victim and his family and further reduce the victim's self-esteem. Changes in personality and emotion, for example, short temper and increased anger, can put additional strain on intimate relationships. Many of these consequences are readily recognized as risk factors for relationship aggression, suggesting that head-injured males may be at increased risk for battering.

Several recent studies of male batterers support the conclusion that batterers are significantly more likely than nonbatterers to have suffered a closed head injury (Rosenbaum et al., 1994; Rosenbaum & Hoge, 1989), further fueling speculation that head-injured males may be at risk for battering. The results of the present investigation provide equivocal support for this hypothesis.

On one hand, analysis of the CTS data, which specifically assessed relationship aggression, failed to show differences between head-injured men and orthopedically injured men. Thus, one cannot conclude that there was more postinjury relationship aggression among head-injured men. This was true based upon both male self-report data and the report of the female partners.

On the other hand, there were between-group differences on many of the variables that might be expected to co-occur with battering. Specifically, head-injured males and their female partners were more likely to show status incompatibility, with the female partner having the higher status job. Head-injured males reported more postinjury problems with their temper, reduced self-control, more arguments both with the female partner and with others, and more yelling. These post-injury changes were confirmed by their female partners, who also felt that the head-injured men were more likely to "smash" things and to get into more frequent fights. The female partners of head-injured subjects also reported more postinjury verbal abuse by the men. Head-injured men, by both self and partner report, also had lower self-esteem, more difficulty communicating, and more difficulty expressing themselves verbally.

Alcohol use has been implicated as a factor in aggression, in general, and although it is unclear whether alcohol plays a central role in the production of marital aggression, it is clearly an important factor for many batterers (Kantor & Straus, 1986). Head-injured men more often than orthopedically injured men reported that they were drinking more since the injury and also that they were more affected by the alcohol (i.e., got drunk on fewer drinks). The latter, but not the former, finding was corroborated by partner report.

Finally, more of the head-injured men and their female partners reported that the men were more depressed and angry since
the injury, that they had experienced more negative changes in
the relationship, and that they felt less close to each other. Many
of these findings are congruent with those reported by
Rosenbaum and Najenson (1976) for men who had received
penetrating head injuries.

How can one account for the fact that, despite the presence of
differences between head-injured men and their orthopedically
injured counterparts on a host of risk factors for relationship
aggression, between-group differences were not obtained on the
CTS? One possible explanation concerns the amount of time
elapsed between the injury and the assessment. The mean number
of years between the injury and the assessment was 2.85 years for
the head-injured men and 5.12 years for the orthopedically
injured men. Although these means are not significantly different,
it is possible that given a longer time frame, more aggression
could occur among the head-injured men, especially considering
the numbers of risk factors and negative relationship changes that
were reported.

A second possibility concerns the average age of the sample.
Relationship aggression is most common in younger couples, with
the majority of batterers being in their 20s and 30s. Our sample is
at the upper end of that range, with a mean of almost 40 years.
Replication with younger samples might produce different results.

A third possibility concerns the most serious limitation of the
investigation, namely, the significant self-selection bias in the sample. Of the almost 1,000 potential subjects identified by the search
of medical records, only 235 were able to be contacted. Of these,
only 130 returned the questionnaires and only 75 were complete
and met inclusion criteria. It is likely that trauma victims who
made the most successful recoveries are overrepresented in the
sample. Individuals experiencing aggression problems may have
been disinclined to participate in the study. This is especially likely considering the stigma attached to battering.

Although the results of this investigation fail to support the hypothesized association between head injury and relationship aggression, the ancillary findings concerning the presence of relationship dysfunction and known risk factors associated with battering in the head-injured group alert us to the possibility that this population may be at increased risk for relationship aggression. Since the present investigation suffers from several methodological weaknesses, additional research examining this phenomenon is necessary before this hypothesis can be rejected.

Head injury is not the only biological factor associated with aggression. There is a substantial body of both animal and human research that suggests that reductions in levels of neurotransmitters, especially serotonin, may relate to aggression (Brown & Linnoila, 1990). Much of the research conducted to date supports a relationship between reduced concentrations of 5-hydroxyindoleacetic acid in the cerebrospinal fluid (an indirect marker of serotonin levels) and aggression, irritability, and hostility (Coccaro et al., 1989). The relationship between serotonergic activity and relationship aggression is the subject of research currently being conducted by the second author.

The possibility that physiological factors may play some role in the facilitation of aggression in relationships suggests that biological interventions have the potential to augment our current psychoeducational intervention strategies. If head-injured men are indeed at risk for battering, preventive strategies may be usefully incorporated into post-head-injury rehabilitation protocols, thus circumventing the development of relationship aggression.

Finally, there is the possibility that a link between physiological factors, such as head injury, and battering may be interpreted as a threat to models that focus on power, control, and sociocultural influences. However, just as the majority of men, irrespective of their sociocultural background and upbringing, are not batterers, neither are all head-injured individuals aggressive. Head injury may be one of a number of factors (e.g., alcohol and drug use) that reduce an individual's ability to control aggressive impulses and thereby increase the probability of an aggressive response under certain circumstances, for example when an individual is angered or feels provoked. Since such circumstances are influenced by learning history, cognitive schema, and sociocultural influences, biological factors may have heuristic value for understanding the complex dynamics of battering. However, they do not absolve the batterer of responsibility for his behavior.

Acknowledgment.
This research was supported by NIMH Grant #MH44812 to Alan Rosenbaum, PhD.

REFERENCES

Adams, D. (1984). *Stages of anti-sexist awareness and change for men who batter.* Paper presented at the annual convention of the American Psychological Association, Toronto, Canada.

Adams, J. H., Mitchell, D. E., Graham, D. I., & Doyle, D. (1977). Diffuse brain damage of immediate impact type. *Brain, 100,* 489–502.

Bach-y-Rita, G., Lion, J. R., Climent, C. E., & Ervin, F. (1971). Episodic dyscontrol: A study of 139 violent patients. *American Journal of Psychiatry, 127,* 1473–1478.

Barnett, O. W., & Hamberger, L. K. (1992). The assessment of maritally violent men on the California Psychology Inventory. *Violence and Victims, 7,* 15–27.

Bond, M. R. (1986). Neurobehavioral sequelae of closed head injury. In I. Grant & K. M. Adams (Eds.), *Neuropsychological assessment of neuropsychiatric disorders* (pp. 347–373). New York: Oxford University Press.

Brooks, D. N., & McKinlay, W. (1983). Personality and behavior change after severe blunt head injury—A relative's view. *Journal of Neurology, Neurosurgery and Psychiatry, 46,* 336–344.

Brown, G. L., & Linnoila, M. I. (1990). CSF serotonin metabolite (5-HIAA) studies in depression, impulsivity, and violence. *Journal of Clinical Psychiatry, 51,* 31–41.

Coccaro, E. F., Siever, K. J., Klar, H. M., Maurer, G., Cochrane, K., Cooper, T. B., Mohs, R. C., & Davis, K. L. (1989). Serotonergic studies in patients with affective and personality disorders: Correlates with suicidal and impulsive aggressive behavior. *Archives of General Psychiatry, 46,* 587–599.

Coen, C. W. (1985). *Functions of the brain.* New York: Oxford University Press.

Detre, T., Kupfer, D. J., & Taub, J. D. (1975). The nosology of violence. In W. S. Fields & W. H. Sweet (Eds.), *Neural bases of violence and aggression* (pp. 294–316). St. Louis: Green.

Elliott, F. A. (1982). Clinical approaches to family violence: Biological contributions to family violence. *Family Therapy Collections, 3,* 35–58.

Fahy, T. J., Irving, J. H., & Millac, P. (1967). Severe head injuries: A six year follow-up. *Lancet, 2,* 475–479.

Fitch, F. J., & Papantonio, M. (1983). Men who batter: Some pertinent characteristics. *Journal of Nervous and Mental Disease, 171,* 190–192.

Geffner, R. A., Jordan, K., Hicks, D., & Cook, S. K. (1985, August). In R. A. Geffner (Chair), *Violent couples: Current research and new directions for family psychologists.* Symposium conducted at the Annual Meeting of the American Psychological Association, Los Angeles.

Goldstein, D., & Rosenbaum, A. (1985). An evaluation of self-esteem in maritally violent men. *Family Relations, 34,* 425–428.

Hastings, J. E., & Hamberger, L. K. (1988). Personality characteristics of spouse abusers: A controlled comparison. *Violence and Victims, 3,* 31–48.

Hollingshead, A. B. (1975). *Four factor index of social status.* Unpublished manuscript, Yale University, New Haven, CT.

Hornung, C. A., McCullough, B. C., & Sugimoto, T. (1981). Status relationships in marriage: Risk factors in spouse abuse. *Journal of Marriage and the Family, 43,* 675–692.

Jennett, B. (1972). Late effects of head injuries. In M. Critchley, B. Jennett, & J. O'Leary (Eds.), *Scientific foundations of neurology* (pp. 441–451). London: Heinemann.

Jouriles, E. N., & O'Leary, K. D. (1985). Interspousal reliability of reports of marital violence. *Journal of Consulting and Clinical Psychology, 53,* 419–421.

Kantor, G. K., & Straus, M. A. (1986, April). *The drunken bum theory of wife beating.* Paper presented at the National Alcoholism Forum Conference on Alcohol and the Family, San Francisco.

LaViolette, A. D., Barnett, O. W., & Miller, C. L. (1984). *A classification of wife abusers of the BEM sex-role inventory.* Paper presented at the Second Conference on Research on Domestic Violence, Durham, NH.

Levin, H. S., Benton, A. L., & Grossman, R. G. (1982). *Neurobehavioral consequences of closed head injury.* New York: Oxford University Press.

Lewis, D. O., Pincus, J., Bard, B., Richardson, E., Prichep, L., Feldman, M., &

Yeager, C. (1988). Neuropsychiatric, psychoeducational, and family characteristics of 14 juveniles condemned to death in the United States. *American Journal of Psychiatry, 145,* 584–589.

Lewis, D. O., Pincus, J. H., Feldman, M., Jackson, L., & Bard, B. (1986). Psychiatric, neurological, and psychoeducational characteristics of 15 death row inmates in the United States. *American Journal of Psychiatry, 143,* 838–845.

Lishman, W. A. (1978). *Organic psychiatry.* Oxford: Blackwell.

Locke, H. J., & Wallace, K. M. (1959). Short marital adjustment and prediction tests: Their reliability and validity. *Marriage and Family Living, 21,* 251–255.

Lundholm, J., Jepsen, B. N., & Thornval, G. (1975). The late neurological, psychological and social aspects of severe traumatic coma. *Scandinavian Journal of Rehabilitation Medicine, 7,* 97–100.

Maiuro, R., Cahn, T., & Vitaliano, P. (1986). Assertiveness deficits and hostility in domestically violent men. *Violence and Victims, 1,* 279–289.

McKinlay, W. W., Brooks, D. N., Bond, M. R., Martinage, D. P., & Marshall, M. M. (1981). The short-term outcome of severe blunt head injury, as reported by the relatives of the injured persons. *Journal of Neurology, Neurosurgery and Psychiatry, 44,* 285–293.

Miller, H., & Stern, G. (1965). The long-term prognosis of severe head injury. *Lancet, 1,* 225–229.

O'Leary, K. D., & Turkewitz, H. (1978). Methodological errors in marital and child treatment research. *Journal of Consulting and Clinical Psychology, 46,* 747–758.

Panting, A., & Merry, P. (1972). The long-term rehabilitation of severe head injuries with particular reference to the need for social and medical support for the patient's family. *Rehabilitation, 38,* 33–37.

Price, B. H., Daffner, K. R., Stowe, R. M., & Mesulam, M. M. (1990). The comportmental learning disabilities of early frontal lobe damage. *Brain, 113,* 1383–1393.

Raine, A., & Scerbo, A. (1991). Biological theories of violence. In J. S. Milner (Ed.), *Neuropsychology of aggression* (pp. 1–25). Boston: Kluwer Academic.

Rimel, R. W., & Jane, J. A. (1983). Characteristics of the head injury patient. In M. Rosenthal, E. R. Griffith, M. R. Bond, & J. D. Miller (Eds.), *Rehabilitation of the head injured adult.* Philadelphia: F. A. Davis.

Rosenbaum, A., & Hoge, S. K. (1989). Head injury and marital aggression. *American Journal of Psychiatry, 146,* 1048–1051.

Rosenbaum, A., Hoge, S. K., Adelman, S., Warnken, W. J., Fletcher, K., & Kane, R. (1994). Head injury in partner-abusive men. *Journal of Consulting and Clinical Psychology, 62* (6), 1187–1193.

Rosenbaum, A., & O'Leary, K. D. (1981). Marital violence: Characteristics of abusive couples. *Journal of Consulting and Clinical Psychology, 41*, 63–71.

Rosenbaum, M., & Najenson, T. (1976). Changes in life patterns and symptoms of low mood as reported by wives of severely brain-injured soldiers. *Journal of Consulting and Clinical Psychology, 44*, 881–888.

Shukla, S., Cook, B. L., Mukherjee, S., Godwin, G., & Miller, M. G. (1987). Mania following head trauma. *American Journal of Psychiatry, 144*, 93–95.

Straus, M. A. (1979). Measuring intrafamily conflict and violence: The Conflict Tactics (CT) Scale. *Journal of Marriage and the Family, 41*, 75–88.

Thompson, R. F. (1985). *The brain: An introduction to neuroscience.* New York: W. H. Freeman.

Thomsen, I. V. (1974). The patient with severe head injury and his family. *Scandinavian Journal of Rehabilitation Medicine, 6*, 180–183.

Volkow, N. D., & Tancredi, L. (1987). Neural substrates of violent behavior: A preliminary study with positron emission tomography. *British Journal of Psychiatry, 151*, 668–673.

Williams, D. (1987). *An exploration study of the subjective perceptions of closed head injury.* Unpublished doctoral dissertation, Antioch/New England Graduate School, Keene, NH.

Wood, R. L. (1984). Behavior disorders following severe brain injury: Their presentation and psychological management. In N. Brooks (Ed.), *Closed head injury* (pp. 195–215). New York: Oxford University Press.

Yeudall, L. T. (1978). *The neuropsychology of aggression.* Clarence Hinks Memorial Lecture, University of Western Ontario, London, Ontario.

Yeudall, L. T., & Flor-Henry, P. (1975). *Lateralized neuropsychological impairments in depression and criminal psychopathy.* Paper presented at the Conference of the Psychiatric Association of Alberta, Calgary, Canada.

6

Patriarchy and Wife Assault

The Ecological Fallacy

Donald G. Dutton

During the late 1970s a number of single-factor explanations for male assaultiveness toward women were proffered. These included sociobiology (Daly, Wilson, & Weghorst, 1982), psychiatric disorders (Faulk, 1974), and patriarchy (Dobash & Dobash, 1979; Yllo, 1988). Sociobiological explanations were based on the premise that the primary motive of men is to maximize their contribution to the gene pool (Daly & Wilson, 1988). By extension, male rage over sexual threat was viewed by sociobiologists as having "survival value" (Wilson, 1975). Dutton (1988) argued that socially learned notions of anger and violence added explanatory power to the individual variation in behavioral responses to sexual threat and that the source of rage in intimate relationships was not kinship per se, but ego identity factors naturally confounded with kinship. In elaborating the ontogeny of rage behaviors, Dutton (1994) was able to account for individual variation among males in response to a common stimulus, which sociobiology could not do.

Dutton (1988) also argued that psychiatric "explanations" were not actually explanatory since they did no more than link assaultiveness to existing diagnostic categories without etiological explication (see also Pantony & Caplan, 1991). They also frequently overlooked important contextual factors that contributed to assault causation.

Dutton (1988) argued that no single-factor explanation for wife assault sufficiently elucidated the available data and proposed instead a nested ecological theory examining interactive effects of the broader culture (macrosystem), the subculture (exosystem), the family (microsystem), and individually learned characteristics (ontogeny). Attempts to explain individual behavior solely through aggregate social categories have been termed the *ecological fallacy* by Dooley and Catalano (1984). By this they mean that more within-category individual variation exists than the categorical view acknowledges. Below I shall examine several data sources that demonstrate, in my opinion, the ecological fallacy in feminist views of wife assault. In general, the purpose of this chapter is to examine several new data sources in the area of wife assault that are problematic from a feminist perspective. The argument is made that feminism needs to give greater weight to male individual difference variables and how these variables might interact with socialization.

Feminist Views of Woman Assault

According to Bograd (1988), there are some defining features that are central to most feminist analyses of the phenomenon of woman assault. All feminist researchers, clinicians, and activists address a primary question: "Why do men beat their wives?" This question "directs attention to the physical violence occurring in heterosexual relationships" (p. 13) and distinguishes feminists from others who ask, "What psychopathology leads to violence?" or "Why are people involved in violent interactions in families?" Since the phrasing of a question always directs attention toward something and away from something else, the causes of "beating of wives" must perforce reside in "men." As Bograd goes on to write: "Feminists seek to understand why *men in general* use physical force against their partners and what functions this serves for a society in a given historical context" (p. 13). When an ideological focus decides to question the use of violence by "men in general," it will necessarily emphasize broader social forces that differentiate men from women and will deemphasize differences among men. This orientation has manifested itself in a feminist focus on patriarchy, male concern for power (Walker, 1989), and macrosystem factors, rather than on ontogenetic factors that might differentiate one male from another.[1]

Bograd describes several dimensions of analysis that are common to feminist perspectives on wife abuse. These include the explanatory utility of the constructs of gender and power and the analysis of the family as a historically situated social institution.

From the first of these analytic dimensions, wife assault is seen to be a systematic form of domination and social control of women by men. All men can potentially use violence as a powerful means of subordinating women. Men as a class benefit from how women's lives are restricted because of their fear of violence. Wife abuse reinforces women's dependence and enables all men to exert authority and control. The reality of domination at the societal level is the most crucial factor contributing to, and maintaining, wife abuse at the individual level. In other words, the maintenance of patriarchy and patriarchal institutions is the main contributor to wife assault. Wife assault is mainly "normal" violence committed, not by madmen who are unlike other men, but by men who believe that patriarchy is their right, that marriage gives them unrestricted control over their wife, and that violence is an acceptable means of establishing this control (Dobash & Dobash, 1979, p. 57).[2] The claim from a feminist analytical perspective, therefore, is twofold: that society is patriarchal and that the use of violence to maintain male domination is accepted. As Dobash and Dobash (1979) put it, "Men who assault their wives are actually living up to cultural prescriptions that are cherished in Western society— aggressiveness, male dominance and female subordination—and they are using physical force as a means to enforce that dominance" (p. 24).

This feminist view implicates patriarchy as the major cause of wife assault rather than an inducement that interacts with other causes. Bograd (1988) claims that "the reality of domination at the social level is the most crucial factor contributing to and maintaining wife abuse at the personal level" (p. 14). As Smith (1990) puts it, "any theoretical work that claims to be feminist probably must sooner or later seriously address the concept of patriarchy" (p. 257). Domination of women is viewed, from the feminist perspective, as a cultural prescription, and violence against women as a means to that end. This emphasis on the cultural is reflected in the feminist distrust of psychological causes of male violence (Goldner, Penn, Sheinberg, & Walker, 1990) as potentially "exonerative" of male violence and by the lack of empirical studies of putative interactive causes conducted within a feminist perspective. Indeed, much feminist analysis (Bograd, 1988) argues that an emphasis on psychopathology in explaining wife assault is misguided because wife assault results from "normal psychological and behavioral patterns of most men" (p. 17) and that "trait theories tend to excuse the abusive man through reference to alcohol abuse or poor childhood histories" (p. 17).[3]

The result of the feminist analysis of wife assault has been the acknowledgment of the powerful and complex role of social factors in creating the context in which violence occurs. As Walker (1989) points out, feminist analysis puts research findings back into the context from which they were deracinated by scientific abstraction. For example, as Rosewater (1987) has shown, Minnesota Multiphasic Personality Inventory scores on battered women were typically read out of context and misdiagnosed. Post hoc scores that indicated anger, anxiety, and confusion in response to battering were misinterpreted as indicating a preexisting "personality problem" such as paranoia. Similarly, Dutton and Painter (1981) and Dutton (1983) demonstrated how contextual features of battering formed paradoxical attachments that made leaving a battering relationship difficult and led to erroneous interpretations of battered women as masochistic. Further, Browne and Williams (1989) demonstrated how female-perpetrated homicide decreased when criminal justice system resources became more available to women in abusive relationships, a pattern that was distinct from male homicide.

Browne (1992) also showed conclusively that the Conflict Tactics Scale (CTS) (Straus, 1979) could not be used to compare male and female violence. Every assessed act on the CTS is different when performed by a man. The reasons have to do with the greater force of the action, the relative strength of perpetrator and target, the point of impact of the action, and the target's ability to resist or escape. Browne's argument shows the dangers of removing context from the measurement process and leads to a reassessment of using the CTS to compare male with female violence out of context. As the above examples demonstrate, feminist focus on the context of violence has led to some valuable reassessments of research findings.

Despite these impressive accomplishments, however, it is difficult to reconcile other key research findings with the feminist approach. Indeed, close reading of feminist theory and research on the problem of wife assault reveals what Kuhn (1965) referred to as a paradigm. Paradigms direct research but also serve to deflect critical analysis of the paradigms' own central tenets through diverting attention from contradictory data. A worldview develops (Janis, 1982) whereby attention is redirected from potential contradictory information. The predominant, almost exclusive, focus of feminist research on cultural determinants has left psychopathology unexamined and not systematically connected to cultural markers. The result has been an analysis characterized by broad statements about male privilege and male dominance in the face of clear evidence for heterogeneous male behaviors in intimate relationships. Hence, feminist researchers draw conclusions about "men's violent reactions to challenges to their authority, honor and self-esteem" based on studies of male criminals

(Dobash, Dobash, Wilson, & Daly, 1992, p. 75) or talk of the "androcentric need for power" (Walker 1989, p. 696), while simultaneously rejecting equally simplistic stereotyping of women.

Direct Tests of Patriarchy

Some direct empirical tests of patriarchal norms on assaultiveness have been reported in the literature. Yllo and Straus (1990) attempted a quantitative analysis of the relationship between patriarchy and wife assault by assessing the latter with the CTS and the former with (U.S.) state-by-state economic, educational, political, and legal indicators of the structural inequality of women. A composite Status of Women Index resulted, with Alaska having the highest status (70) and Louisiana and Alabama the lowest (28). An ideological component of patriarchy was also assessed: the degree to which state residents believed that husbands should be dominant in family decision making (patriarchal norms).

A curvilinear (U-shaped) relationship was found between structural indicators and wife assault rates, with the lowest and highest status of women states having the highest rates of severe wife assault. Structural indicators and patriarchal norms had a correlation of near zero. Patriarchal norms were related to wife assault in that states with the most male-dominant norms had double the wife assault rate of states with more egalitarian norms.

Yllo and Straus explain their data by arguing that high violence rates in states where the status of women is highest are caused by a breakdown of patriarchal norms and males resorting to violence to bolster threatened masculinity. This explanation assumes that the structural changes came initially and that family patriarchal norms lagged behind, thus generating conflict. However, no independent evidence to support this temporal relationship is presented.

Since low status states also have high rates of wife assault, the authors explain this as due to "greater force being necessary to keep women in their place and because women in these states have fewer alternatives to violent marriage" (p. 394). It is not clear why "greater force" in such states is necessary because alternatives to marriage are few.

The implication of this study is that in low status states, women are more likely to be trapped in abusive marriages, whereas in high status states, women feel freer to leave, but males are more threatened. However, trapping women in marriage through lessened opportunity should produce higher violence frequency scores within violent couples, but not necessarily higher incidence scores. That is, it accounts for why women could not leave an abusive marriage, but still does not supply a motive for male violence.

A final problem is that structural inequality and patriarchal norms were not associated in this study. In fact, the reported correlation was "near zero" (op. cit. p. 395). This result is problematic for feminist analysis because patriarchal structure is frequently implicated as a cause of assaultiveness, yet still must operate through the ideology of individual men. The "slippage" between structural patriarchy and individual male ideology is an example of the *ecological fallacy* (Dooley & Catalano, 1984) described above. Broad macrosystem features cannot strongly predict the thoughts or actions of individuals "nested" under the system. Moderating variables from the exosystem, from the microsystem, and from the individuals'own developmental history are necessary to complete the predictive picture. With the Yllo and Straus (1990) study, a safer conclusion is that societal power imbalances are associated with more violence against women. The mechanism whereby that violence is generated is unknown.

Smith (1990) also conducted a test of patriarchy by asking 604 Toronto women to guess their male partner's response to a series of questions about "patriarchal beliefs" and then correlating these responses with socioeconomic factors and, finally, with that woman's responses to the CTS measure of wife assault. Through this method, Smith argued that he was assessing "patriarchal ideology" and that this measure, in combination with sociodemographic factors, could predict wife assault. However, the responses that these women supplied for their male partners described a very nonpatriarchal group of males, with the majority disagree-ing with the patriarchal statements of the measure in all cases except one, that "sometimes it's important for a man to show his partner that he's the head of the house." One conclusion that could be drawn from these attitudinal data (as with Yllo & Straus's data) is that the patriarchal structure of North American society has a weak effect on the "patriarchal ideology" of most men. Smith does not draw this conclusion. As Smith puts it, "When all the socioeconomic risk markers and indexes of patriar-chal ideology were combined in a single model assessing the extent to which these variables predicted wife beating, the com-bination of husband's educational attainment, patriarchal beliefs and patriarchal attitudes parsimoniously explained 20% of the variance in wife beating" (p. 268).

It seems to me that such a conclusion clearly accentuates the paradigmatic aspect of current family violence research. A pre-dictive study using women's CTS self-reports on husband vio-lence by Dutton, Saunders, Starzomski, and Bartholomew (1994) found that a brief (16-item) assessment of the husbands' anger and identity problems also explained 20% of wife assault (and 50% of domination) reported by one sample of battered wives. In other words, some brief measures of psychological factors have as much or greater predictive weight than the attitudinal and sociodemographic assessments of "patriarchal ideology" report-ed by Smith (1990).

Cross-Cultural Studies

If feminist analysis is correct, we should expect greater violence directed toward women in more patriarchal cultures. However, this prediction is not supported. Sorenson and Telles (1991), for example, found that a Mexican-born Hispanic sample ($n = 705$) reported wife assault rates that were about half the rate reported by a sample ($n = 1,149$) of non-Hispanic whites, despite Hispanic cultures being gen-erally more patriarchal than American culture (Davis, 1992).

Campbell (1992) reports that "there is not a simple linear correlation between female status and rates of wife assault" (p. 19). Female status is not a single variable. Levinson (1989) found family-related female status (economic, decision-making, and divorce restrictions) to be more predictive of wife beating than societal level variables (control of premarital sexual behavior, place of residence, property inheritance). The exception to this finding was female economic work groups, whose presence correlated negatively with wife assault incidence.

Campbell (1985, 1992) also points out that feminist notions that male sexual jealousy is an expression of a cultural norm that women are male property are not supported by cross-cultural studies of jealousy and wife assault. Except in extreme cases, jealousy varies widely between cultures and appears unrelated to variations in wife assault incidence.

Acceptance of Violence

A survey by Stark and McEvoy (1970) found that 24% of men and 17% of women approved of a man slapping his wife "under appropriate circumstances." Hence, only a minority of men and women approved of a man slapping his wife under any circumstances. Viewed from another perspective, the survey result tells us that the majority believe slapping is never appropriate. Second, the wording of the question was ambiguous. The phrase "appropriate circumstances" loads the question; we do not know what egregious transgressions may be conjured up by respondents as necessary before a slap is appropriate. Also, the question tells us nothing about the degree of violence that is acceptable. Although 25% of men may approve of slapping a wife, fewer may approve of punching or kicking a wife and still fewer may approve of beating or battering a wife.

Also, many men who have been convicted of wife assault do not generally believe that what they did was acceptable (Dutton, 1986; Dutton & Hemphill, 1992). Instead they feel guilty, deny and minimize the violence, and try to exculpate themselves in the manner of one whose actions are unacceptable to oneself. The feminist view would lead us to expect the opposite: that no guilt and evasion would follow from violence used in the course of justifiable control and domination. As Bugenthal, Kahn, Andrews, and Head (1972) demonstrated in a survey study, violence is considered acceptable when it is in the service of an accepted social objective.

Survey Findings

If patriarchy is the main factor contributing to wife assault, then a large percentage, if not the majority, of men raised in a patriarchal system should exhibit assaultiveness. If the number of men who are assaultive diminishes, then noncultural factors figure more prominently in assault causation. In five major surveys of incidence of wife assault implemented to date, the vast majority of men are nonassaultive for the duration of their marriage (Kennedy & Dutton, 1989; Schulman, 1979; Straus & Gelles, 1985; Straus, Gelles, & Steinmetz, 1980; Straus & Kantor, 1994).

In surveys conducted by female interviewers of female respondents using strategies to maximize disclosure, only one of eight couples reported acts from the Severe Violence subscale of the CTS occurring at any time in their marriage, and only 27.8% reported any kind of violence (including pushes and slaps) occurring at any time in their marriage (Straus et al., 1980, p. 43). Furthermore, this finding does not seem to be related to a desire on the female respondents' part to image manage through underreporting. Dutton and Hemphill (1992) found that women's reports of violence committed against them were unrelated to social desirability factors (unlike male perpetrators).

This result is hard to explain if one considers patriarchy as the main cause of wife assault. If social license determines violent behavior, we would expect a majority of men to be violent, but only a minority actually are. Also, as the violence becomes more extreme, the size of this minority group of perpetrators shrinks.

The type of actions that might be called "wife beating" occur in only about 11% of marriages at any time during the marriage. A clearer picture of the incidence of violence in marriage is that serious assaults do not occur in 90% of marriages, they occur once in another 7%, and they occur repeatedly in about 3% (Kennedy & Dutton, 1989; Straus et al., 1980; Straus & Gelles, 1985). What kind of causal weight does patriarchy have if 90% of the men raised under it are nonassaultive? Do these men all dominate their wives using nonviolent means? To answer this question we must examine the literature on dyadic family power and violence.

Power and Violence

Sociopolitical power is not positively related to wife assault in males. Working-class males have higher wife assault rates than middle-class males (Straus et al., 1980), and black males have higher wife assault rates than white males (Julian & McKenry, 1993).

Dyadic family power is nonlinearly related to use of violence. Coleman and Straus (1986) found that there was no main effect of power on violence. The highest rates of "minor" violence (male to female, female to male) were found in female-dominant couples, followed by male-dominant, and violence was mitigated by attitudes toward power sharing. Hence, couples who agreed to a gender-dominant arrangement were less violent than those who disagreed. In that study, a decision-making "final say" measure was made of power. By this measure, male-dominant couples made up only 9.4% of the total and female-dominant made up 7.5%. The more typical power arrangements were "divided power" (54%) and "egalitarian" (29%). The main contributor to marital conflict and violence was lack of consensus about power sharing. Where the couple agreed, both conflict and violence were low, regardless of marital power arrangement. To a feminist perspective, the notion of a male-dominant marriage where both parties agree to that power-sharing arrangement is unacceptable. However, it is not a sufficient cause of violence. When we compare the survey results in the preceding section with the Coleman and Straus results above, we see that 90% of men are nonassaultive and 91% are nondominant. In other words, the large majority of men raised under patriarchal norms are both nonassaultive and nondominant. This perspective is lost when we ask why men in general beat their wives. It is these data that indicate the *ecological fallacy* of feminist approaches to wife assault: that patriarchal structure and male socialization are sufficient to produce dominance and assaultiveness.

Control and Violence

Another tenet of feminist thought is that male violence is part of a wider repertoire of control tactics men use to dominate women. In the literature on "feminist therapy" (Adams, 1988), emphasis is placed on "male control and domination." However, in one of the few studies to examine controlling behaviors and psychological abuse, Kasian and Painter (1992) found that females were more jealous, more verbally abusive, and more controlling than males in a sample of 1,625 dating undergraduates.[4] Use of controlling behaviors and verbal abuse appears to be bidirectional in intimate relationships. If controlling behaviors are bidirectional and feminist therapy seeks to reduce control tactics in men who already feel powerless in intimate relationships, a positive therapeutic outcome is contraindicated.

Feminist definitions of power and status can be an impediment to understanding male assaultiveness because these definitions are based on and often restricted to the sociopolitical. Feminist analysts are acutely aware of the sociopolitical powerlessness of women and have taken important steps to initiate a remedy. However, what defines powerlessness for a politicized woman and what defines it for a nonpoliticized man are not the same.

For a man, sociopolitical comparisons with women or with a woman are irrelevant. What is experienced, especially in intimate relationships, is the power advantage women appear to have in their ability to introspect, analyze, and describe feelings and process. Transference from early relationships in which a female (mother) had apparently unlimited power still affects male assessments of power in adult relationships (Dutton & Ryan, 1992). Hence, assaultive males report feeling powerless in respect to their intimate partners (Dutton & Strachan, 1987). One is reminded of Eric Fromm's definition of sadism as the conversion of feelings of impotence to feelings of omnipotence. Although batterers may appear powerful in terms of their physical or sociopolitical resources, they are distinctly impotent in terms of their psychic and emotional resources, even to the point of depending on their female partner to maintain their sense of identity (Dutton, 1994).[5] I do not suggest by this that we should excuse or exonerate batterers. However, to view men's violence simply as a defense of sociopolitical power is erroneous. Only a minority of batterers are misogynisitic (Dutton & Browning, 1986), and few are violent to nonintimate women; a much larger group experiences extreme anger about intimacy. If there is a politic at work, it exists primarily in the microsystem of the dyad.

Homosexual Relationships

The prevalence of violence in homosexual relationships, which also appear to go through abuse cycles, is hard to explain in terms of men dominating women (Bologna, Waterman, & Dawson, 1987; Island & Letellier, 1991; Lie & Gentlewarrior, 1991; Renzetti, 1992). Bologna and colleagues (1987) surveyed 70 homosexual male and female college students about incidence of violence in the most recent relationship. Lesbian relationships were significantly more violent than gay relationships (56% vs. 25%). Lie and Gentlewarrior (1991) surveyed 1,099 lesbians, finding that 52% had been a victim of violence by their female partner, 52% said they had used violence against their female partner, and 30% said they had used violence against a nonviolent female partner. Finally, Lie, Schilit, Bush, Montague, and Reyes (1991) documented, in a survey of 350 lesbians (who had had prior lesbian and heterosexual relationships), that reported rates of verbal, physical, and sexual abuse were all significantly higher in their prior lesbian relationships than in their prior heterosexual relationships: 56.8% had been sexually victimized by a female, 45% had experienced physical aggression, and 64.5% experienced physical/emotional aggression. Of this sample of women, 78.2% had been in a prior relationship with a man. Reports of violence victimization by men were all lower than reports of violence victimization in prior relationships with women (sexual victimization, 41.9% [vs. 56.8% with women]; physical victimization 32.4% [vs. 45%]; and emotional victimization 55.1% [vs. 64.5%]).

These are two findings that are difficult to accommodate from a feminist perspective: why violence rates are so high in lesbian relationships and why they are higher for past relationships with women than for past relationships with men. Walker (1986) has tried to explain higher rates of violence in lesbian relationships as being due to equality of size and weight, fewer normative restraints on fighting back, and tacit permission to talk about fighting back. However, Coleman and Straus (1986) found that power equalization produced less violence. The focus on fighting back overlooks the fact that a woman initiated the violence in these lesbian couples. It might also be argued that lesbians adopt the values of the dominant patriarchal culture and that a dominance-submissiveness relationship may exist in a lesbian relationship, whereby the "functional male" (i.e., the dominant member) is the abuser. The problem with this argument is that even in heterosexual relationships, as Coleman and Straus showed, a variety of power relations exist. The "functional male" theory maps a stereotype onto lesbian relationships that has no data support. What is important about the data of Lie and her colleagues (1991) is that they assess abuse for past lesbian and heterosexual relationships reported by these women. Hence, each subject becomes, in effect, her own control, and sample selection issues (for comparisons with other groups) are minimized.

Browne (1993) cites Saakvitne and Pearlman (1993) as arguing that lesbians may internalize misogyny and homophobia, which they then project onto their female partners. Lesbian battering is consistent with another view on intimate violence: that intimacy generates dependency, jealousy, and anger, which is sometimes expressed violently (Dutton, 1988; Dutton & Browning, 1986; Dutton et al., 1994). In fact, Renzetti (1992) found the main contributors to lesbian battering in her study to be dependency and jealousy, two psychological factors related to intimacy. These two factors also show up as predictors in heterosexual wife assault studies (Dutton, 1994; Dutton & Painter, 1993). This explanation has the advantage of being parsimonious; it applies to both heterosexual and lesbian battering without needing recourse to separate models of explanation. Separate explanatory models for two types of battering have an added danger when developed from a feminist paradigm: Female violence is "explained away" using psychological notions such as projected misogyny (Saakvitne & Pearlman, 1993), while male violence is refused psychological examination on the grounds of it being potentially exonerative (Goldner et al., 1990). A double standard for explanation results.

Female Violence

The question of why men beat women precludes any notion of female violence, and as Browne (1992) has pointed out, gender comparisons using the CTS can be misleading. The focus of a feminist paradigm is on males as transgressors, and feminists have avoided, with good reason, victim-blaming explanations that locate in women victims the causes of violence performed by males. Given their advantages in strength and power, most males, it is believed, can avoid physical conflict with women under all but the most extenuating circumstances. Nevertheless, research shows that only minor differences exist between male and female aggression (Frodi, Macaulay, & Thome, 1977; Hyde, 1984). In an extensive review of the literature on aggression, Hyde (1984) concluded via a meta-analysis that gender accounts for only 1% of the variance in aggression in college students (and only 7% in children under 6).[6]

Walker (1989) claims that "women usually use violence as a reaction to men's violence against them" (p. 696). However, in Bland and Orn's (1986) study, 73.4% of a sample of 616 women said they were the first to use physical violence. An argument is also made that female violence is a "preemptive strike" designed to terminate an escalating abuse cycle. However, Stets and Straus (1990) compared couples where the violence pattern was male-severe/female-minor, with those where this pattern was reversed. They found the female-severe/male-minor pattern to be significantly (three to six times) more prevalent than the male-severe/female-minor pattern regardless of whether the couple was dating, cohabiting, or married.

With these data, the use of severe violence by females was not in reaction to male violence or as a preemptive strike since the female partner in each couple reported only minor violence from her male partner despite using severe violence herself. Similarly, couples in which only the female was violent were significantly more common (39.4% of dating couples, 26.9% of cohabiting couples, 28.6% of married couples) than couples in which only the male was violent (10.5% of dating couples, 20.7% of cohabiting couples, 23.2% of married couples). Although men may use more multiple aggressive acts during a single incident (Browne, 1993), the data above suggest that in some couples, female violence may be serious and may not be in response to male violence.

Psychopathology

Questions of psychopathology are deemphasized by feminist analysis because such questions might "maintain that violent acts and violent relationships have a psychology" and "once again let batterers off the hook" (Goldner et al., 1990, p. 345) and also because psychopathological analyses imply that only some men who are atypical generate violence against women (Bograd, 1988).

Nevertheless, there is strong evidence that the majority of men who are either court referred or self-referred for wife assault do have diagnosable psychological pathology. In studies of assaultive males, about 80%–90% of both court-referred and self-referred men exhibited diagnosable psychopathology, typically personality disorders (Dutton, 1994; Dutton & Starzomski, 1994; Hamberger & Hastings, 1986, 1989; Hart, Dutton, & Newlove, 1993; Hastings & Hamberger, 1988; Saunders, 1992). Estimates of personality disorder in the general population would be more in the 15%–20% range (Kernberg, 1977; Zimmerman & Coryell, 1989). As violence becomes more severe and chronic, the likelihood of psychopathology in these men approaches 100% (Dutton, 1994; Dutton & Hart, 1992a, 1992b; Hastings & Hamberger, 1988), typically with extreme scores on borderline personality organization BPO, narcissism, antisocial behavior, and aggressive-sadistic personality.

To say that violent batterers are psychopathological neither "lets them off the hook" nor exculpates social forces in shaping their rage. Dutton (1994) has argued that men with severe identity problems and intense dependency on women may seek out aspects of the culture to direct and justify abuse. For example, the primitive defenses of BPO in males, which involve splitting "good objects" from "bad objects" (Mahler, 1971), are reinforced by cultural judgments about female sexuality. Cultures that divide women into "madonnas and whores" provide a sanctioned reinforcement of the object split in the assaultive borderline male. Cultures that socialize men and women to expect the woman to be responsible for relationship outcome provide a rationale for the borderline personality's expectation that his intimate partner should maintain both his ego integrity and euphoric affect. Any dysphoric stalemates that occur are then viewed as her fault. Hence, attachment-derived anger is projected toward the individual woman partner. Through this view, the personality pattern contains emotional demands, which it directs and justifies through drawing on the ambient culture.

Hence, patriarchy does not elicit violence against women in any direct fashion. Rather, it may provide the values and attitudes that personality-disordered men can exploit to justify their abuse of women. This distinction is an important one: It explains why the majority of men remain nonviolent and how they differ in at least one essential and nontautological aspect from violent men.

Walker (1989) describes a "socialized androcentric need for power." However, a need for power, in itself, does not predict violence or even dominance in social relationships. Winter (1973) and McClelland (1975) have demonstrated how power motivation varies from one man to the next and how it translates into a variety of behavioral forms, including stamp collecting and running for public office. It is only when power needs are combined with identity diffusion, so that the intimate other becomes necessary for one's identity integrity, that these needs begin to focus exclusively on that person. In a culture that isolates men emotionally and alienates them from their ability to sense and know their own feelings, dependency on a female who is perceived as a conduit to one's inner self will remain problematic.

Therapy and Policy Implications

Feminist therapists criticize anger-management approaches for focusing on stress reduction, anger management, and coping skills, while not paying enough attention to gender politics (Adams, 1988). At the same time, they criticize insight therapy for focusing on identity deficits to offer labels instead of explanations and for not emphasizing male responsibility for violence and control. I have argued above that patriarchy is another label that does not explain violence. If patriarchy "causes" violence, how can we hold men individually responsible for their violence?

Feminist therapists want to focus on power and control issues and on misogynistic attitudes toward women in what they call resocialization models (Adams, 1988; Gondolf & Russell, 1986). The problem with these models is that the relationship between attitudes and violence is weak (Browning, 1983; Dutton, 1988; Neidig & Friedman, 1984). Furthermore, there is a problem in delivering these models to court-directed men who may resent female power, who exist in a subculture that does not share feminist values, and who resist attempts to decrease their use of control tactics when they already feel a sense of diminished control. Such approaches may develop backlash in clients if they do not address the felt powerlessness that drives control tactics and seek to develop remedial negotiation skills.

My view is that anger and anxiety provide the psychological substratum for control. Males try to control the things they fear, and intimate relationships are a source of great fear (Pollack & Gilligan, 1982). Hence, a complete understanding of anger does not only reflect on outbursts of anger but also on chronic resentments and control of another. It also renders the "case" against "anger control" treatment for assaultive males artificial. It is not an issue of "anger versus control" as Gondolf and Russell (1986) put it; anger and control stem from the same origin: terror of intimacy.

When feminists ask "Why do men beat their wives?" their answer will necessarily exaggerate differences between males and females and minimize differences among males. The categories of study are framed by the question. However, what is required for a more complete analysis is to answer why some but not all men beat their wives. A complete explanation for wife assault must also distinguish men who habitually and severely assault their wives from men who do so sporadically, as response to extreme stressors, and from men (the majority) who remain nonviolent throughout their marriages. This leads necessarily to psychological explanations in order to differentiate these men.

Put in nested ecological terms (Dutton, 1988), distal macrosystem influences such as patriarchal structure, seem to have little effect on rates of individual wife assault; they are poorly related both to individual male patriarchal beliefs and to violence. Exosystem factors, especially subcultural norms for assaultiveness, have a somewhat stronger effect, whereas microsystem and ontogenetic factors seem strongest of all. Powerlessness rather than power seems to be implicated in male use of intimate violence, and intimacy itself rather than gender politics seems to be the most crucial factor in such violence. If we wish to both understand and diminish violence in society, we must resist the temptation to easily classify perpetrators in broad social terms. Our response to violence can be improved by focusing clearly on those psychopathological features that interact with culture in order to ultimately reduce the risk of violence for women.

Notes

[1]To this extent, feminist analysis of wife assault has been almost exclusively sociological and not psychological. Exceptions exist, to be sure. These would include Lenore Walker's (1984) profile of battering husbands, based on descriptions of women in shelters, and Anne Ganley's (1989) attempt to reconcile feminism and social learning theory. Also, Pantony and Caplan (1991) proposed a "delusional dominating personality disorder" as a response to what Caplan saw as sexism in the proposed *DSM-IIIR* category "self-defeating personality disorder," and which could theoretically distinguish men who were generally abusive in intimate relationships from other men (although the authors saw this personality disorder as a response to "rigid masculine socialization"). Despite these exceptions, the focus of feminist analysis has been, as Bograd put it, on the question of "why men *in general* beat their wives." Hence, there is a necessary deemphasis on the possibility of individual differences among men.

[2]It could be argued that from a feminist perspective violence will not necessarily be normal but will only occur when other forms of male control of women have failed. This premise should lead to the prediction that when men have large socially conferred power advantages, they need not be violent. This prediction is not supported by empirical examination (Campbell, 1992; Coleman & Straus, 1985). Feminism ends up arguing both that violence occurs as a "last resort" for domination (when men are otherwise powerless) and when domination is ensured by the social structure (when men are otherwise powerful). In the latter case, the violence is said to occur because there are no sanctions against it, but this "explanation" does not supply a motive for violence.

[3]To be fair to Bograd, she does also say that "wife abuse may be linked to psychopathology in either partner" and that feminism seeks to "connect our psychological analyses with understandings of the patriarchal social

context" (op. cit. p. 17). My point, however, is that feminism has offered no "psychological analysis" because its focus has been on the question of why "men in general use physical force against their partners." Bograd has not, to my mind, seen the implications of her own question. For this reason, her statement about psychopathology reads like an afterthought.
⁴The criticisms that Browne made of the CTS do not apply in this study because reports for each gender were for verbal, not physical, abuse. Although physical "hits" are different when performed by a man against a smaller woman, there is no evidence that verbal abuse has less serious consequences as a function of gender.
⁵It is a paradox of power in dyads that each member can feel powerless vis-à-vis the other. Women, for example, report feeling disempowered by male physical strength, violence potential, and sociopolitical power (French, 1985), whereas men report being disempowered by female emotional access, verbal skills, sexuality, and self-containment as well as by intense unresolved transference issues (Dutton, 1994; Dutton & Strachan, 1987; Goldberg, 1987). No consensus has yet been reached on dyadic power, and "final say" measures such as that used by Coleman and Straus (1986) are limited in that one member may allow the other to make decisions in specific areas, generating an appearance of equality (Huston, 1983).
⁶It is curious why so little interest has developed in reconciling the consistent finding of lab and field studies of aggression that little difference exists that is attributable to gender with the larger gender difference in homicide statistics (e.g., Browne, 1993, and Browne & Williams, 1989, found that of spousal homicide victims, 61% were women and 39% were men). One possibility is that males use extreme violence more when experiencing intimacy-rage (Dutton et al., 1994), which transfers more readily for males during intimacy dissolutions. As Browne and Williams have pointed out, female-perpetrated homicides are more likely to have been responses to prior abuse by their partner.

REFERENCES

Adams, D. (1988). Treatment models of men who batter: A profeminist analysis. In K. Yllo & M. Bograd (Eds.), *Feminist perspectives on wife abuse* (pp. 176–199). Beverly Hills: Sage.

Bland, R., & Orn, H. (1986, March). Family violence and psychiatric disorder. *Canadian Journal of Psychiatry, 31,* 129–137.

Bograd, M. (1988). *Feminist perspectives on wife abuse: An introduction.* In M. Bograd & K. Yllo (Eds.), *Feminist perspectives on wife abuse* (pp. 11–26). Beverly Hills: Sage.

Bologna, M. J., Waterman, C. K., & Dawson, L. J. (1987). *Violence in gay male and lesbian relationships: Implications for practitioners and policy makers.* Paper presented at the Third National Conference of Family Violence Researchers, Durham, NH.

Browne, A. (1992). *Are women as violent as men?* Unpublished manuscript, University of Massachusetts, Worcester, MA.

Browne, A. (1993). Violence against women by male partners: Prevalence, outcomes and policy implications. *American Psychologist, 48,* 1077–1090.

Browne, A., & Williams, K. (1989). Exploring the effect of resource availability and the likelihood of female perpetrated homicides. *Law and Society Review, 23,* 75–94.

Browning, J. J. (1983). *Violence against intimates: Toward a profile of the wife assaulter.* Unpublished doctoral dissertation, Department of Psychology, University of British Columbia, Vancouver.

Bugenthal, M. D., Kahn, R. L., Andrews, F., & Head, K. B. (1972). *Justify violence: Attitudes of American men.* Ann Arbor, MI: ISR.

Campbell, J. (1985). The beating of wives: A cross-cultural perspective. *Victimology, 10,* 174–180.

Campbell, J. (1992). Prevention of wife battering: Insights from cultural analysis. *Response, 80, 14,* 18–24.

Coleman, D. H., & Straus, M. A. (1986). Marital power, conflict, and violence. *Violence and Victims, 1*(2), 141–157.

Daly, M., & Wilson, M. (1988). *Homicide.* New York: Aldine De Gruyter.

Daly, M., Wilson, M., & Weghorst, S. J. (1982). Male sexual jealousy. *Ethology and Sociobiology, 3,* 11–27.

Davis, L. V. (1992). Attitudes toward wife abuse in a cross-cultural context: A comparison of Colombian and American Human Service students. In E. Viano (Ed.), *Intimate violence: Interdisciplinary perspectives* (pp. 229–243). Washington, DC: Hemisphere Publishing.

Dobash, R. E., & Dobash, R. P. (1979). *Violence against wives: A case against the patriarchy.* New York: Free Press.

Dobash, R. E., Dobash, R. P., Wilson, M., & Daly, M. (1992). The myth of sexual symmetry in marital violence. *Social Problems, 39,* 71–91.

Dooley, D. G., & Catalano, R. (1984). The epidemiology of economic stress. *American Journal of Community Psychology, 12,* 387–409.

Dutton, D. G. (1983). *Masochism as an "explanation" for traumatic bonding: An example of the "fundamental attribution error."* Boston: American Orthopsychiatric Association.

Dutton, D. G. (1986). Wife assaulters' explanations for assault: The neutralization of self-punishment. *Canadian Journal of Behavioural Science, 18,* 381–390.

Dutton, D. G. (1988). *The domestic assault of women: Psychological and criminal justice perspectives.* Boston: Allyn & Bacon.

Dutton, D. G. (1994). Behavioral and affective correlates of borderline personality organization in wife assaulters. *International Journal of Law and Psychiatry, 17*(3), 265–279.

Dutton, D. G., & Browning, J. J. (1986). Power struggles and intimacy anxiety as causative factors in wife assault. In G. Russell (Ed.), *Violence in intimate relationships.* Great Neck, NY: PMA Publishing.

Dutton, D. G., & Hart, S. G. (1992a). Risk markers for family violence in a federally incarcerated population. *International Journal of Law and Psychiatry, 15,* 101–112.

Dutton, D. G., & Hart, S. G. (1992b). Evidence for long-term, specific effects of childhood abuse and neglect on criminal behavior in men. *International Journal of Offender Therapy and Comparative Criminology, 36*(2), 129–138.

Dutton, D. G., & Hemphill, K. J. (1992). Patterns of socially desirable responding among perpetrators and victims of wife assault. *Violence and Victims, 7,* 29–40.

Dutton, D. G., & Painter, S. L. (1981). Traumatic bonding: The development of emotional attachments in battered women and other relationships of intermittent abuse. *Victimology: An International Journal, 6,* 139–155.

Dutton, D. G., & Painter, S. L. (1993). Emotional attachments in abusive relationships: A test of traumatic bonding theory. *Violence and Victims, 8*(2) 105–120.

Dutton, D. G., & Ryan, L. (1992). *Antecedents of borderline personality organization in wife assaulters.* Unpublished manuscript.

Dutton, D. G., Saunders, K., Starzomski, A., & Bartholomew, K. (1994). Intimacy-anger and insecure attachment as precursors of abuse in intimate relationships. *Journal of Applied Social Psychology, 24*(15), 1367–1386.

Dutton, D. G., & Starzomski, A. (1994). Psychological differences between court-referred and self-referred wife assaulters. *Criminal Justice and Behavior, 21*(2) 203–222.

Dutton, D. G., & Strachan, C. E. (1987). Motivational needs for power and dominance as differentiating variables of assaultive and non-assaultive male populations. *Violence and Victims, 2,* 145–156.

Faulk, M. (1974). Men who assault their wives. *Medicine, Science and Law, 14,* 180–183.

French, M. (1985). *Beyond power.* New York: Ballantine.

Frodi, A., Macaulay, J., & Thome, P. (1977). Are women always less aggressive than men? *Psychological Bulletin, 84,* 634–660.

Ganley, A. (1989). Integrating feminist and social learning analyses of aggression . In P. L. Caesar & L. K. Hamberger (Eds.), *Treating men who batter* (pp. 196–235). New York: Springer Publishing Company.

Goldberg, H. (1987). *The inner male: Overcoming roadblocks to intimacy.* New York: New American Library.

Goldner, V., Penn, P., Sheinberg, M., & Walker, G. (1990). Love and violence: Gender paradoxes in volatile attachments. *Family Process, 29,* 343–364.

Gondolf, E., & Russell, D. (1986). The case against anger control treatment for batterers. *Response, 9,* 2–5.

Hamberger, L. K., & Hastings, J. E. (1986). *Characteristics of male spouse abusers: Is psychopathology part of the picture?* Paper presented at American Society of Criminology, Atlanta, GA.

Hamberger, L. K., & Hastings, J. E. (1989). Counseling male spouse abusers: Characteristics of treatment completers and dropouts. *Violence and Victims, 4,* 275–286.

Hart, S. D., Dutton, D. G., & Newlove, T. (1993). The prevalence of personality disorder among wife assaulters. *Journal of Personality Disorders, 7*(4), 1721–1740.

Hastings, J. E., & Hamberger, L. K. (1988). Personality characteristics of spouse abusers: A controlled comparison. *Violence and Victims, 3,* 31–48.

Huston, T. L. (1983). Power. In H. H. Kelley (Ed.), *Close relationships* (pp. 169–219). New York: Freeman.

Hyde, J. S. (1984). How large are gender differences in aggression? A developmental meta-analysis. *Developmental Psychology, 20,* 722–736.

Island, D., & Letellier, P. (1991). *Men who beat the men who love them.* New York: Harrington Park Press.

Janis, I. (1982). *Victims of groupthink.* Boston: Houghton-Mifflin.

Julian, T. W., & McKenry, P. C. (1993). Mediators of male violence toward female intimates. *Journal of Family Violence, 8,* 39–56.

Kasian, M., & Painter, S. (1992). Frequency and severity of psychological abuse in a dating population. *Journal of Interpersonal Violence, 7,* 350–364.

Kennedy, L. W., & Dutton, D. G. (1989). The incidence of wife assault in Alberta. *Canadian Journal of Behavioural Science, 21,* 40–54.

Kernberg, O. (1977). The structural diagnosis of borderline personality organization. In P. Hartocollis (Ed.), *Borderline personality disorders: The concept, the syndrome, the patient* (pp. 87–121). New York: International Universities Press.

Kuhn, T. S. (1965). *Structure of scientific revolutions.* Chicago: University of Chicago Press.

Levinson, D. (1989). *Family violence in a cross-cultural perspective.* Newbury Park, CA: Sage Publications.

Lie, G., & Gentlewarrior, S. (1991). Intimate violence in lesbian relationships: Discussion of survey findings and practice implications. *Journal of Social Service Research, 15,* 41–59.

Lie, G., Schilit, R., Bush, J., Montague, M., & Reyes, L. (1991). Lesbians in currently aggressive relationships: How frequently do they report aggressive past relationships? *Violence and Victims, 6,* 121–135.

Mahler, M. (1971). A study of the separation-individuation process and its possible application to borderline phenomena in the psychoanalytic situation. *Psychoanalytic Study of the Child, 26,* 403–424.

McClelland, D. C. (1975). *Power: The inner experience.* New York: John Wiley & Sons.

Neidig, P. H., & Friedman, D. H. (1984). *Spouse abuse: A treatment program for couples.* Champaign, IL: Research Press.

Pantony, K. L., & Caplan, P. (1991). Delusional dominating personality disorder. *Canadian Psychology, 32,* 120–135.

Pollack, S., & Gilligan, C. (1982). Images of violence in thematic apperception test stories. *Journal of Personality and Social Psychology, 42,* 159–167.

Renzetti, C. M. (1992). *Violent betrayal: Partner abuse in lesbian relationships.* Newbury Park, CA: Sage.

Rosewater, L. B. (1987). The clinical and courtroom application of battered women's personality assessments. In D. J. Sonkin (Ed.), *Domestic violence on trial: Psychological and legal dimensions of family violence* (pp. 86–94). New York: Springer.

Saakvitne, K. W., & Pearlman, L. A. (1993). The impact of internalized misogyny and violence against women on feminine identity. In E. P. Cook (Ed.), *Women, relationships and power* (pp. 247–274). Alexandria, VA: American Counselling Association.

Saunders, D. (1992). A typology of men who batter: Three types derived from cluster analysis. *American Journal of Orthopsychiatry, 62,* 264–275.

Schulman, M. (1979). *A survey of spousal violence against women in Kentucky.* Washington, DC: U.S. Department of Justice, Law Enforcement.

Smith, M. (1990). Patriarchal ideology and wife beating: A test of feminist hypothesis. *Violence and Victims, 5,* 257–273.

Sorenson, S. B., & Telles, C. A. (1991). Self-reports of spousal violence in a Mexican-American and non-Hispanic white population. *Violence and Victims, 6,* 3–16.

Stark, R., & McEvoy, J. (1970). Middle class violence. *Psychology Today, 4,* 107–112.

Stets, J., & Straus, M. (1990). Gender differences in reporting marital violence and its medical and psychological consequences. In M. Straus & R. Gelles (Eds.), *Physical violence in American families* (pp. 151–166). New Brunswick, NJ: Transaction Publishers.

Straus, M. A. (1979). Measuring family conflict and violence: The Conflict Tactics Scale. *Journal of Marriage and the Family, 41,* 75–88.

Straus, M. A., & Gelles, R. J. (1985, November). *Is family violence increasing? A comparison of 1975 and 1985 national survey rates.* Paper presented at the American Society of Criminology, San Diego, CA.

Straus, M. A., Gelles, R. J., & Steinmetz, S. (1980). *Behind closed doors: Violence in the American family.* Garden City, NY: Anchor Press/Doubleday.

Straus, M. A., & Kantor, G. K. (1994). Change in spouse assault rates from 1975 to 1992: A comparison of three national surveys in the U.S. Paper presented at the 13th World Congress of Sociology, Bielefeld, Germany, July.

Turner, C., Fenn, M., & Cole, A. (1981). A social psychological analysis of violent behavior. In R. B. Stuart (Ed.), *Violent behavior: Social learning approaches.* New York: Brunner/Mazel.

Walker, L. (1984). *The battered woman syndrome.* New York: Springer.

Walker, L. (1986). Battered women's shelters and work with battered lesbians. In L. Kobel (Ed.), *Naming the violence: Speaking out about lesbian battering.* Seattle: Seal Press.

Walker, L. (1989). Psychology and violence against women. *American Psychologist, 44,* 695–702.

Wilson, E. O. (1975). *Sociobiology.* Cambridge: Harvard University Press.

Winter, D. G. (1973). *The power motive.* New York: The Free Press.

Yllo, K. (1988). Political and methodological debates in wife abuse research. In K. Yllo & M. Bograd (Eds.), *Feminist perspectives on wife abuse.* Beverly Hills: Sage.

Yllo, K., & Straus, M. (1990). Patriarchy and violence against wives: The impact of structural and normative factors. In M. Straus & R. Gelles (Eds.), *Physical violence in American families.* New Brunswick, NJ: Transaction Publishers.

Zimmerman, M., & Coryell, W. (1989). DSM-III personality disorder diagnoses in a nonpatient sample. *Archives of General Psychiatry, 46,* 682–689.

7

Psychopharmacological Treatment of Aggressive Behavior

Implications for Domestically Violent Men

Roland D. Maiuro and
David H. Avery

Although sociocultural and social learning approaches have exerted a major influence upon the development of both etiological and intervention models for domestic violence, psychobiological variables have received relatively little attention (Rosenbaum & Maiuro, 1989). Perpetrators and victims of spouse abuse have, by and large, been the domain of the criminal-justice and social service systems, thus gaining the attention of criminologists, sociologists, and other social scientists. Only recently have health care disciplines begun to mainstream domestic violence as a public health problem (American Medical Association, 1992a; Randall, 1990). In an attempt to further improve our understanding and response to domestic violence, a number of investigators have begun to prioritize the development of specialized diagnostic and intervention methods from a biomedical perspective

(American Medical Association, 1992b; Maiuro & Sugg, in press). The potential use of selectively prescribed and carefully monitored medications to reduce violence would be an important step toward mainstreaming the treatment of domestically violent men into the realm of modern medicine and health care.

However, the idea of employing psychopharmacological interventions for domestically violent men also raises a number of philosophical and conceptual issues. psychopharmacological approaches to violent behavior, which are primarily biological forms of interventions, are sometimes criticized as being "reductionistic" and tied to "disease models" of etiology. It may be argued that such approaches run the risk of oversimplifying and underestimating the scope of interpersonal violence, promoting the disavowal of personal responsibility because of "diminished capacity," as well as ignoring important sociocultural and psychological bases for such behavior (Breggin, 1980; Dobash & Dobash, 1987).

Although such concerns may be legitimate, they assume a univariate and nonintegrated model of intervention that emphasizes biological factors as superordinate. This need not be the case. Moreover, legitimate criticisms can provide a basis for sharpening our thinking about personal accountability and models of etiology and intervention. The presence of a classifiable syndrome or disorder and what a defense attorney attempts to make of it in a court of law are two different things. Well-chosen caveats, concerns, and words of caution can assist the development of more sensitive and sophisticated models and protocols.

More important, critical acknowledgement of limitations associated with any approach does not provide a rational basis for its exclusion in cases in which it can be justified. With regard to psychopharmacological intervention, such justification might include the identification of an etiological factor or component of risk (i.e., a demonstrable syndrome, a diagnosable condition, or a comorbid pattern of symptoms or complaints); which is known to be amenable to medication-assisted intervention. Although much work remains in understanding the specific linkages and mechanisms between psychobiology and aggressive and violent behavior, there is a growing body of basic and clinical research that has important potential for expanding our intervention efforts for domestically violent men. The purpose of this chapter is to review this research in relation to current efforts to understand and treat domestically violent men. A biopsychosocial model that incorporates selective and adjunctive psychopharmacological treatment within the context of cognitive-behavioral 'and social systems' interventions is proposed.

Violent and Abusive Behavior: Relationship to "Psychiatric Disorder"

To date, the vast majority of studies investigating the use of psychopharmacological compounds for violent behavior have appeared in the general psychiatric literature. Often there is an assumption of a specific disorder as defined by behavioral, emotional, and, sometimes, biological markers that conform to the Diagnostic and Statistical Manual *(DSM-IV)* classification utilized by the mental health field (American Psychiatric Association, 1994). This classification is a descriptive nosology comprised of meaningful and replicable clusters of antecedent events, maladaptive reactions, cognitive and behavioral deficits and excesses, and associated intrapersonal and interpersonal conflicts. The diagnostic clusters included in the schema are validated by consensus among recognized experts on the basis of the existing literature and appropriate field studies. Although violent and abusive behavior per se is not considered a disorder, there are many diagnosable syndromes and disorders that are associated with the increased likelihood of such behavior. At the present time, violent behavior is listed as an essential diagnostic feature for antisocial personality disorder, borderline personality disorder, intermittent explosive disorder, and sexual sadism. However, in reviewing the clinical literature on violence and intermittent explosive disorder,

Maiuro (1993) found a broader spectrum of classifiable disorders to be implicated in violent behavior. These disorders ranged from adjustment disorders, defined as significant but temporary maladaptive reactions to situational stressors, to major forms of mental illness. In a recent, large-scale empirical study based upon the Diagnostic Interview Schedule (Robins, Helzer, Croughan, & Ratcliff, 1981) used in the National Institute of Mental Health's Epidemiologic Catchment Area project, Swanson, Holzer, Gonju, & Jono (1990) also found a variety of commonly diagnosed clusters (e.g., anxiety-related disorders, obsessive-compulsive disorder, depressive or affective disorders) to be associated with an increased risk of violent behavior. A significant interaction effect was found between the presence of psychiatric disorder and both alcohol and drug abuse, yielding a notably higher likelihood of violence.

Unlike many other studies in the psychiatric literature, Swanson et al. (1990) made specific inquiry regarding a variety of forms of violent behavior, including domestic violence ("Did you ever hit or throw things at your wife/husband/partner?...Have you ever spanked or hit a child hard enough so that he or she had bruises or had to stay in bed or see a doctor?"). The results for spouse abuse and child abuse mirrored the pattern of increased risk for violence in general for the Axis I disorders (e.g., mood disorders, anxiety disorders, thought disorders, alcohol and substance abuse) studied. Given that violent behavior is an essential feature of a variety of Axis II disorders (e.g., antisocial and borderline personality disorders), one might expect the rates of violence to have been much higher had a comprehensive assessment been made of these diagnostic classifications as well.

Domestic Violence and "Psychopathology" The degree to which domestic violence is associated with psychopathology has been debated over the years. In the foreword to an early text by Gelles (1972), Straus stated that "individual pathology is but a minor element" and that "few, if any, of the people he [Gelles] studied can be considered as suffering from any gross abnormality" (p. 16).

Indeed, the national survey data later reported by Straus and Gelles (1986) confirmed the notion that domestic violence was not confined to a small, disturbed segment of the community but a relatively large percentage of the American population.

However, in recent years, increased attention has been given to the role of individual characteristics as contributing factors to domestic violence episodes. Despite the commonality of the problem and the facilitating influence of cultural factors, it should be remembered that most men do not engage in violent and abusive behavior toward their domestic partners. Moreover, although lifetime prevalence figures that include mild manifestations among a broad segment of the population are important, it is probably the repeated, escalating, injurious, multiply featured, and possibly more psychopathological, cases that create the most concern for families and social systems.

In a comprehensive review of existing research on risk factors for domestic violence by men, Hotaling and Sugarman (1986) concluded that the data pointed toward enduring patterns of maladjustment in many cases. They suggested that the cluster of behavioral-emotional characteristics described in the literature appeared to be consistent with some form of personality disorder. A cross-validated study of 198 spouse abusers by Hamberger and Hastings (1986) found that 88% of the men evaluated evidenced discernable psychopathology when systematically assessed with the Million Clinical Multiaxial Inventory (MCMI), Novaco Anger Scale, and Beck Depression Inventory. The investigators found that schizoidal/borderline, narcissistic/antisocial, and dependent/compulsive disorders were particularly represented. In a follow-up study that employed a comparison group methodology lacking in their earlier studies, Hastings and Hamberger (1988) failed to replicate the same three personality factors. However, they found that domestically violent men scored significantly higher than nonviolent men in the areas of borderline symptomatology and negative, passive-aggressive tendencies.

Citing the controversy that often emerges in the literature between the emphasis on individual psychopathology and social structural variables (Pagelow, 1993), Dutton and Starzomski (1993) applied the construct of borderline personality organization (BPO) to the study of domestically violent men. Borrowing from Gunderson (1984) the authors suggested that a dimensional model of dysfunction that manifests itself primarily in the context of attempts to establish intimate relationships might help "depathologize" the perpetrator profile of wife abuse. The three essential characteristics of BPO include (1) a proclivity to form intense conflicted relationships marked by intermittent attempts to undermine, manipulate, and mask dependency; (2) poorly developed identity and loss of boundaries characterized by intolerance of being alone attended by abandonment anxiety; and (3) intense anger, demandingness, and impulsivity, sometimes attended by substance abuse or promiscuity.

Dutton and Starzomski's results supported the idea that BPO constituted a central feature of a domestic abuse profile, accounting for a significant amount of variance related to both psychological and physical abuse. The investigators also reported a replication of Maiuro, Cahn, Vitaliano Wagner, and Legree's (1988) findings of affective instability in domestically violent men in the form of depression and anger dyscontrol. Anger dyscontrol was also found to independently contribute to the examined, abuse profiles which the investigators developed from independently derived victim reports on standardized measures.

Other studies have questioned the clinical meaning of the psychopathological categorizations derived from dimensional measures, such as MCMI scores, and have suggested that a significant number of false positives could result (Wonderlich, Hart, Dutton, & Newlove, 1993; Else, Beatty, Christie, & Staton, 1993). Nonetheless, when more conservative diagnostic interview protocols are employed, domestically violent men still evidence higher rates of psychopathology than the general population. In this regard, Bland and Orn (1986) used the Diagnostic Interview

Schedule (DIS) and found that the odds for diagnosable antisocial personality disorder increased by a factor of 8.2 among wife abusers drawn from a general community sample. Dinwiddie (1992) employed the Home Environment and Lifetime Psychiatric Evaluation Record and replicated and extended the results of Bland and Orn by finding higher rates of major depression as well.

Thus, when the methodology involves direct assessment of domestically violent men and systematic use of psychological and psychiatric measures, a significant number, but not all, appear to have some type of classifiable, maladaptive syndrome recognizable to mental health professionals. Although domestically violent men seldom evidence generalized or major forms of mental illness, there is strong evidence of more circumscribed problems associated with mood or affective disorder, impulse control disorder, substance abuse, and personality disorders. Of course, the presence of such disorders need not imply a cause-and-effect relationship in which spouse abuse is viewed as a simple by-product of psychopathology. Rather, psychological disorders may be more appropriately and productively viewed as individual vulnerability factors. Thus, in interaction with a host of other proximal and distal variables, the presence of psychiatric disorder may potentiate or increase the probability of acts of violence when the men are faced with interpersonal conflict, perceived threats associated with intimacy, or challenges to personal control (cf. Hambergerand Lohr, 1989; Rosenbaum & Maiuro, 1989). In any event, the identification of diagnosable syndromes as contributing factors to the behavior of at least some domestically violent men opens the possibility of expanding current treatment paradigms to include psychopharmacological forms of intervention.

Biological Systems and Psychopharmacological Intervention

To date, at least four biological systems have been implicated in the genesis of aggressive behavior, which may have implications for the treatment of domestically violent men. The first system is a neurophysiological pathway associated with electrical activity in the brain and seizurelike foci in the form of "kindling" patterns and epilepsy. The other three are neurotransmitter systems. These include the gamma-aminobutyric acid (GABA-ergic) system, the noradrenergic system, and, of more recent interest, the serotonergic system. Although these systems are discussed independently, actual human behavior may involve complex interactions among them. Similarly, although the psychopharmacological interventions presently reviewed may be theoretically linked primarily to one system, data suggest that multiple receptor sites and multiple systems can be involved at the biochemical level (Manji, Potter, & Lenox, 1995).

Neurophysiological System

In early clinical studies, Monroe (1970, 1975) reported that patients with "episodic dyscontrol syndrome" improved after treatment with anticonvulsants. Characteristics of the dyscontrol syndrome included behavioral impulsivity, anger, and moodiness that frightens others; not feeling responsible for one's own behavior; and a sense of loss of control, verbal screaming, physically attacking others, smashing things, and impulses to kill oneself or others, as well as alcohol related aggression. Given the intermittent and explosive quality of the aggressive behavior exhibited by the sample he studied, Monroe speculated that some of these patients, particularly those with signs of maturational lag in their EEG rhythms, had a subclinical neurological basis for their behavior. He also concluded that many had no demonstrable neurological pathology but, instead, evidenced psychodynamic mechanisms for their aggressive episodes.

The notion that neurophysiolgical or structural abnormalities are associated with heightened levels of anger and aggression in humans has been a controversial topic. Diagnostic studies of aggressive patients frequently yield histories of head injury, soft neurological signs, and abnormal EEG results (Lewis, Lovely,

Yeager, & Femina, 1988). Rosenbaum and Hoge (1989) assessed the occurrence of severe head injury in the medical histories of 31 domestically violent men and found that 18 (61%) reported having experienced a head injury severe enough to have produced a loss of consciousness or to have been diagnosed as a concussion. However, it is often difficult to tell whether such abnormalities are the cause of aggressive behavior or the result of the subject's history of abuse or physically violent encounters. In Chapter 5, Warnken, Rosenbaum, Fletcher, Hoger, and Adelman investigated relationship changes in men with head injuries. They compared head-injured and orthopedically injured samples without prior histories of domestic violence on a variety of abuse and risk indices. Although the groups did not differ on physically abusive behavior at the time of assessment, the head injured sample evidenced greater verbal abuse, temper problems, arguments, and dyscontrol episodes and were rated as more dependent on their domestic partners. The results were interpreted as suggesting the presence of greater risk or vulnerability among head-injured men, mediated by intervening emotional and relationship changes, as opposed to a direct, neurological cause and effect.

Early psychopharmacological work with the anticonvulsant phenytoin has been supplanted by the use of carbamazepine, which numerous investigators have found effective in reducing both irritability and behavioral tantrum sometimes associated with chronic epilepsy (Dalby, 1975; Monroe, 1975). However, a number of studies suggest that carbamazepine may be effective in reducing aggressiveness in patient populations regardless of neurological diagnostic status. Such findings suggest the possibility of symptomatic, but not diagnostic, specificity with the use of such compounds. In nonblind studies, Luchins (1983, 1984), reported carbamazepine to reduce violent behavior in 19 violent patients (15 of these were diagnosed as schizophrenic) on neuroleptics. The 11 patients with normal EEGs responded as well as the 8 patients with abnormal findings. Mattes (1984) and Mattes, Rosenberg, and Mayes (1984) randomly assigned patients with rage outbursts to carbamazepine or to a β-blocker (propranolol). Although carbamazepine significantly reduced aggressiveness, therapeutic benefit was not related to neurological diagnosis, EEG, or other evidence of neurological dysfunction. Motles and associates however, did not employ a placebo group to control for nonspecific treatment effects.

Thus, the available data suggest that anticonvulsants may sometimes work for reasons other than the hypothesized mechanisms of neurophysiological abnormality. In this regard, carbamazepine has also been reported to be efficacious in mania (Ballenger and Post, 1980) and in nonepileptic children with symptoms of attention deficit disorder and hyperactivity (Groh, 1976; Kuhn-Gebhart, 1976; Puente, 1976; Remschmidt, 1976). Such findings suggest the possibility of emotional and arousal "dampening" properties for the drug, which, in turn, decrease the likelihood of aggression. Mood and arousal disorders, with and without histories of head injury, are commonly seen in domestically violent men (Rosenbaum & Maiuro, 1989). Evidence supporting the use of carbamazepine as an adjunctive treatment component in such cases could have significant implications for the treatment of both physical and psychological abuse.

GABA-ergic System

The general psychiatric literature suggests that benzodiazepines can be useful in the management of acutely agitated and aggressive patients. These psychopharmacological compounds (e.g., diazepam, lorazepam, oxazepam, and chlordiazepoxide) operate by enhancing the gamma-aminobutyric acid (GABA) neurotransmitter system, which, in turn, inhibits various types of aggression including both attack and defensive behavior.

In an early clinical study, Monroe (1970) reported that patients with "episodic dyscontrol syndrome" improved after treatment with either benzodiazepines (chlordiazepoxide) or anticonvulsant compounds. Additional studies of both outpatient (Lion, 1979) and incarcerated populations (Brown, Goodurn, Ballenger, Goyer, &

Major, 1979) have reported successful drug treatment with oxazepam of a broad range of patients having both "anxious and hostile" features. Targeted aggression indices have included assaultive behavior, verbal abuse, property destruction, temper tantrums, and general feelings of hostility and irritability (Lion, 1979). A significant limitation of benzodiazepine treatment relates to its strong sedating and relaxant side effects. In fact, intramuscular doses of lorazepam have been used in emergent situations to attenuate aggressive behavior in out-of-control patients. Although there is evidence that the sedating side effects of benzodiazepines diminish with repeated administration (File, 1985), it is possible that those domestically violent men with a rigidly developed need for control might respond poorly or become noncompliant because of these effects.

Along these lines, it should be noted that "paradoxical rage" reactions have been observed in a minority of patients who have been administered benzodiazepine drugs. A number of case reports document reactions in which there is actually an increase in agitation, hostility, and physically assaultive behavior (Lion, Hill, & Madden, 1975; Lipman et al., 1986). Other potential problems include the development of tolerance to the drug and abusive and addictive use of medications, particularly in patients identified as having personality disorders (Soloff, 1994). Some writers (Eichelman, 1987) indicate that such reactions have been reported only for specific benzodiazepine compounds (e.g., for diazepam and chlordiazepoxide but not for oxazepam) and only for patients who exhibit features of panic disorder (Rosenbaum, Woods, Groves, & Klerman, 1984). Thus, the benzodiazepine class of drugs may act differently, depending upon the specific compound employed and the preexisting emotional, and possibly biochemical, reactivity of the subject. When taken together, these data suggest a more complex mechanism than the specific receptor related "taming effect" initially postulated. Indeed, more recent research suggests that there may be at least 15 different subsites of the GABA-benzodiazepine complex with the potential for more diverse and selective pharmacological effects (Miczek, Werts, Haney, & Tidey, 1994).

Of potential interest to clinical researchers exploring the prevalence and dynamics of domestic violence is the possible action of alcohol upon the GABA-benzodiazepine receptor. Specifically, a variety of animal studies have linked aggressogenic effects of alcohol to this receptor site in the brain (Miczek et al., 1994). Studies that have explored the interaction between illicit drug use and violence have found alcohol to be, by far, the most commonly associated factor for frequent and severe patterns of spouse abuse. Although incidence rates vary widely depending on the sampling procedures employed, more common estimates range from about 40% to 50% (Byles, 1978; Gelles, 1974; Fagan, Stewart, & Hansen, 1983). In their review of 15 studies reporting on the alcohol-wife abuse link, Kantor and Straus (1986) found that all six studies which provided statistical comparisons with a nonabusive sample reported significantly more alcohol use among abusers. Moreover, in dividing their own sample (the 1985 national probability sample of 4,032 households) by level of alcohol use, they found rates of wife abuse by high and binge drinkers that were 2.3 to 3 times higher than the rates for moderate drinkers. Although the exact mechanism(s) by which alcohol enhances the likelihood of spousal violence is still debated, a recent clinical study of alcohol abusing, domestically violent men indicated that alcohol use independently contributes to the frequency and severity of both physical and psychological abuse beyond personality and behavioral-emotional dispositions (Maiuro, Vitaliano, & Cowden, 1995).

If alcohol use or withdrawal is assessed as a contributing factor to episodes of violence, some clinicians advocate the use of benzodiazepines (Conn & Lion, 1984). Benzodiazepines appear to be functionally cross-tolerant with alcohol and may mitigate or block some of the aggressogenic effects of alcohol in violence-prone individuals. Benzodiazepines may also be useful in the treatment of aggressive behavior associated with toxic drug use (e.g., phencyclidine or PCP). Although alcohol abuse may be neither necessary nor sufficient for domestic violence to occur in such cases, it is possible that selective and cautious use of benzodiazepines may lower the risk of violence and abuse and decrease the duration and severity of episodes. To date, however, our knowledge in this area is limited to analogue laboratory studies and clinical case reports.

Noradrenergic System

The noradrenergic system regulates the level of norepinephrine (NE) in the brain. For many years now, it has also been implicated in the "flight or fight" syndrome observed in humans in which both defensive and aggressive behaviors commonly occur in response to stress, challenge, and threat (Selye, 1956). The notion that violence-prone individuals may have unusually high NE activity was first documented by Brown et al. (1979). In a study of military personnel rated as highly aggressive by a composite index of nine lifestyle indicators, the investigators found a significant and positive correlation with elevated levels of the norepinephrine metabolite 3-methoxy-4-hydroxyphenylglycol (MHPG) in cerebral spinal fluid (CSF) assays. Sandler et al. (1979) similarly found elevated levels of phenylethylamine, an endogenous amphetamine-like compound, in the blood of aggressive prisoners.

Lithium carbonate is a standard treatment for manic-depressive disorders that are commonly characterized by emotional lability, excitability, instrusive violation of the personal boundaries of others, belligerence, impulsiveness, and, at times, physically assaultive behavior. Although available research indicates that lithium carbonate has multiple molecular targets and systems of action (e.g., serotonergic, noradrenergic), its therapeutic effect appears to stem, in part, from decreasing the effects of norepinephrine (Manji, et al., 1995). Early studies by Sheard, Marini, Bridges, and Wagner (1976) demonstrated that lithium carbonate could decrease aggressive acts in personality-disordered violent patients as well as in those formally diagnosed as manic-depressive. Sheard's initial placebo-controlled investigation involved 12 male volunteer prisoners who were given lithium 3 times a day.

Decreases in assaultive behavior as well as verbal hostility were documented by prison staff. Sheard's work (Sheard, 1984)was replicated and extended with a larger sample of 66 highly aggressive prisoners in a double-blind design. Other investigators have reported benefits from lithium treatment similar to those reported by Sheard (Tupin et al., 1973).

Potential problems involved with lithium treatment stem from the fact that it requires close monitoring of blood levels to ensure adequate dosing to achieve therapeutic levels. Too low a dosage results in little effect and too high a dosage can create common side effects such as motor tremor and nausea. Thus, while lithium may offer potential benefits to some, such data also suggest the possibility of compliance problems with significant subsamples of domestically violent men who have difficulty adhering to treatment programs.

β-adrenergic antagonists also act to decrease the effect of norepinephrine. Based on case studies, various clinical researchers have reported that β-blockers such as propranolol, metoprolol, pindolol, and nadolol may decrease a variety of relevant target behaviors including irritability, property damage, and different forms of violent and assaultive behavior. Originally developed to treat arrhythmia and hypertensive symptoms of cardiovascular disease, these compounds have now been used with a variety of difficult and resistant patient populations, including the organically impaired, mentally retarded, psychotic, and personality disordered. In a recent comparative study, Mattes (1990) randomly assigned 51 of 80 patients who experienced "rage outbursts" to propanolol or carbamazepine (a commonly prescribed anticonvulsant) treatments. Although study results supported the efficacy of both compounds, a diagnosis of attention deficit disorder statistically predicted a preferential response to propanolol. A diagnosis of intermittent explosive disorder predicted a preferential, albeit not exclusive, response to carbamazepine. Because sideeffects may include fatigue, insomnia, and depression in some cases (Sheard, 1984), one might hypothesize that β–blockers would yield better outcomes in cases where hyperarousal and impulsivity was present and not be the treatment of choice in depressed subsamples of domestically violent men.

It is well known that intense arousal can interfere with higher cortical functioning and interpersonal problem solving during stressful encounters (Mandler, 1982). As a result, most treatment programs for domestically violent men include a variety of arousal reduction strategies, such a progressive muscle relaxation, cognitive imagery, deep breathing exercises, or "time out" training. Clinicians believe that such "self-control" techniques can help increase the probability that a domestically violent client will be in a state of body and mind that is conducive to good communication and rational problem solving. Despite the common use of β-blocker compounds in cases of hyperarousal, anxiety disorder, Type A hostility, and generally violent populations, there have been no studies of β-blocker assisted arousal and violence reduction reported for individuals specifically identified as domestically violent.

Serotonergic System

Sometimes referred to as a "civilizing neurohumor" in the early literature, serotonin has probably been the neurotransmitter that has been most carefully explored in clinical studies of violent behavior. Initial studies were based on autopsy studies of individuals who had committed suicide. Lower-than-expected levels of serotonin (5-HT) or its metabolite, 5-hydroxylindoleacetic acid (5-HIAA), were found in various parts of the central nervous system (CNS). Asberg, Thoren, and Traskman (1976) and Asberg, Traskman, and Thoren (1976) replicated and extended these findings in living subjects with affective disorders, finding low levels of 5-HIAA in the CSF to be associated with violent, self-destructive behavior.

In a landmark series of investigations, Brown et al. (1979) reported CSF 5-HIAA levels to be inversely correlated with violent behavior directed toward others as well. The study sample comprised men in the military facing discharge because of a repeated history of uncontrolled, violent, and aggressive acts. A similar negative and highly significant correlation was found between the Minnesota Multiphasic Personality Inventory psychopathic deviance scale, a subscale associated with a cluster of angry, aggressive, impulsive attitudes and behaviors as well as conflict in family of origin. In a subsequent investigation, Brown et al. (1982) again found low CSF 5-HIAA levels in young adult males who had a childhood history of dishonesty, fits of rage, fighting, and property damage. The investigators interpreted their data to suggest the possibility of a psychobiolgical vulnerability in the form of a serotonergic deficit ("serotonin syndrome") in some violence-prone individuals.

In a comparative study of depressed patients with and without low CSF 5-HIAA, Van Praag (1986) reported that the low 5-HIAA subjects had higher levels of anger and aggression, more arguments with spouse, more contacts with police, more self-destructive behavior, more conflict on the job, as well as greater interview rated hostility. Decreased central serotonin neurotransmission has now been implicated in the mediation of "impulsive aggression" in a wide variety of patients labelled as prone to episodic alcohol abuse, dysphoric, and personality disordered, particularly borderline and antisocial types (Coccaro, 1989; Coccaro, 1989; Coccaro & Murphy, 1990).

Studies employing a fenfluramine challenge (an intravenous procedure that provides an active peripheral measure of 5-HT system activity by stimulating the release of prolactin through the anterior pituitary) have strengthened the support for the notion of a psychobiological vulnerability in such individuals. Coccaro et al. (1989) have specifically found blunted or reduced prolactin response consistent with lower serotonergic functioning in individuals exhibiting a cluster of depression, personality disorder, and "impulsive aggression." However, the strongest correlates with low 5-HIAA were angry irritability as measured by the Buss-Durkee Hostility Inventory and impulsive aggression, as opposed to premeditated or instrumental acts of violence.

It should be noted that all of the behavioral and emotional features associated with low serotonergic functioning in Van Praag's and Coccaro et al.'s studies have been also been reported for domestically violent men. In a comparative study, Maiuro, et al. (1988) examined anger and depression in domestically violent men relative to two groups of demographically matched, generally assaultive men as well as nonviolent controls. Similarly high levels of trait anger and aggressivity were found for domestically violent men in comparison with generally assaultive men. The investigators concluded that the similarity of the trait anger and hostility scores of domestically violent men to those of other assaultive men challenged the notion of circumscribed, situationally, or victim provoked anger. Rather, in keeping with the construct of a trait being more of a subject-based propensity, it suggested the presence of a "predisposition" to respond in this manner as part of a dysfunctional personality or coping profile on the part of the abusive man.

Maiuro, et al. (1988) also found a significantly greater incidence of clinical levels of depression in domestically violent men when compared to both generally assaultive samples and nonviolent controls. Although all of the domestically violent men did not evidence depression, two thirds of the sample scored within the clinical range. These findings were interpreted as consistent with dynamics related to low self-esteem, psychological themes of attachment, abandonment, loss, and "rejection hypersensitivity," and dysfunctional use of anger to reestablish a sense of power and control. The authors also suggested that further assessment of potential grief reactions or more long standing vulnerability in the form of a dysthymic or affective disorder may improve the understanding and treatment of domestically violent men. A number of recently conducted studies have produced similar results (Beasely & Stoltenberg, 1992; Dutton & Starzomski, 1993; Else, et al., 1993; Flournoy & Wilson, 1991), finding domestically violent men to score significantly higher on a cluster of personality disorder indices, trait anger measures, and depression. Moreover, in an ongoing investigation of serotonergic functioning in domestically violent men, Rosenbaum (personal communication July 1995) has obtained data consistent with the notion of a psychobiological vulnerability to aggression. In this regard, Rosenbaum has reported preliminary findings of reduced or blunted prolactin response in a sample of domestically violent men undergoing a fenfluramine challenge.

In recent years, a number of investigators have begun to conduct clinical trials of serotonin-enhancing compounds for anti-aggressive effects. An early study by Morand, Young, and Ervin (1983) explored the use of orally administered tryptophan (an essential amino acid that acts as a precursor to serotonin in the body) with a small sample of severely aggressive men diagnostically classified as schizophrenic. The investigators employed a double-blind placebo crossover and observed a significant decrease in depressed mood, hostility, and ward-related aggressive incidents in the treated group after 4 weeks when compared to placebo controls. Interestingly, the authors noted that the treatment effect was observed only for a subgroup of patients who initially evidenced a cluster of frequent aggressive episodes, high anger and hostility scores, and normally reactive galvanic skin response.

A number of studies also suggest that recently developed selective serotonin reuptake inhibitors (SSRIs) may also be effective in treating a cluster of behavioral-emotional features commonly found in domestically violent men. Initially introduced as a new form of antidepressant, SSRI compounds such as fluoxetine and paroxetine have begun to receive clinical study as treatments for angry and aggressive behavior. For example, there are reports that patients classified with borderline personality disorder who are treated with fluoxetine not only evidence improvements in depressed mood but also experience decreases in rejection sensitivity, impulsive behavior, self-destructive behavior, and hostility toward others (Coccaro et al., 1989; Cornelius, Soloff, Perel, et al., 1990; Norden, 1989). In a 13-week double-blind study, Salzman et al. (1995) assigned subjects closely resembling Dutton and Starzomski's (1993) classification of BPO to either fluoxetine or placebo conditions. Although significantly greater decreases in anger, depression, and aggression were found in the medicated sample, the investigators observed the greatest changes in the area of angry mood.

In a similar series of studies with depressed outpatients, Fava, Anderson, and Rosenbaum (1990) found a subsample with what they described as "anger attacks." The subsample comprised both men and women who experienced intermittent episodes of rage at home and/or at work characterized by high levels of autonomic arousal, verbal abuse, throwing things, and fighting. Although similar, the sample did not meet the full criteria for intermittent explosive disorder owing to the absence of clearly articulated reports of serious violent episodes. Many subjects expressed subsequent regret for their actions and disowned their angry and aggressive behavior as uncharacteristic or unintended in nature. In an uncontrolled but double-blind study of fluoxetine treatment with 56 depressed individuals exhibiting such anger attacks, Fava et al. (1993) reported that 71% of the sample had significant reductions in anger, depression, and generally aggressive behavior after 8 weeks of treatment. However, no direct assessments were made of domestic violence in the cases studied.

Although the available studies have important implications for the potential use of SSRIs with domestically violent men, there have been no published treatment studies specifically focused on this population. In an ongoing clinical pilot study investigating the adjunctive use of paroxetine with domestically violent men evaluated and treated by the Harborview Anger Management and Domestic Violence Program in the Department of Psychiatry and Behavioral Sciences at the University of Washington School of Medicine, we have recorded behavioral and emotional changes that appear to be similar to those reported with other samples. Decreases have been observed on indices of anger, depression, and both psychological and physical abuse. There are also subjective reports of increased "reflective delay" before responding when the men are confronted with an emotional challenge within intimate relationships. However, given the combined use of cognitive-behavioral and drug treatments in the clinic's current protocol, it is difficult to attribute the changes observed to the medication as opposed to the ongoing psychosocial interventions or possible placebo effects.

The fact that an impressive array of cross-culturally conducted studies have implicated low 5-HIAA to both self-directed and other-directed acts of violence (Lidberg, Tuck, Asberg, Scalia-Tomba, & Bertillson, 1985) may also be important to intervention efforts with some of the highest risk cases of domestic violence; those that evolve to the point of homicide and suicide. A number of investigators have found similarities in emotional state between suicidal and assaultive men (Brown et al., 1982; Maiuro, O'Sullivan, Michael, & Vitaliano, 1989; Van Praag, Plutchik, & Apter, 1990). Early clinical work (Walker, 1979) as well as more recently conducted, large scale studies (Wilson & Daly, 1993) have indicated that some domestically violent men are at particularly high risk for homicide and/or suicide in battering relationships in which the woman exits or seeks divorce or separation. Although many of these cases are appropriately discussed in terms of morbid jealousy, narcissistic injury, exit-blocking, and power and control motives, the possible presence of pathological grief reactions and affective disorders in these men are often overlooked as a focus of treatment. The acute, often emergent nature of these cases suggests that fast-acting interventions for both victim and perpetrator are in order. Customary psychosocial, legal case management, and crisis intervention techniques may be inadequate. It is possible that the adjunctive and strategic use of serotonin-enhancing compounds, as well as some of the other medications discussed in this review, might improve the outcome in some of these cases by mitigating dysthymia and impulses toward violent and self-destructive behavior. Ironically, few studies presently exist that offer information relevant to intervention with cases of severe and life-threatening forms of domestic violence. As noted by Browne (1993), such cases appear to have been resistant to many of the intervention efforts made over recent years and require new approaches.

A Biopsychosocial Approach To Domestic Violence

A number of writers have begun to challenge the "either/or thinking" associated with debates about sociocultural versus individual factors in domestic violence (see Renzetti & Hamberger, Introduction; Rosenbaum & Maiuro, 1989). Existing evidence indicates that spousal abuse is a difficult and complex problem that has, despite strong polemics on the topic, not proven to be explained or solved by one particular philosophy or model of intervention. In a review of developments in research on aggression by an international group of investigators, Maiuro and Eberle (1989) suggested that an integrated, biopsychosocial perspective that includes, but not necessarily centers on, biological influences may be be helpful in generating more powerful and comprehensive approaches to violent behavior. Although most human behavioral phenomena are considered increasingly from a biopsychosocial perspective, the potential role of physiological factors in spouse abuse has been relatively unexplored.

Sophisticated models of spousal abuse suggest the need to attend to multiple issues during intervention. The available evidence suggests that psychopharmacological interventions may be most useful in emergent situations or when complicating depression, irritability, impulsivity, hyperarousal, toxicity, or organic disorders are present (Table 7.1). Indeed, modification of biological substrata may be required to make some patients amenable to additional therapy. In other cases, it may result in more rapid or more comprehensive amelioration of interpersonal violence and other abusive behaviors.

Table 7.1 Biopsychosocial Intervention For Spousal Abuse and Domestic Violence

Potential Targets for Psychopharmacological Intervention
Depressed mood
Pathological grief reactions
Irritable temperament
Hyeperreactivity
Impulsivity
Emotional lability
Pathological anxiety
Obsessiveness and compulsivity
Postconcussive/Other Organic Syndrome

Potential Targets for Cognitive-Behavioral Intervention
Minimization and denial
Projection of blame and responsibility
Denigrating/abusigenic attitude toward women
Power and control expectancies
Personal acceptance/justification of violence
Lack of awareness of destructive and self-defeating impact of abusive behavior
Anger management
Assertiveness and communication skills
Nonviolent conflict resolution skills
Enhanced stress and coping skills
Family of origin modelling influences
Posttraumatic sequelae
Relationship enhancement skills
Relapse prevention skills

Potential Targets for Social Intervention
Cultural/community acceptance of violence
Public accountability for the perpetration of violence
Mandated intervention for perpetrators
Legal support for victim's right to safety and health
Comprehensive police protection for victims
Victim shelter resources
Prioritization of social and health care services for perpetrators and victims of abuse
Sex role conditioning conducive to spouse abuse and violence
Gender inequality in sociopolitical power and access to resources
Preventive education in schools
Improved surveillance methods
Modelling and desensitizing influences in the media

At the same time, it is essential to acknowledge that domestic violence and spouse abuse is largely a result of learned behaviors. Although psychopharmacological interventions may increase the number of therapeutic tools available to stop violence and abuse, it is equally important that the problem not be "biologized" in a manner that oversimplifies it or ignores critical psychosocial determinants. A variety of cognitive-behavioral treatment programs now exist for domestically violent men, and preliminary results indicate that positive outcomes can be achieved in many cases with these methods (Edleson & Tolman, 1992; Rosenbaum & Maiuro, 1989). In this regard, cognitive-behavioral methods may have a greater likelihood of changing attitudes, imparting new emotional coping strategies, developing healthier conflict resolution skills, more positive interpersonal relationships, and engineering relapse prevention strategies, that is, alternatives to violence and abuse (Table 7.1). As aptly put by one of our cognitive-behavioral therapists at the Harborview Anger Management and Domestic Violence Program, "There are no skills with pills." As aptly understood by one of the domestically violent men enrolled in both cognitive-behavioral and drug treatment components of the program, "If there was a shot in the ass or a pill I could take to cure this problem, I would do it...but it is not that simple...so I have joined the specialized group that the clinic also offers for men who abuse their wives..."

It is important to note that the use of psychopharmacological interventions is not inconsistent or incompatible with the cognitive-behavioral and social learning approaches currently applied by many clinicians and researchers. Bandura (1973) posits that specific forms of aggressive behavior are acquired through learning. Thus, men who have learned spousal aggression through modelling influences in their families of origin might be primed or disinhibited for this type of behavior. Bandura further states that all people have the neurophysiological capacity to behave aggressively but do not do so without appropriate stimulation. He asserts that this is a dynamic and interactive process subject to cognitive mediation and the availability of nonviolent coping strategies in an individual's behavioral repertoire. Thus, people can either exacerbate or mitigate their neurophysiological potential for violence and abuse by cognitive and behavioral means.

Consistent with this dynamic model, psychopharmacological intervention would decrease the probability of domestic abuse by directly modifying psychobiological substrata conducive to (a) irritable or dysthymic temperament; (b) hot or impulsive reactivity; (c) labile or unstable reactivity; and/or (d) anhedonic or under-reactive temperament or depressive mood. The net result would be a decrease in the likelihood of interpersonal negativity, and poorly thought out responses, an increased capacity for joy and positive response, and an increased threshold of stimuli necessary to trigger aggressive behavior of either a defensive or offensive nature.

A comprehensive biopsychosocial approach also acknowledges the importance of the dyadic, social environmental and larger sociocultural contexts in which domestic violence occurs. Thus, both immediate and longer-term interventions to decrease the vulnerability of potential victims is the first line of defense in ending and preventing the perpetration of spouse abuse. This not only includes police protection, legal support, and political advocacy but also treatment in some cases. Failure to deal with disabling post-traumatic symptoms and depression can undermine the victimized individuals' right to safety and health. Restoration, or in some case, habilitation of the victim's balance of power and independence through referral to community resources is also critical. Changes in the balance of power can lead to the development of different socioenvironmental contingencies for domestically violent men. These changes can modify the "force field" surrounding domestic abuse by actively limiting the pathological reinforcement of abusive power and control tactics by the man.

Many practitioners and applied researchers feel that violence and abuse in the individual case may be better explained and modified by accessing proximal, situational, and subject-related variables (see Dutton, Chapter 6). Nonetheless, a broad-based biopsychosocial approach would also include a preventative focus on distal social factors. Such factors establish community norms and define what is culturally appropriate and tolerable, as well as provide healthy models of social adjustment. In this manner, intervention may also include a public health partnership between the provider and various social institutions, such as schools, to help modify cultural acceptance of violence and foster preventive education.

Given the presence of mandatory arrest laws regarding domestic assault in most jurisdictions, a significant number of referrals may come as court-mandated for treatment. Contrary to the speculation still offered by some investigators that these men may represent a more antisocial and less treatable subsample (e.g., Gottman et al., 1995), we have observed court-referred men to be quite heterogeneous in profile and capable of similar levels of change to those who arrive as self-referred. Moreover, we have also observed that mandated treatment often enhances treatment compliance. Thus, it is important that the practitioner not exclude such cases from consideration when it comes to adjunctive psychopharmacological treatment because the recommended biopsychosocial approach may also involve a collaborative relationship with the court system. Many domestic violence specialists feel that the best outcomes are obtained through a combination of criminal-justice and rehabilitative interventions (Rosenbaum & Maiuro, 1989).

Psychopharmacological Intervention As An Adjunctive Treatment Strategy

Eichelman (1988) has offered the following suggestions to clinicians considering psychopharmacological approaches to violent behavior: (1) use the most benign intervention when beginning treatment; (2) select the medication that most closely addresses the primary diagnosable disorder, because the violence and dyscontrol episodes may be a by-product of this problem; (3) have some quantifiable means of assessing efficacy and side effects (repeated structured interviews or psychometrics); and (4) institute drug trials systematically by applying one intervention at a time, assessing its impact, and monitoring therapeutic levels through routine lab work.

Given the special risks associated with the treatment of domestically violent men, it is also important that intervention be empirically guided by a comprehensive assessment that is not only oriented toward the patient but also the spouse or partner and available children. It should be carefully monitored and evaluated to determine the actual impact of the treatment employed. Care must be taken to avoid mislabelling the man's violence as a biochemical problem, thus diffusing personal responsibility for the attitudes and behavioral choices that constitute abusive behavior. In our own work, it is also clear that, even in cases in which there appears to have been a beneficial effect, drug treatment in no way provides a panacea for domestic violence and abuse. Because there are as yet no definitive studies that indicate that drug treatment improves the efficacy of existing methods of intervention for domestically violent men, it is the present authors' view that psychopharmacological treatment of domestically violent men be conducted only in the context of a more comprehensive specialized treatment program for spouse abuse (Rosenbaum & Maiuro, 1990). This clearly sends the message that the psychopharmacological treatment is an adjunctive rather than primary treatment. It also allows for the efficacy to be more reliably measured through behavioral observations conducted under the challenge of intensive group therapy, conjoint sessions with the spouse, and/or individual psychotherapy sessions.

Over the past few years, we have clinically observed, with some concern, a small but apparent increase in the number of cases in which the referred party already has a prescription from a family physician for one of the classes of medication discussed in this chapter. In some of these cases, the basis for this prescription was only briefly assessed and only intermittently monitored. Given the exploratory and relatively untried status of this work, it is important that these methods be employed in a cautious and closely monitored fashion to assess intended effects as well as potentially undesirable or negative side effects. As is customary for all health care interventions, informed consent for drug treatment also necessitates a frank discussion of the potential benefits and drawbacks of such intervention, along with the alternatives available. In this regard, the clinician is advised to assume a public health role in such cases and to become acquainted with existing community treatment programs for domestically violent men as well as shelter and advocacy programs for victims of domestic violence.

Comments and Conclusions

As with other forms of intervention for interpersonal violence, psychopharmacological approaches are still in a developmental stage. Accordingly, many of the medication treatment studies reviewed presently suffer from a number of methodological limitations that prevent us from generalizing with a high degree of confidence to domestically violent men. As many studies have been conducted in applied research settings with a primary focus upon clinical service, there is often a lack of staffing to permit the use of double-blind methods and an absence of experimental comparison groups that control for other case management strategies and placebo effects. Perhaps more important, however, is the issue of study samples. Although there are undoubtedly spouse-abusing patients within some of the study samples described in the psychiatric literature, it is often difficult to know what percentage of the sample are actually or exclusively domestically violent. Ironically, the target or victim of the aggressive behavior is seldom mentioned in the descriptions provided for the participants of psychopharmacological studies for violent behavior.

Part of the problem appears to stem from the exclusive use of a diagnostic or syndrome model of inquiry. In this regard, participants are commonly defined only in terms of demographics and the diagnostic category assigned to them or in terms of the emotional features associated with the problem behavior (e.g., "rage outbursts," "anger attacks"). Most studies are published without reference to situational, interpersonal, or important intergender dynamics. In fact, until recently, much of this literature has referred to violence as a "symptom" of a disorder as opposed to a problem in and of itself. Although it is probably true that domestic violence can be conceptualized as either a cause or outcome, most specialists in the field consider it to be a special problem with an attending recognizable pattern or syndrome in its own right; that is, domestic violence or spouse abuse is the problem. Moreover, sophisticated studies of violent behavior clearly indicate that specification of situational and interpersonal dynamics is crucial to the prediction and understanding of different forms of violent behavior (Monahan, 1981; Wilson & Daly, 1993).

The development of adequate conceptual and assessment methods has been a long-standing problem for our understanding of angry, hostile, aggressive, and abusive behaviors (Biaggio & Maiuro, 1985; Eichelman, 1992). Despite the additional predictive power and potential clinical utility gained from the recognition of diagnosable syndromes (Dutton & Starzomski, 1994; Hamberger & Hastings, 1986; Hastings & Hamberger, 1988; Swanson et al., 1990), there continues to be dissatisfaction with the adequacy of the currently developed diagnostic and statistical system on both philosophical and empirical grounds. The national trend toward increased criminalization of spouse abuse and other forms of family violence appears to have fueled the fires of an old debate regarding whether it is more appropriate to view perpetrators of violence as "mad or bad." Moreover, as in the lay community, there appears to be a significant amount of stigmatization and lack of awareness regarding what constitutes a psychological or psychiatric disorder among some researchers and practitioners working in the area of domestic violence. Some clinical researchers have argued for the use of a more inclusive, dimensional coding system for psychobiological factors related to violent behavior as an alternative to the currently used categorical diagnostic system (Dutton & Starzomski, 1993; Eichelman & Hartwig, 1993). From a scientific perspective, the appropriateness of any diagnostic system ultimately comes down to a question of utility, that is, what such nosological systems offer us in our ability to explain and intervene in domestic violence.

It should be noted that the issue of diagnostic versus behavioral or other forms of classification for violent and abusive behavior is not simply a matter of conceptual paradigm. At the present time, there are no antiaggression medications explicitly indicated for violent or aggressive behavior in the absence of a recognizable diagnostic entity. Therefore, careful assessment and documentation of an associated symptom cluster, syndrome, or psychiatric disorder is important for the selection and the prescription of a specific drug that may have beneficial effects. Many of the biochemical markers (e.g., low 5-HIAA) and antiaggressive compounds reviewed appear to have "symptomatic" as opposed to diagnostic specificity. The current literature indicates that some drug interventions may work in the absence of a fully developed or classifiable diagnostic condition within existing schema. Moreover, it is possible that such interventions may add to the efficacy of treatment in the absence of currently known methods for identifying biochemical markers or deficits. Perhaps the emergence of public health models of domestic violence will facilitate the development of specialized diagnostic paradigms that acknowledge the unique parameters of this type of violence. Knowing the traumatic, injurious, and, at times, life-threatening quality of domestic violence, it would be difficult to argue against the inclusion of both perpetration and victimization-related syndromes as distinct entities within new nosological systems and related health plans.

The use of adjunctive psychopharmacological interventions for violence and abuse may also facilitate the development and differentiation of better typologies for domestically violent men. Although there are some common features among domestically violent men, it is increasingly clear that they are all not the same. Although differing profiles may result in part from the ideology, methodology, and the sampling procedures used by investigators (Dutton, 1988), they also reflect the complex etiology and multifaceted nature of this type of assault (Holtzworth-Monroe & Stuart, 1994; Rosenbaum & Maiuro, 1989). The trend toward identifying subgroups of domestically violent men on a variety of personality (Dutton & Starzomski, 1993; Hamberger & Hastings, 1986), behavioral (Gondolf, 1988) biological (Gottman et al., 1995; Warnken et al., 1994), and background (Caesar, 1988) variables is a promising development, given the need to evolve more refined and effective interventions. There appears to be more than one pathway into this pattern of behavior and, undoubtedly, there may be more than one pathway to change and recovery. Interestingly, there appears to be convergence of thought in the existing psychopharmacological and domestic violence literature that some perpetrators may present profiles that are more amenable (affectively disordered, Type II, angry, impulsive) or less amenable (predatory, Type I, sadistically hostile, premeditated) to treatment (Gottman et al., 1995; Holtzworth-Monroe & Stuart, 1994; Maiuro, 1989). More controlled studies investigating the applicability and efficacy of existing psychopharmacological treatments for domestically violent men are needed to help answer these questions.

Acknowledgements.
The authors would like to thank Jane Eberle and Ruth White for their assistance during the preparation of this chapter.

REFERENCES

American Medical Association. (1992a). American Medical Association diagnostic and treatment guidelines on domestic violence. *Archives of Family Medicine, 1,* 39-47.

American Medical Association: Council on Ethical and Judicial Affairs. (1992b). Physicians and domestic violence: Ethical considerations. *Journal of the American Medical Association, 267,* 3190-3193.

American Psychiatric Association. (1994). *Diagnostic and statistical manual of mental disorders* (4th ed.). Washington, DC: Author.

Asberg, M., Thoren, P., & Traskman, L. (1976). "Serotonin depression"—A biochemical subgroup within the affective disorders? *Science, 191,* 478-480.

Asberg, M., Traskman, L., & Thoren, P. (1976). 5-HIAA in the cerebrospinal fluid: A biochemical suicide predictor? *Archives of General Psychiatry, 33,* 1193-1197.

Ballenger, J. C., & Post, R. M. (1980). Carbamazepine in manic-depressive illness: A new treatment. American. *Journal of Psychiatry, 137,* 782-790.

Bandura, A. (1973). *Aggression: A social learning analysis.* Englewood Cliffs, NJ: Prentice-Hall.

Beasely, R., & Stoltenberg, C. D. (1992). Personality characteristics of male spouse abusers, *Professional Psychology: Research & Practice, 23,* 310-317.

Biaggio, M. K., & Maiuro, R. D. (1985). Recent advances in the assessment of anger. In C. D. Spielberger & J. N. Butcher (Eds.), *Advances in personality assessment: vol. 5* (pp. 71-111). Hillsdale, NJ: LEA.

Bland, R., & Orn, H. (1986). Family violence and psychiatric disorder. *Canadian Journal of Psychiatry, 31,* 129-137.

Breggin, P. R. (1980). In E. S. Valenstein (Ed.) *The psychosurgery debate: Scientific, legal and ethical perspectives* (pp. 467-493). San Francisco: W. H. Freeman and Company.

Browne, A. (1993). Violence against women by male partners. *American Psychologist, 48,* 1077-1087.

Brown, G. L., Ebert, M. H., Goyer, P. F., Jimerson, D. C., Klein,W. J., Bunney, W. E., Jr., & Goodwin, F. K. (1982). Aggression, suicide, and serotonin: Relationships to cerebrospinal fluid amine metabolites. *American Journal of Psychiatry, 139,* 741-746.

Brown, G. L., Goodwin, F. K., Ballenger, J. C., Goyer, P. F., & Major, L. F. (1979). Aggression in humans correlates with cerebrospinal fluid amine metabolites. *Psychiatry Research, 1,* 131-139.

Byles, J. A. (1978). Violence, alcohol problems, and other problems in disintegrating families. *Journal of Studies on Alcohol, 39,* 551-553.

Caesar, P. L. (1988). Exposure to violence in the families-of-origin among wife abusers and maritally nonviolent men. *Violence and Victims, 3,* 49-63.

Coccaro, E. F. (1989). Central sertonin and impulsive aggression. British *Journal of Psychiatry, 155,* 52-62.

Coccaro, E. F., Astill, J. L., Herbert, J., & Shut, A. G. (1989). Fluoxetine treatment of impulsive aggression in DSM-III-R personality disorder patients. *Journal of Clinical Psychopharmacology, 10,* 373-375.

Coccaro, E. F., & Murphy, D. L. (1990). (Eds.) *Serotonin in major psychiatric disorders.* Washington, DC: American Psychiatric Press.

Conn, L. M., & Lion, J. R. (1984). Pharmacologic approaches to violence. *Psychiatric Clinics of North America, 7,* 879-886.

Coccaro, E. F., Siever, L. J., Klar, H. M., Maurer, G., Cochrane, K., Cooper, T. B., Mohs, R. C., & Davis, K. L. (1989). Serotonergic studies in affective and personality disorder patients: Correlates with suicidal and impulsive aggressive behavior. *Archives of General Psychiatry, 46,* 587-599.

Cornelius, J. R., Soloff, P. H., Perel, J. M., & Ulrich, R. F. (1990). Fluoxetine trial in borderline personality disorder. *Psychopharmacology Bulletin, 26,* 151-154.

Dalby M.A. (1975). Behavioral effects of carbamazepine. *Advances in Neurology, 11,* 331-334.

Dinwiddie, S. H. (1992). Psychiatric disorders among wife batterers. *Comprehensive Psychiatry, 33,* 411-416.

Dobash, R., & Dobash, R. (1987). *Theoretical underpinnings of family violence.* Paper presented at the meeting of the Association for the Advancement of Behavior Therapy, New York, NY.

Dutton, D. G. (1988). *The domestic assault of women: Psychological and criminal justice perspectives.* Boston: Allyn & Bacon.

Dutton, D. G., & Starzomski, A. (1993). Borderline personality in perpetrators of psychological and physical abuse. *Violence and Victims, 8,* 327-337.

Dutton, D. G., & Starzomski, A. (1994). Psychological differences between court-referred and self-referred wife assaulters. *Criminal Justice and Behavior, 21,* 203-222.

Edleson, J.L. & Tolman, R.M. (1992). *Intervention for men who batter: An ecological approach.* Newbury Park: Sage Publications.

Eichelman, B. (1987). Neurochemical and psychopharmacologic aspects of aggressive behavior. In H. Y. Meltzer (Ed.), *Psychopharmacology: The third generation of progress* (pp. 697-704). New York: Raven Press.

Eichelman, B. (1988). Toward a rational pharmacotherapy for aggressive behavior. *Hospital and Community Psychiatry, 39,* 31-39.

Eichelman, B. (1992). Aggressive behavior: From laboratory to clinic: Quo vadit? *Archives of General Psychiatry, 49,* 488-492.

Eichelman, B., & Hartwig, A. (1993). The clinical psychopharmacology of violence: Toward a nosology of human aggressive behavior. *Psychopharmacology Bulletin, 29,* 57-63.

Else, L., Wonderlich, S. A., Beatty, W. W., Christie, D. W., & Staton, R. D. (1993). Personality characteristics of men who physically abuse women. *Hospital and Community Psychiatry, 44,* 54-58.

Fagan, J. A., Stewart, D. K., & Hansen, K. V. (1983). Violent men or violent husbands? In D. Finkelhor, R. J. Gelles, G. T. Hotaling, & M. A. Straus (Eds.), *The dark side of families: Current family violence research.* Beverly Hills, CA: Sage.

Fava, M., Anderson, K., & Rosenbaum, J. F. (1990). "Anger attacks": Possible variance of panic and major depressive disorders. *American Journal of Psychiatry, 7,* 867-870.

Fava, M., Rosenbaum, J. F., Pava, J. A., McCarthy, M. K., Steingaid, R. J., & Bouffides, E. (1993). Anger attacks in unipolar depression. Part 1: clinical correlates and response to fluoxetine treatment. *American Journal of Psychiatry, 150,* 1158-1167.

File, S. E. (1985). Tolerance to the behavioral actions of benzodiazepines. *Neuroscience and biobehaviorial reviews, 9,* 113-121.

Flournoy, P. S., & Wilson, G. L. (1991). Brief research report: Assessment of MMPI profiles of male batterers. *Violence and Victims, 6,* 309-320.

Gelles, R. J. (1972). *The violent home: A study of physical aggression between husbands and wives.* Beverly Hills, CA: Sage.

Gelles, R. J. (1974). *The violent home: A study of physical aggression between husbands and wives.* Sagemark edition. Beverly Hills, CA: Sage.

Gondolf, E. W. (1988). Who are these guys? Toward a typology of batterers. *Violence and Victims, 3,* 187-203.

Gottman, J. M., Jacobson, N. S., Rushe, R. H., Short, J. W., Babcock, J., La Taillade, J. J., & Waltz, J. (1995). The relationship between heart rate reactivity, emotionally aggressive behavior and general violence in batterers. *Journal of Family Psychology, 9* (3), 227–248.

Groh, C. (1976) The psychotropic effect of Tegretol in non-epileptic children, with particular reference to the drug's indications. In W. Birkmayer (Ed.), *Epileptic seizures-behavior-pain* (pp. 259-263). London: University Park Press.

Gunderson, J. G. (1984). *Borderline personality disorder.* Washington, DC: American Psychiatric Press.

Hamberger, L. K., & Hastings, J. E. (1986). Personality correlates of men who abuse their partners: A cross-validation study. *Journal of Family Violence, 1,* 323—341,

Hamberger, L. K., & Lohr, J. M. (1989). Proximal causes of spouse abuse: A theoretical analysis for cognitive-behavioral interventions. In P. L. Caesar & L. K. Hamberger (Eds.), *Treating men who batter: Theory, practice, and programs* (pp. 53-76). New York: Springer.

Hart, S. D., Dutton, D. G., & Newlove, T. (1993). The prevalence of personality disorder among wife assaulters. *Journal of Personality Disorders, 7,* 329-341.

Hastings, J. E., & Hamberger, L. K. (1988). Personality characteristics of spouse abusers: A controlled comparison. *Violence and Victims, 3,* 31-48.

Holzworth-Munroe, A., & Stuart, G. L. (1994). Typologies of batterers: Three subtypes and the differences among them. *Psychological Bulletin, 116,* 476-497.

Hotaling, G. T., & Sugarman, D. B. (1986). An analysis of risk markers in husband to wife violence: The current state of knowledge. *Violence and Victims, 1,* 101-124.

Kantor, G. K., & Straus, M. A. (1986). *The drunken bum theory of wife beating.* Paper presented at the National Alcoholism Forum Conference of Alcohol and the Family, San Francisco.

Kuhn-Gebhart, V. (1976). Behavioral disorders in non-epileptic children and treatment with carbamazepine. In W. Birkmayer (Ed.), *Seizures-Behavior-Pain* (pp. 264-267). London: University Park Press.

Lewis, D. O., Lovely, R., Yeager, C., & Femina, D. D. (1988). Toward a theory of the genesis of violence: A follow-up study of delinquents. *Journal of the American Academy of Child and Adolescent Psychiatry, 28,* 431-436.

Lidberg, L., Tuck, J. R., Asberg, M., Scalia-Tomba, G. P., & Bertillson, L. (1985). Homicide, suicide, and CSF 5-HIAA. *Acta Psychiatrica Scandinavica, 71,* 230-236.

Lion, J. R. (1979). Benzodiazepines in the treatment of aggressive patient. *Journal of Clinical Psychiatry, 40,* 70-71.

Lion, J. R., Hill, J., & Madden, D. J. (1975). Lithium carbonate and aggression: A case report. *Diseases of the Nervous System, 36,* 557-558.

Lipman, R. S., Covi, L., Rickels, K., McNair, D. M., Downing, R.,Kahn, R. J., Lasseter, V. K., & Faden, V. (1986). Imipramine and chlordiazepoxide in depressive and anxiety disorders. *Archives of General Psychiatry, 43,* 68-77.

Luchins D. J. (1983) Carbamazepine for the violent psychiatric patient. *Lancet, 1,* 766.

Luchins, D. J. (1984) Carbamazepine in violent non-epileptic schizophrenics, *Psychopharmacology Bulletin, 20,* 569-571.

Maiuro, R.D. (1993). Intermittent explosive disorder. In D. L. Dunner (Ed.), *Current psychiatric therapy* (pp. 482-489), Philadelphia: W. B. Saunders.

Maiuro, R.D. (1989). *The sadistic hostility questionnaire.* Unpublished manuscript.

Maiuro, R. D., Cahn, T. S., Vitaliano, P. P., Wagner, B. C., & Zegree, J. B. (1988). Anger, hostility, and depression in domestically violent versus generally assaultive men and nonviolent control subjects. *Journal of Consulting and Clinical Psychology, 56,* 17-23.

Maiuro, R. D., & Eberle, J. A. (1989). New developments in research on aggression: An international report. *Violence and Victims, 4,* 3-15.

Maiuro, R. D., O'Sullivan, M. J., Michael, M. C., & Vitaliano, P. P. (1989). Anger, hostility, and depression in assaultive versus suicide attempting males. *Journal of Clinical Psychology, 45,* (4), 531–541.

Maiuro, R. D., & Sugg, N. (Eds.). (in press). *Handbook on family violence for health care professionals.* New York: Springer.

Maiuro, R. D., Vitaliano, P. P., & Cowden, L. (1995, July). *Psychosocial profiles of domestically violent alcohol abusing men: Implications for evaluation and treatment.* Paper presented at the Fourth International Family Violence Research Conference, Durham, N.H.

Mandler, G. (1982). Stress and thought processes. In L. Goldberger & S. Breznitz (Eds.), *Handbook of stress.* New York: Free Press/Macmillan.

Manji, H. K., Potter, W. Z., & Lenox, R. H. (1995). Signal transduction pathways: Molecular targets for lithium's actions. *Achives of General Psychiatry, 52,* 531-543.

Mattes, J. A. (1984). Carbamazepine for uncontrolled rage outbursts. *Lancet 2,* 1164-1165.

Mattes, J. A. (1990). Comparative effectiveness of carbamazepine and propranolol for rage outbursts. *Journal of Neuropsychiatry and Clinical Neurosciences, 2,* 159-164.

Mattes, J.A., Rosenberg, J., & Mayes, D.. (1984). Carbamazepine vs. propranolol in patients with uncontrolled rage outbursts: A random assignment study. *Psychopharmacology Bulletin, 20,* 98-100.

Miczek, K. A., Weerts, E., Haney, M., & Tidey, J. (1994). Neurobiological mechanisms controlling aggression: Preclinical developments for pharmacotherapeutic interventions. *Neuroscience and Biobehavioral Reviews, 18,* 97-110.

Monahan, J. (1981). *The clinical prediction of violent behavior.* U.S. Department of Health and Human Services, Washington, DC: ADAMHA.

Morand, C., Young, S. N., & Ervin, F. R. (1983). Clinical response of aggressive schizophrenics to oral tryptophan. *Biological Psychiatry, 18,* 575-578.

Monroe, R.R. (1970). *Episodic Behavioral Disorders.* Cambridge, MA: Harvard University Press.

Monroe, R. R. (1975) Anticonvulsants in the treatment of aggression. *Journal of Nervous and Mental Disorders, 160,* 119-126.

Norden, M. J. (1989). Fluoxetine in borderline personality disorder. *Progress in Neuro-Psychopharmacology and Biological Psychiatry, 13,* 885-893.

Pagelow, M. D. (1993). Response to Hamberger's comments. *Journal of Interpersonal Violence, 8,* 137-139.

Puente, R. M. (1976). The use of carbamazepine in the treatment of behavioral disorders in children. In W. Birkmayer (Ed), *Epileptic seizures-behavior-pain* (pp. 243-258). London: University Park Press.

Randall, T. (1990). Domestic violence intervention calls for more than treating injuries. *Journal of the American Medical Association, 264,* 939-944.

Remschmidt H. (1976). The psychotropic effect of carbamazepine in non-epileptic patients, with particular reference to problems posed by clinical studies in children with behavioral disorders. In W. Birkmayer (Ed.), *Epileptic seizures-behavior-pain* (pp. 253-258). London: University Park Press.

Robins, L. N., Helzer, J. E., Croughan, J., et al. (1981). National Institute of Mental Health Diagnostic interview Schedule: Its history, characteristics, and validity. *Archives of General Psychiatry, 38,* 381-389.

Rosenbaum, A., & Hoge, S. K. (1989). Head injury and marital aggression. *American Journal of Psychiatry, 146,* 1048-1051.

Rosenbaum, A., & Maiuro, R. D. (1989). Eclectic approaches with men who batter. In Caesar P. L. & Hamberger, L. K. (Eds.), *Treating men who batter: Theory, practice, and programs.* New York: Springer.

Rosenbaum, A., & Maiuro, R. D. (1990). Treatment of spouse abusers. In R. T. Ammerman & M. Hersen (Eds), *Treatment of Family Violence: A Sourcebook.* New York: John Wiley & Sons, Inc..

Rosenbaum, J. F., Woods, S. W., Groves, J. E., & Klerman, G. L. (1984). Emergence of hostility during alprazolam treatment. *American Journal of Psychiatry, 141,* 792-793.

Salzman, C., Wolfson, A. N., Schatzberg, A., Looper, J., Henke, R., Albanese, M., Schwartz, J., & Miyawaki, E. (1995). Effect of fluoxetine on anger in symptomatic volunteers with borderline personality disorder. *Journal of Clinical Psychopharmacology, 15,* 23-29.

Sandler, M., Ruthven, C. R. J., Goodwin, B. L., Field, H., & Rhys, M. (1979). Phenylethylamine overproduction in aggressive psychopaths. *Lancet, 12/16,* 1269-1270.

Selye, H. (1956). *The stress of life.* New York: McGraw-Hill.

Sheard, M. H. (1984). Clinical pharmacology of aggressive behavior. *Clinical Neuropharmacology, 7,* 173-183.

Sheard, M. H., Marini, J.L, Bridges, C.I., Wagner, E. (1976). The effect of lithium on impulsive aggressive behavior in man. *American Journal of Psychiatry, 133,* 1409-1413.

Soloff, P. H. (1994). Is there any drug treatment of choice for the borderline patient? *Acta Psychiatrica Scandinavica, 89,* 50-55.

Straus, M., & Gelles, R. (1986). Societal change and change in family violence from 1975 to 1985 as revealed in two national surveys. *Journal of Marriage and the Family, 50,* 281-291.

Swanson, J. W., Holzer, C. E., Ganju, V. K., & Jono, R. T. (1990). Violence and psychiatric disorder in the community: Evidence from the Epidemiologic Catchment Area surveys. *Hospital and Community Psychiatry, 41,* 761-770.

Tupin, J. P., Smith, D. B., Clanon, T. L., Kim, L. I., Nugent, A., & Groupe, A. (1973). The long-term use of lithium in aggressive prisoners. *Comprehensive Psychiatry, 14,* 311-317.

Van Praag, H. M. (1986). (Auto) aggression and CSF 5-HIAA in depression and schizophrenia. *Psychopharmacology Bulletin, 22,* 669-673.

Van Praag, H. M., Plutchik, R., & Apter, A. (Eds.). (1990). _Violence and suicidality: Perspectives in clinical and psychobiological research._ New York: Brunner/Mazel.

Walker, L. E. A. (1979). _The battered woman._ New York: Harper & Row.

Wilson, M., & Daly, M. (1993). Spousal homicide risk and estrangement. _Violence and Victims, 8,_ 3-16.

8

Expanding the Boundaries

Toward a More Inclusive and Integrated Study of Intimate Violence

Susan L. Miller

This book, stemming from a special issue of the journal *Violence and Victims* (1994, 9, 2), is devoted to examining the complexities and subtleties regarding intimate violence by focusing on an expansive array of diverse research topics. As a whole, the authors question the paradigmatic assumptions and issues related to intimate violence, challenges us to reconceptualize some of our theoretical frameworks, and explores alternative samples, diverse methodologies, and consequences of new legal intervention policies. What is striking about this collection is the compatibility and complementary nature with such different chapters "fit" together. On the one hand, the authors acknowledge that violence extends to all kinds of human relationships; none is immune. On the other hand, just as there is no monolithic "batterer" nor monolithic "victim," the authors suggest that relying on narrow explanatory theories that are gender based or essentially sociocultural is too limiting in our study of relationship aggression. The use of different methodologies, ideologies, and foci in this volume provides a provocative forum that can guide future development of more inclusionary models and programs.

Some common themes emerge. All of the contributing authors challenge and push the limits of existing theories and models used in intimate violence research. A recurrent criticism raised by the authors highlights the assumptions of gender-based models, which not only reduce battered victims to unidimensional representations that exclude victims in same-sex relationships (Letellier, Chapter 1, and Coleman, Chapter 4), but also overgeneralize about the nature of violent relationships and ignore the variety in abusers (Dutton, Chapter 6). A related interest, discussed by Coleman (Chapter 4), Vivian and Langhinrichsen-Rohling (Chapter 2), and Warnken et al. (Chapter 5) is the importance of personality, neurological, and psychological variables in models of relationship aggression. An expansion of current criminal justice policies is introduced by Hamberger and Potente (Chapter 3) in their evaluation of the Kenosha, Wisconsin, experiment: arrest models that result in dual arrests, and push the boundaries of too narrow a conceptualization of the law enforcement role in combatting intimate violence. And Maiuro and Avery (Chapter 7) discuss the potential for including psychopharmacological methods of treating domestically violent men. Drawing from diverse areas of research, treatment and policy, issues are advanced by the authors that reflect more inclusive conceptualizations of what factors are part of the dynamics of intimate violence and how these vary or remain constant across different populations.

Critique of Sociopolitical and Gender-Based Theories

Many of the contributors acknowledge that, unlike some areas of psychological or sociological inquiry, "research in relationship aggression...has political and legal ramifications" (Warnken et al., p. 103; see others in this book). Dutton's chapter will be examined initially and more thoroughly for it raises some important controversial issues and deals with concepts that are also reflected in other chapters. Dutton begins by identifying what he sees as an ideological transgression characteristic of feminist analysis because of a devotion to viewing patriarchy as the direct cause of "wife assault." Dutton identifies this (misguided) focus as the problem of "ecological fallacy"—meaning that aggregate social categories are incorrectly used to explain individual behavior (Dooley & Catalano, 1984). Specifically, Dutton argues that unidimensional explanations of battering that anchor battering as the kingpin of patriarchy perpetuate reductionist models as well as monolithic depictions of male abusers. Feminist analyses are further flawed by not adequately capturing the complex variations in violent relationships and the range of factors that contribute to violent behavior. To bolster his contentions, Dutton points out that (according to self-reported or official data) far more men do not beat their intimate partners than men who do, clearly indicating to him that battering involves more complex dynamics than simply sociocultural factors.

Yet, at the same time Dutton is excoriating feminists for too broadly casting the explanatory net, he likewise makes the same mistake by lumping together and castigating all feminist research as if there is only one kind of feminism (ignoring the different philosophies and goals of liberal, socialist, marxist, radical, and postmodern feminisims). In fact, much of the recent compelling feminist scholarship on domestic violence steers clear of blaming patriarchy as the sole or direct causal factor, while maintaining that gender remains a crucial key explanatory variable. Rather, patriarchy provides a historical and contemporary foundation to assist in explaining the pervasive and enduring quality of (white, middle-and-upper class, heterosexual) male privilege and power that has created and defined our systems of laws, courts and law enforcement as well as other social institutions and interactions (Farr, 1988; Hoff, 1991; Smart, 1989).

Despite Dutton's brief discussion of Kuhn's paradigmatic shifts in knowledge production and how paradigms are used to deflect contradictory information, what Dutton omits in his own analysis is a historical and ideological grounding of the battered women's movement and the placement of feminist research and practice (with their attendant financial and political exigencies). The initial goals of the battered women's movement were twofold: (1) to create safe shelter and provide resources focused on the immediacy of victims' problems, and (2) to challenge the patriarchal structure of social institutions that created and perpetuated male domination over women in both the public and private spheres (Schechter, 1982). The abusers' problems were viewed as tangential to the early phases of the movement so as not to dilute the goals of the battered women's movement or to deflect attention away from women's problems (Dobash & Dobash, 1992). As the movement evolved, particularly in the last decade, innovative programs involving prevention and education have been introduced, as well as an increase in court-mandated counseling programs for abusers. Even unidimensional portraits of battered women themselves are being challenged; although most battered women share similar battering experiences, their interpretations, reactions, and actions to the violence are further shaped by their own diverse cultural, racial, ethnic, class, and sexual orientation experiences and expectations (Miller, 1989; Rasche, 1991). Dutton's ahistorical and superficial critique of feminist analyses is precisely why feminist analyses are crucial: Human behavior is anchored by sociocultural beliefs shaped by genderpolitics.[1]

To his credit, Dutton (1988) presents a promising solution in his nested ecological model that essentially connects both macro-and micro-level variables in explaining intimate violence, including the interactive effects of the broader culture, the subculture, the family, and individually learned characteristics. The interest in generating more inclusive models that integrate social as well as psychological factors is reflected in chapters in this volume (Coleman; Vivian Langhinrichsen-Rohling; and Warnken et al.). Dutton also stresses that individual characteristics of male batterers vary and understanding this variation may help us to differentiate between habitual versus sporadic abusers. In a related vein, Letellier (Chapter 1) also explores individual uniqueness of men in his discussion of psychological traits and male socialization and how these relate to battered gay men.

Dutton marshals "evidence" to "prove" that feminist analyses of wife assault that implicate patriarchy are shortsighted. He argues that if patriarchy directly causes wife assault, the greater frequency of lesbian battering reported in the literature vis-a-vis heterosexual battering is inexplicable. Similar claims are made in the Coleman and Letellier chapters. We should take caution, however, to not over-state the comparability of rates of heterosexual and homosexual relationship violence. Typically, rates from nationally representative samples of heterosexual couples (28%–50%) are compared to studies on violent lesbian and/or gay couples (with rates ranging from 25%–48%). The authors prematurely conclude that homosexual battering is equal or in some cases higher than heterosexual battering. Obtaining accurate incidence estimates for gay and lesbian battering is difficult, particularly given the double "taboo" of being a domestic violence victim as well as a homosexual. Sample limitations also increase the unreliability of estimates, including nonrandomness, self-selected samples (snowball, convenience, referrals through newspaper recruitment or fliers, contracts with therapists), and samples that overrepresent white, well-educated, and middle- and upper-class respondents. Additionally, research on lesbian relationship violence (and gay male violence) is in its infancy, and as Coleman points out in her literature review, methodological problems have not yet been resolved. Because Letellier's sample is based on his own clinical and personal experiences, there is a clear need for replication of studies.

Dutton's discussion of cross-cultural variation is not fully informed by the extant literature. Measurement of intimate violence can be significantly affected by how different racial, ethnic, or cultural minority groups define "abuse," reflecting cultural prohibitions against "loss of face" or honor for oneself or one's family, language barriers, unwillingness to expose a racial or ethnic group in a way that might reinforce negative images or stereotypes, or by how much trust one places in the criminal justice system (Rasche, 1988).

Dutton also challenges a fundamental feminist assertion that within a patriarchal society, the practice of male violence committed against women contributes to maintaining male dominance and that this practice is widely—albeit tacitly—accepted. Although he offers survey results reporting that a majority of respondents believe violence is inappropriate, several points are missing in his analysis. First, the survey question fails to take into account the contextual circumstances of when violence is or is not considered appropriate, which may vary by gender of respondent. Second, there may be "social desirability" operating, in which respondents tailor their responses to please the researcher or to some perceived image of acceptability (Babbie, 1992). Third, asking batterers in treatment if they think their actions are acceptable obfuscates the point. Dutton maintains that a feminist interpretation would expect no guilt or evasion from batterers when confronted with their behavior; yet the feminist research on the cycle of violence clearly states the opposite expectation because batterers are trying to "win" back their partners and will do/say anything to prevent their departure (Walker, 1979). Men's responses may also differ depending on whether they volunteered for treatment or treatment was court-ordered. Finally, the dating violence literature suggests that many individuals believe mild violence—like slapping—is acceptable and can even be interpreted as an expression of love (Levy, 1991; Sugarman & Hotaling, 1989). In addition, Dutton neglects a whole area of research that examines the role that male peer support plays in reinforcing collective definitions of masculinity and dominance and how these social support networks relate to male violence (DeKeseredy, 1988; Sanday, 1990; Warshaw, 1988) although he does include subcultural norms in the exosystem part of his nested ecological model.

Overall, Dutton dismisses "gender politics," finding no relationship to intimate violence. He sees the powerlessness of men (e.g., their inability to have the "power advantage" women have in their ability to "introspect, analyze, and describe feelings and process" pp. 136–137) as playing a more important role than men's power in terms of their "physical or sociopolitical resources." The dichotomy of power/powerlessness and how it relates to intimate violence is far more complicated than Dutton leads us to believe and is beyond the scope of this chapter. The theme of gender politics and its relationship to power and control is reflected in many of the chapters and is explored further in the next section.

The Continued Importance of Examining the Role of a Capitalist, Patriarchal Society

Both Coleman's and Letellier's articles elaborate on Dutton's mention of the issues of heterosexism and exclusion: the very existence of battering in lesbian and gay male relationships challenges the early guiding tenets of the battered women's movement that stipulate abuse to be committed by men against their female partners, grounded by sociopolitical theories involving male domination and control over subordinate women, with gender roles maintained by the threat or actual presence of violence. Given these gender-based assumptions, both Coleman and Letellier argue that there is no room in the picture for same-sex violence in relationships. We should note, however, that essential to our conceptualization of American society are the capitalist, patriarchal structures that demarcate the choices, patterns, and behaviors for both genders in society. This sets the stage for both market (public) and familial/intimate (personal) social relations. The dominant relationship is characterized by the physical and economic power men wield over women. Within heterosexual relationships, gender (male privilege) is more obvious, yet power (both personal and economic) characterizes lesbian and gay relationships as well

(Blumstein & Schwartz, 1983). It is simplistic to dismiss patriar-chal-based feminist theories of intimate violence as being falsely deterministic or unrelated to intimate violence when examining same-sex relationships.

Both men and women are raised in a patriarchal society and learn therefore to behave in gender-appropriate ways that are fur-ther reinforced by other socializing agents and institutions (Coleman, Chapter 4). Desire for control over resources and deci-sions in relationships knows no sexual orientation boundaries (Blumstein & Schwartz, 1983). Hart (1986) argues that power to make the decisions and the violence that can "assure" it when "control is resisted" and, in fact, "the same elements of hierarchy of power, ownership, entitlement and control exist in lesbian fam-ily relationships." As the authors in this book point out, social stress, social isolation, low socioeconomic status, and rigid sex roles increase the likelihood of violence in heterosexual couples and families (Weidman, 1986); these same factors are related to les-bian battering (Coleman, 1990; Renzetti, 1992). Feminist theory in general focuses on unequal power distribution in relationships and gender-power matters: "Gay men can suffer when one partner has a larger income...having more money gives a [gay] man sym-bolic—and therefore real—advantages over his partner" (Blumstein and Schwartz, 1983, pp.59, 110). Women's earning power is less than men's, which can cause even greater financial stress for lesbian couples.

Both Coleman and Letellier correctly state that early feminist writings regarding the battered women's movement helped to ren-der same-sex intimate violence invisible; however, this invisibility is changing and a feminist analysis concerned with power and control continues to significantly contribute to explaining violent relationship dynamics and should not be dismissed and discarded for being implacably heterosexist. Again, integrated theories are necessary: ones that are gender neutral and include societal and interpersonal factors as well as psychological characteristics. These same concerns are raised by other authors in this book, and remain especially important for same-sex intimate violence since there is such a dearth of empirical research exploring this population.

New Directions: Additional Variables, Concepts, and Alternative Models

Expanding sociocultural models of relationship aggression and developing integrated models of explanation to better guide research, policy, and intervention is the next step. Although some researchers have expressed a reluctance in including individual-level factors that could be used to inappropriately excuse violent behavior, the researchers in this book welcome the inclusion. At this point, it is widely recognized that people are profoundly shaped by many features: biological, neurological, environmental, and familial, and these features may interact or correlate with other enduring components that affect one's psychological makeup. For example, Coleman (Chapter 4) argues: "trauma experienced by children as a result of family violence has significant implications in the development of personality characteristics and disorders which become problematic in adolescence and adulthood."

Prior empirical work with male batterers indicate that levels of psychopathology, and physiological and neurological factors may play a more important role in battering than traditionally acknowledged and may help explain variations in individual relationship aggression (Coleman, pp. 80–85; see also chapters by Vivian and Langhinrichsen-Rohling, Dutton, and Letellier). Studies examining heterosexual male batterers using a variety of personality tests found that various personality traits/profiles are associated with battering (see pp. 83–85) in Coleman and other chapters for brief reviews of these studies).

Coleman provides just such an integration of personality traits and disorders to explain the phenomenon of battering, looking specifically at a sample of lesbians. Previous lesbian violence studies indicate similar personality traits that have exerted effects in heterosexual battering models may be operating: drug/alcohol abuse, powerlessness, low self-esteem, overdependency, jealousy (Renzetti, 1992). Additionally, both gender and sex-role socialization play a part in the development of different personality characteristics. Coleman's work looks particularly at borderline personality disorder and narcissistic personality disorder because these disorders may result from childhood trauma and "consequential failures in normal development." Coleman believes that women are more likely to have been victims of childhood sexual and physical abuse that is complicated by female socialization that emphasizes identification with others and interrelatedness rather than the "male" characteristics of autonomy and independence (see also Gilligan, 1982).

For lesbian batterers with borderline or narcissistic personality disorders, these issues are compounded because lesbian couples are often more "intrapsychically merged," which is reinforced by greater intimacy between partners, the closed nature of lesbian communities because of their small size, minority status, and the possibility that friends could potentially become lovers. For "merger hungry personalities," the closeness is desired but also it magnifies the potential for abandonment, which could stimulate conflict and control in an attempt to create distance (pp. 89–90). Coleman also discusses the projection of bad qualities (such as shame or powerlessness resulting from internalized homophobia and misogyny) onto one's partner and how that shapes the possibility of violence. Lesbian batterers with narcissistic personality disorders would engage in battering to increase their self-esteem that has been lost, and this impotence needs to be replaced "with omnipotence and grandiosity... as a means to exert power and control" over her partner (p. 94).

Coleman provides some excellent treatment strategies to increase effective counseling for lesbian batterers, including addressing the social conditions of homophobia, misogyny, and sex-role socialization as well as more specific strategies for those with borderline and narcissistic personality disorders that remain sensitive to the dynamics in lesbian relationships.

Personality Changes as a Result of Head Trauma

Although the research conducted by Warnken et al. (Chapter 5) is not directly concerned with sociocultural models, it suggests that the possible link between physiological factors (such as head injury) and relationship aggression provide a "threat" to models which focus on power and control (p. 120). Similar to other contributors, Warnken et al. favor expanding etiological models of relationship aggression to include both biological factors and neurological dysfunction. They look specifically at traumatic head injury, which affects more than 7 million people annually and shares common characteristics with relationship violence. They set out to test whether damage to the brain (as the site of cognition, emotion, behavior, and memory) affects interpersonal relationships and functioning. Warnken et al. provide an insightful discussion of the implications of their findings as well as a discussion of the study's limitations. It is important for people working in the field to be cognizant of the increased risk of relationship aggression for head-injured males. Treatment implications include biological interventions and the incorporation of specific treatment into posthead injury rehabilitation protocols.

Psychopharmacological Treatment of Aggressive Behavior

Maiuro and Avery's chapter explores biological forms of intervention for domestically violent men using psychopharmacological treatment. Their reasoning is solid: Since many factors contribute to violent behavior, it is thus reductionist to ignore one facet, such as the biological, because of its potential controversy. At the same time, they mention—albeit briefly—the ethical and conceptual problems this inclusion introduces, namely, that men's accountability for their violent behavior is alleviated, and male offenders may become recast as victims of their (out-of-control) biologically driven urges and forces. The danger, however, in Maiuro and Avery's interpretation here is that men would not be labeled as crazy, whereas women who are more often seen as hostage to their (out-of-control) hormones, *are* viewed as crazy. The reconceptualization of men as victims is potentially overdeterministic, for it gives short shrift to the social structural context of which intimate violence is a part.

It is deeply problematic to speak about male violent aggression as biologically driven and uncontrollable. Violent men often *only* target their current or former female partners and are somehow able to "control" their aggression outside of their intimate relationships. Maiuro and Avery, however, avoid a discussion of male power and gender politics when they address sociocultural factors. Recent research by Saunders (1993) suggests that there are multiple profiles of men who assault their female partners, thus requiring multiple kinds of interventions. He identifies three groups: generalized aggressor, family only, and emotionally volatile. Just as these men may differ in their responsiveness to criminal justice and counseling interventions, so might their differences affect drug intervention.

From a policy perspective, the issue of court-mandated treatment must also be considered. Maiuro and Avery (p. 177) promote a "collaborative relationship with the court system," similar to mandated treatments following arrest in place already for batterers. Hamberger and Hastings (1993) have reviewed the limited research on compliance with court-mandated counseling treatment and found that support for this use is mixed, often hinging on demographic factors and abuse severity, although more mandated offenders enter and complete counseling than nonmandated offenders. They also review the 28 major research evaluations of treatment outcome, finding, for example, that recidivism measures are unclear or unreported, and studies suffer from small sample sizes, nonrandom assignment to treatment, attrition, follow-up intervals, and poor outcome measures (see Hamberger and Hastings 1993). Psychopharmacological approaches to intervention for interpersonal violence, as suggested by Maiuro and Avery (p.), may also be plagued by similar problems. In addition, as noted by Maiuro and Avery, unintended or opposite consequences may result from chemical interventions with violent men. In fact, earlier studies that have attempted to reduce the sexual aggression of men with "chemical castration," find the overall treatments ineffective (Fausto-Sterling, 1985).

Maiuro and Avery's clarion call echoes those of the other contributors: to expand our knowledge and repertoire available to deal with aggressive behavior toward one's intimate partner by adopting multifaceted approaches. Maiuro and Avery propose a balanced approach that is not oversimplistic, deterministic, or ignorant of social learning and cognitive-behavioral treatment models. They argue that being cognizant of the larger sociocultural environments in which battering occurs mandates the inclusion of *all* kinds of immediate and longer-term interventions, including strengthening criminal justice and legal responses. They envision a "broad-based biopsychosocial approach [which] would also include a preventative focus on distal social factors" (p. 177). In following this concern, Maiuro and Avery provide general guidelines that can to be used to empirically ground treatment plans.

Gender and Couple Differences

Vivian and Langhinrichsen-Rohling's research examines gender and couple differences in partner aggression using a clinical couple sample. Through their use of multiple indices of victimizations (such as frequency, severity, psychological impact, and physical injury), they identified three conceptually distinct subgroups of mutually victimized couples. Vivian and Langhinrichsen-Rohling also include the often-neglected psychological component of abuse, an interest that is surfacing in the literature as well (cf Retzinger, 1991), particularly given that high levels of verbal/psychological aggression in both spouses is predictive of the beginning of physical aggression in couples during the first 3 years of marriage (Murphy & O'Leary, 1989; p. 24 in Vivian and Langhinrichsen-Rohling).

Their findings add further confirmation to the recurring debate (see Hamberger & Potente, Chapter 3 over husband, or mutual, victimization, finding that context and gender continue to influence effects of aggression: "even when aggression is bidirectional it may not be symmetrical, as wives are affected more negatively than husbands." Additionally, even when wives appear to be the primary perpetrators, the wives still experience more distress and dysphoria than when men are the primary perpetrators. Vivian and Langhinrichsen-Rohling propose that relationship diversity and individual differences facilitate the need to test multiple models of marital aggression that incorporate contextual and individual variables and use multidimensional assessment tools to capture the full picture of marital aggression. Appropriate treatment and interventions need to be linked to both gender and couple differences, and these differences should be considered when developing typologies that reflect variations between couples.

Variations in Male Offenders

In his discussion of gay male battering, Letellier looks at a less familiar angle by examining how being male affects the interpretations and responses of a gay male victim. Men are socialized to be the protectors, the victors, the problem solvers, and the survivors. To see themselves as the "victim" in a variety of situations such as incest or battering can threaten their male identity and complicate their willingness to seek help, unless the man is injured quite severely. This disassociation with male victimization is exacerbated by the exclusion of same-sex relationships in larger society as evidenced by the lack of programs, laws, and shelters, thus contributing to the victim's social isolation and to his remaining in a violent relationship.

Using his clinical experience working with battered gay and bisexual men, Letellier illuminates the concept of "mutual combat." As stated earlier, women are socialized to resolve conflict through peacemaking, while men absorb cultural messages that the use of physical force against an attacker is appropriate. The greater likelihood that male victims will respond to physical violence with self-defensive or retaliatory violence, however, should not be interpreted to mean that same-sex battering is mutual. Similar to what is urged elsewhere in this volume, the context of the relationship must be taken into account to determine the motivation and power dynamics that activate the violent action. Letellier also raises the possibility that "victims identify as perpetrators regardless of the motivation for their violence" because the role is more socially acceptable or because the victim feels that he is equally responsible. These interpretative differences must be taken into account when treatment and intervention programs are designed, particularly given the social isolation from traditional sources of help that are designed primarily for heterosexuals that so many gay men encounter.

Letellier suggests that future research should examine the correlation between homophobia and same-sex battering as well as the social blaming of gays for the AIDS epidemic and how these beliefs may fuel relationship violence. For instance, gay victims of battering who have internalized homophobia and society's hostility may feel that the violence is justified punishment for being gay. Although Letellier does not raise any issues specifically pertaining to bisexuals, his emphasis on examining how gay men respond to violence and trauma should stimulate future empirical endeavors and guide criminal justice and social service practitioners.

Complexities of Criminal Justice Policy

Until this point, the research presented in this book has focused on theoretical issues and special populations, such as head-injured males and gay men and lesbians. Chapter 3 by Hamberger and Potente raises important issues concerning treatment programs for heterosexual women arrested for domestic violence. This kind of treatment dilemma is the consequence of a dramatic shift in law enforcement response to domestic violence, namely, the initiation of proarrest or mandatory arrest policies.[2] This policy shift was promulgated by the Minneapolis Domestic Violence Experiment; which reported that arrest of batterers was more effective in deterring subsequent violence than the more traditional informal police actions (Sherman & Berk, 1984). A possible consequence is that an augmented enforcement response would "widen the net," thus increasing the likelihood that "victims," typically women, would be arrested with the batterers. In Chapter 3, Hamberger and Potente present the consequences of new mandatory arrest legislation enacted in Kenosha, Wisconsin: women experienced a 12-fold increase in arrests while men experienced only a twofold increase. Although Hamberger and Potente acknowledge that there are some violent women who act similarly to men and may use violence to dominate and control, women's culpability and consequences of their actions differ from men: most women cause less injury, and their violence rates are lower, particularly when motives and context are taken into account (Marshall & Rose, 1990). Following this reasoning, Hamberger and Potente introduce the neutral term "domestically violent" women to describe and label women who assault their partners, a term they feel is context descriptive without relying on politically or value-laden pejorative connotations of power and injury associated with terms used to describe male batterers of women (see also Hamberger, 1991).

The dilemmas of a court-ordered treatment program for "domestically violent" women are obvious, particularly if the majority of women act out of self-defense or in retaliation for previous attacks upon them. Traditional legal definitions of self-defense, however, were designed to encompass situations *men* were most likely to experience: a fight between equally sized opponents—usually strangers—occurring in a public place and the ability to retreat or escape (Gillespie, 1989). These same legal parameters do not apply equally to a typical battered woman's situation: the abuser is not a stranger, the violence occurs in private, the violent incident is most often not a fair fight among equals since they are not the same size, strength, or fighting ability, and there is often no ability to retreat (Gillespie, 1989). Hamberger and Potente recognize that the battered women arrested under the new legislation were viewed as culpable within the legal bounds of self-defense even though the majority were battered themselves and clearly different from their male counterparts. Most of these women, however, had not previously used battered women advocacy services, so providing these services through court order was viewed as an opportunity to connect them with the local shelters, to decrease their isolation, and to provide them with community resources and support services (see also Nurius, Furrey & Berliner, 1992).

Despite the initial—and lingering—concerns about court-ordered treatment for domestically violent women, in the Kenosha experiment, the majority of women responded positively and wanted to learn techniques for taking responsibility (*not* blame) for their own behavior and to seek nonviolent ways to ensure the safety of themselves and their children. Part of their willingness may reflect the laudable goals and philosophical orientation of the women's violence intervention program and the actual content of the treatment program, described in greater detail in Hamberger and Potente's article. Different goals exist for the men who are court ordered for treatment: they are challenged to stop abusing power and to learn to share power equally with their partners.[3] The program provisions are similar to programs provided in shelters, yet the domestically violent women in this sample had not been exposed to these resources through residential or community outreach programs.

A particular strength of the program involves teaching assertiveness skills, which are introduced within a broader conceptual framework designed to empower women beyond their immediate relationship needs, such as dealing with social welfare system personnel, job training programs, and child protective or mediation services—all institutions that have some bureaucratic characteristics that "can be frustrating, dehumanizing, and disempowering (pp. 69). There is also on-going coordination between respective therapists if the abuser is in his own program. However, Hamberger and Potente caution that although most of the domestically violent women are in treatment for their aggression, their partners may *not* be, thus creating a potentially risky situation. If women are mandated to treatment, however, the counseling services may not appear as threatening to either partner because the interpretation of the event does not have to include her choice or desire; the male partner may then feel less threatened and less retaliatory if it is clear that she has to attend the program regardless of his agreement or involvement.

Hamberger and Potente also maintain that through directly working with domestically violent women, they have "consistently observed that feminist sociopolitical models provide a closer fit with the data. (p. 70)" This sentiment is reminiscent of positions taken by Tolman and Bennett (1990), who believe that personality and psychopathological variables must be linked to important social variables such as the patriarchal social context and unequal power distribution (see also Adams, 1988). These beliefs are in opposition to Dutton's analysis, which may reflect both a difference in philosophical orientation of the authors and a difference in treatment populations for Hamberger and Potente because they are dealing with females while Dutton's work is with male abusers.

Where Do We Go From Here? Toward an Integration of Knowledge

From the authors represented in this collection, a universal theme emerges: multiple levels of explanations are necessary to link developmental and biological characteristics, personalities, subcultural variations, and economic, social, political, and community dimensions in our models of relationship aggression. Increasingly, social science has supported the development of integrated theoretical models of human behavior that identifies individual factors (such as personality) as well as sociocultural factors (Messner, Krohn, & Liska, 1990; Riggs & O'Leary, 1989; Stith & Rosen, 1990). For instance, Eisikovitz and Edleson (1989) introduce an ecological model that uses an "interaction of multiple variables from the individual to the society" and examine these factors across a backdrop of the social inequality of women. Models such as this one and Dutton's (1988) nested model permit greater clarification of offender variation across multiple populations.

Although this book could not capture all of the complex and varied scholarship on relationship aggression in the available space, its content reflects central issues and questions important to research, policy, and intervention. By increasing our collective knowledge of the intricacies and dynamics of violent interpersonal relationships, this book promises to stimulate new areas and kinds of research to further elaborate the themes and issues developed here.

Notes

[1]What is puzzling is that Dutton does recognize important contributions made by feminist researchers (e.g., the problems with using the Conflict Tactics Scale to compare female and male violence, gender differences in homicide rates, and their relationship to available resources).

[2]Particularly for the police, this change is not as altruistic as the words may suggest: by their continued failure to protect the rights of battered women (through trivialization of domestic assault and nonarrest), police departments became vulnerable to civil suits, such as the 1984 case Thurman v. City of Torrington, Connecticut, where a federal jury awarded a battered woman $2.3 million because the police did not protect her from her abusive husband (Zorra, 1992).

[3]These goals could be easily adoptable for treatment programs designed for battered lesbian and gay male couples.

REFERENCES

Adams, D. (1988). Treatment models of men who batter: A profeminist analysis. In K. Yllo and M. Bograd (Eds.) *Feminist perspectives on wife abuse.* Newbury Park, CA: Sage.

Babbie, E. (1992). *The practice of social research,* 6th ed. Belmont, CA: Wadsworth.

Blumstein, P., & Schwartz, P. (1983). *American couples.* New York: William Morrow.

Coleman, V.E. (1990). *Violence between lesbian couples: A between groups comparison.* Unpublished dissertation. University Microfilms International, 9109022.

DeKeseredy, W.S. (1988). *Woman abuse in dating relationships: The role of male peer support.* Toronto, Canada: Canadian Scholars' Press.

Dobash, R.E., & Dobash, R.P. (1992). *Women, violence, and social change.* London: Routledge.

Dooley, D.G., & Catalano, R. (1984). The epidemiology of economic stress. *American Journal of Community Psychology.* 12 (4), 387–409.

Dutton, D.G. (1988). *The domestic assault of women: Psychological and criminal justice perspectives.* Boston: Allyn and Bacon.

Eisikovitz, Z.C., & Edleson, J.L. (1989). Intervening with men who batter: A critical review of the literature. *Social Science Review, 9,* 384–414.

Farr, K.A. (1988). Dominance bonding through the good old boys sociability group. *Sex Roles. 18* (5/6), 259–277.

Fausto-Sterling, A. (1985). *Myths of gender: Biological theories about men and women.* New York: Basic Books.

Gillespie, C.K. (1989). *Justifiable homicide: Battered women, self-defense, and the law.* Columbus, OH: Ohio State University Press.

Gilligan, C. (1982). *In a different voice.* Cambridge, MA: Harvard University Press.

Hamberger, L.K., & Hastings, J.E. (1993). Court-mandated treatment of men who assault their partner: Issues, controversies, and outcomes. In N. Zoe Hilton (Ed.) *Legal response to wife assault: Current trends and evaluation.* Newbury Park, CA: Sage.

Hart, B. (1986). Lesbian battering: An examination. In K. Lobel (Ed.) *Naming the violence: Speaking out about lesbian battering.* Seattle: Seal Press.

Hoff, J. (1991). *Law, gender and injustice: A legal history of U.S. women.* New York: New York University Press.

Levy, B. (1991). *Dating violence: Young women in danger.* Seattle: Seal Press.

Marshall, L.L., & Rose, P. (1990). Premarital violence: The impact of family of origin violence, stress, and reciprocity. *Journal of Family Violence., 5.*

Messner, S.F., Krohn, M.D., & Liska, A.E. (1990). *Theoretical integration in the study of deviance and crime: Problems and prospects.* Albany, NY: SUNY Press.

Miller, S.L. (1989). Unintended side effects of pro-arrest policies and their race and class implications for battered women: A cautionary note. *Criminal Justice Policy Review., 3,* 299–316.

Murphy, C.M., & O'Leary K.D. (1989). Psychological aggression predicts physical aggression in early marriage. *Journal of Consulting and Clinical Psychology, 57,* 579–582.

Nurius, P., Furrey T., & Berliner, L. (1992). Coping capacity among women with abusive partners. *Violence and Victims, 7,* 229–244.

Rasche, C.E. (1988). Minority women and domestic violence: The unique dilemmas of battered women of color. *Journal of Contemporary Criminal Justice, 4,* 150–174.

Renzetti, C.M. (1992). *Violent betrayal: Partner abuse in lesbian relationships.* Newbury Park, CA: Sage.

Retzinger, S.M. (1991). *Violent emotions: Shame and rage in marital quarrels.* Newbury Park, CA: Sage.

Riggs, D., & O'Leary, K.D. (1989). A theoretical model of courtship aggression. In M.A. Pirog-Good & J.E. Stets (Eds.) *Violence in dating relationships.* New York: Praeger.

Sanday, P.R. (1990). *Fraternity gang rape: Sex, brotherhood, and privilege on campus.* New York: New York University Press.

Saunders, D.G. (1993). Husbands who assault: Multiple profiles Requiring multiple responses. In N.Z. Hilton (Ed.) *Legal response to wife assault: Current trends and evaluation.* Newbury Park, CA: Sage.

Schechter, S. (1982). *Women and male violence: The visions and struggles of the battered women's movement.* Boston: South End Press.

Sherman, L.W., & Berk, R.A. (1984). The specific deterrent effects of arrest for domestic assault. *American Sociological Review, 49,* 261.

Smart, C. (1989). *Feminism and the power of law.* London: Routledge.

Stith, S., & Rosen, K. (1990). Overview of domestic violence. In S. Stith, M.K. Williams, & K. Rosen (Eds.) *Violence hits home.* New York: Springer.

Sugarman, D.B., & Hotaling, G.T. (1989). Dating violence: Prevalence, context and risk markers. In M.A. Pirog-Good & J.E. Stets (Eds.) *Violence in dating relationships.* New York: Praeger.

Tolman, R.M. & Bennett, L.W. (1990). A review of quantitative research on men who batter. *Journal of Interpersonal Violence, 5* (1), 87–118.

Walker, L.E. (1979). *The battered woman.* New York: Harper & Row.

Warshaw, R. (1988). *I never called it rape.* New York: Harper & Row.

Weidman, A. (1986). Family therapy with violent couples. *Social casework, 67* (4), 211–218.

Zorza, J. (1992). The criminal law of misdemeanor domestic violence, 1970-1990. *Journal of Criminal Law and Criminology, 83* (1), 46–72.

9

On Dancing With a Bear

Reflections on Some of the Current Debates Among Domestic Violence Theorists

Claire M. Renzetti

A s I read this book, I was simultaneously elated and dismayed. My elation derives from what I see as the substantial progress that has been made in a relatively short period of time in the study of intimate violence. One outstanding example is the growing awareness of the problem of same-sex domestic violence. As Coleman (Chapter 4) and Lettlier (Chapter 1) point out, less than 10 years ago lesbian and gay domestic violence was virtually excluded from academic, clinical, and activist discussions of partner abuse. This is not to say that the problem currently is being addressed with the level of attention or degree of seriousness it warrants. Nevertheless, increasing recognition of same-sex partner abuse, as well as explorations of its potential implications for our understanding of intimate violence generally, stand out to me as major breakthroughs in our field. Related to this is the observation that each of the authors call for the development of integrated, multidimensional theories of intimate violence. This reflects not only the quantity of domestic violence research conducted from diverse perspectives during the past two decades, but also the increasing sophistication of this research, which has revealed complexities in perpetrators' and victims' motivations, interactions, and reactions on both micro and macro levels.

At the same time, however, I am dismayed by what I perceive as persistent, though certainly not insurmountable, obstacles to a fuller understanding of—and, therefore, the development of more effective responses to—intimate violence. Consider, for example, the continuing debate surrounding the question of whether women are as violent as men (see, for instance, Gelles & Loseke, 1993, and, in particular, its essays by Kurz & Straus). The majority of authors in the present book speak to this question, with at least one (Dutton) most clearly joining the once again growing crescendo of voices arguing that women are indeed as violent as—some even more violent than—men. Proponents of this position typically cite statistics that show women's frequency of violence against intimates to be about the same as men's frequency of violence against intimates. Studies showing that women often aggress against their partners first, without provocation or retaliation, are consistently cited, and now that data are available on lesbian battering, these data also are being used to bolster the claim that "women do it too." All of this evidence taken together supposedly undermines the feminist theory of domestic violence, which advocates of the "women are as violent as men" position portray as unitary and invariable, although they also usually pay lip service to the contributions feminist theorists have made in advancing our field.

It is not surprising to me that the data presented by proponents of the "women are as violent as men" argument serve to undermine feminist theory—that is, feminist theory as they have formulated it. However, what is surprising, especially in light of the current diversity within feminism and the explosion of published research written from a variety of feminist perspectives, is that such proponents continue to depict feminism as a single, unified, unchanging paradigm. As Miller (Chapter 8) notes, there is not one, but rather several feminisms. And as she and others (e.g., Messerschmidt, 1993) point out, many feminists have been among the most vocal critics of one-dimensional models of human behavior, including violent behavior.

It is the case that all feminist theories do share the assumption of the centrality of gender as a variable for understanding human behavior. And this is precisely why I am unwilling to follow the calls of Dutton's and others to "move beyond" feminism or to abandon it altogether. Intimate violence *is* gendered, as are individual and institutionalized responses to that violence. A careful review of the extant data collected by both feminist and nonfeminist researchers, for instance, reveals that men are more likely than women to be both the perpetrators and the victims of violent crimes. At the same time, however, women are more likely than men to be injured or killed by an intimate partner (Browne & Williams, 1993; Randall, 1990, U.S. Department of Justice, 1994). That women are sometimes violent in intimate relationships does not diminish the importance of discerning the role gender plays in the etiology of domestic violence. When women use violence against their partners, they are not behaving "like men." A glaring error in the "women are as violent as men" position is that it holds male behavior as normative and evaluates female behavior in terms of this male standard. Yet, as Hamberger and Potente (Chapter 3) and Vivian and Langhinrichsen-Rohling (Chapter 2) show, the violent behavior of women is both quantitatively and qualitatively different from the domestically violent behavior of men. Their research documents gender differences in intimate violence.

This is not to say that individual factors are irrelevant or insignificant in the etiology of domestic violence. The chapters in this book by Coleman, Warnken et al., Maiuro and Avery, and Dutton and others (e.g., O'Leary, 1993) make a strong case for the inclusion of individual variables, such as neurophysiological disorders, head injuries, and personality disorders in any theoretical account of domestic violence. However, feminist theory does not preclude an examination of individual factors, just as such an examination does not lessen the need for an analysis of the role of gender. Indeed, given that the possibility of incurring a head injury as well as the likelihood of being diagnosed with a specific neurophysiological or personality disorder are also gendered phenomena, we are reminded again of the centrality of the gender variable.[1]

But feminist theorists are not unidimensionally focused on gender. A substantial amount of feminist research documents the historical and cultural specificity of particular behaviors and institutional arrangements, including those pertaining to intimate violence (Burbank, 1994; Messerschmidt, 1993). Moreover, an examination of how gender intersects with other status variables, including race, social class, age, and sexual orientation, is becoming a critical component of much feminist research (see, for instance, Hirsch & Keller, 1990).

The extant literature tells us that there are racial, class, and age variations in domestic violence perpetration and victimization. Browne and Williams's (1993) research highlights differences in domestic violence perpetration and victimization not only by gender, but also across types of relationships—married versus unmarried heterosexual couples. We should not be surprised, therefore, when research reveals differences between the domestic violence experiences of lesbians and gay men, as well as between those of homosexual and heterosexual couples. Such differences are explainable within a feminist framework that emphasizes the interrelatedness of sexism and heterosexism and their intersection with other inequalities, especially racism, classism, and ageism. Thus, I must disagree with Letellier's (Chapter 1) assessment of feminist theory as inherently heterosexist. To the contrary, I continue to view feminist theorizing as offering the most fertile ground for the development of a truly integrated, multidimensional theory of domestic violence causation.

That said, it must also be noted that despite the preponderance of evidence documenting significant gender differences in intimate violence, it is the "women are as violent as men" perspective that appears to be garnering the most support, at least in the public consciousness if not in academic and clinical circles (however, see Dobash, Dobash, Wilson, & Daly, 1992, for discussion of how it is also influencing the latter domains). As Schwartz and DeKeseredy (1993, p.249) maintain, "Right now, there is an important battle being waged over the nature of women's behavior and its role in woman abuse." This is a battle whose outcome has serious consequences for battered women, especially in terms of our society's institutionalized responses to their behavior. Battered women's survival strategies increasingly are being stigmatized and, worse, criminalized.

I am reminded, for example, of a recent television viewing experience. While channel surfing one cold Friday night in January 1994, I came upon a segment of the news program, *20/20*, in which reporter Tom Jarrell was discussing the verdict in Lorena Bobbitt's trial. With solemnity, Hugh Downs asked Jarrell if he thought the verdict would motivate other women to violently attack their husbands and subsequently claim a so-called battered woman defense, to which Jarrell responded, with equal solemnity, in the affirmative. When Barbara Walters chided the two men for suggesting that now legions of raging women, battered or not, would be arming themselves with knives and cutting off men's penises, Jarrell responded in an anger-tinged voice that that was precisely what Lorena Bobbitt had done and that she had gotten away with little more than a "slap on the wrist." Just four months later, the focus of another nationally broadcast program was how individuals are increasingly using their previous victimization experiences as an "excuse" for their own violent behavior, and Lorena Bobbitt's case was featured as an example of this tendency.

Setting aside the question of whether confinement in a mental hospital does, in fact, constitute "little more than a slap on the wrist," I wish to consider instead some of the consequences of this framing of the problem of intimate violence. As Schwartz and DeKeseredy (1993) point out, problems such as intimate violence are socially constructed through a process of typification. That is, the social construction of intimate violence as a problem involves not only drawing attention to the phenomenon but also characterizing its essential nature by portraying particular cases as typical. Although the media play a central role in the typification process, they almost always draw on the work of academics to lend to their reports the credibility of science (Loseke, 1989).

Few of us would be willing to argue that the Bobbitt case represents in many respects an example of the "typical" domestic violence scenerio, but the fact remains that the media have used it and other newsworthy domestic violence cases, in conjunction with the academic work of researchers writing from the "women are as violent as men" perspective, to socially construct an image of battered women as culpable partners in relationship violence.[2] Although this is not a new image, it is one that fell into disfavor during the late 1970s. With the resurgence in the last few years of the "women are as violent as men" perspective, this image also has been ressurected (Schwartz & DeKeseredy, 1993).

We see the influence of this resurrection in changing public opinion regarding battered women. More important, its impact is reflected in the criminal justice system's reponses to domestic violence generally and to battered women specifically. For example, as Hamberger and Potente (Chapter 3) show, mandatory arrest laws for domestic violence—laws that supposedly were intended to protect battered women from abusive partners—are resulting in skyrocketing arrest rates for women. Despite the fact that the evidence in these cases almost always indicates that the women were acting in self-defense, they often are being criminally charged and sentenced to jail or to treatment programs. Although the treatment programs, as described by Hamberger and Potente, may be sympathetic to battered women and may have the worthy objective of empowering battered women to free themselves from the violence in their relationships, it is nonetheless the case that the self-defensive behavior of these women has been criminalized while, as Hamberger and Potente note, many of their abusive partners are not receiving treatment or punishment. Similarly, in her anaylsis of appellate decisions involving battered women who killed their abusive partners, Maguigan (1991) found that despite the fact that 75% of the defendants met the standard legal criteria of having acted in self-defense, many trial judges simply refused to apply self-defense law in these cases, usually resulting in convictions for the defendants.

The police, attorneys, and judges frequently argue that the arrest and trial of women who have used violence against their partners represents a gender-neutral application of the law. However, as noted earlier, institutionalized responses to domestic violence, like domestic violence perpetration and victimization, are gendered. Domestic violence continues to be judged by male rules, and women who defend themselves against abusive partners are being forced to pass an increasing number of "tests" to demonstrate that they are "true" victims. Given the typification of battered women as culpable, it is assumed that their violence is the same as men's violence, unless they can prove otherwise. The greater availability of services for battered women is often used against them; they now have fewer "excuses" for staying in an abusive relationship. But even if they are successful in establishing their victimization status, they may still lose in other ways; for example, their children may be taken from them because they are then considered incapable of protecting their children from the batterer.

Proponents of the "women are as violent as men" position maintain that what is needed for a comprehensive understanding of domestic violence and for the establishment of effective prevention and intervention stratgies is a gender-neutral theory. In light of the evidence I have reviewed here, I argue instead that what is needed is a theory that recognizes gender as well as sexual orientation, race, class, and age as interconnected organizing variables in domestic violence perpretation, victimization, and institutionalized response. It is perhaps more difficult to develop a theory that integrates social structural factors that facilitate or support violence with interpersonal dynamics in contrast to one that reduces such violence to individual pathologies, but it appears to be the most promising avenue for advancing our knowledge and our strategies for solving this serious social problem. I am reminded here of a speech given by former Surgeon General Jocelyn Elders (Elders, 1994). To borrow an analogy used by Dr. Elders, developing the most comprehensive and effective approach to domestic violence is like dancing with a bear: You can't sit down when you get tired; you have to wait for the bear to get tired and then you can sit down. Let me conclude, therefore, by urging the contributors to this volume, as well as our readers, to muster the stamina to keep on dancing.

Notes

[1]For instance, Warnken et al. (Chapter 5) note that one of the most common causes of head injury is auto accidents. Males are more likely than females to be involved in serious auto accidents, and researchers have linked this observed difference to gender socialization. Females are socialized to act safely and to avoid risks, whereas males are encouraged from an early age to be adventurous and unafraid of risk taking. Consequently, males, more often than females, are involved in the kinds of dangerous situations that may lead to accidents that cause head injuries (Waldron, 1986). At the same time, there is an extensive research literature that documents gender bias in psychiatric and psychological diagnoses, resulting in males and females having a different likelihood of being diagnosed with a specific mental or emotional disorder. For a review of this literature, see Renzetti and Curran, 1995. Finally, although Maiuro and Avery (Chapter 7) use gender-neutral terms, such as "patients," "subjects," and "violence-prone individuals," the question arises as to whether the research they review included both men and women or men only? What is known about sex differences in the incidence of the neurophysiological conditions they describe? Are men more likely than women to suffer from these and, if so, why? Raising and seeking the answers to such questions assumes that gender is a central organizing variable in the researchers' theoretical framework; failure to ask such questions runs the risk of overlooking important differences in the etiology of men's and women's use of violence.

[2]It was expected, for example, that the murder of Nicole Brown Simpson would draw a more sympathetic response to domestic violence victims than Lorena Bobbitt had, and to some extent this did occur. Nevertheless, the Simpson murder was also seized by proponents of the "women are as violent as men" position as an opportunity to remind the public of women's responsibility for domestic violence. See, for instance, Sherven and Sniechowski, 1994.

REFERENCES

Browne, A., & Williams, K. R. (1993). Gender, intimacy, and violence: Trends from 1976 through 1987. *Gender & Society,7*, 78–98.

Burbank, V. K. (1994). Cross-cultural perspectives on aggression in women and girls: An introduction. *Sex Roles, 30*, 169–176.

Dobash, R. P., Dobash, R. E., Wilson, M., & Daly, M. (1992). The myth of sexual symmetry in marital violence. *Social Problems, 39*, 71–91.

Elders, M. J. (1994, June). *Keynote address.* 16th National Lesbian and Gay Health Conference, New York, NY.

Gelles, R. J., & Loseke, D. R. (Eds.) (1993). *Current controversies on domestic violence.* Newbury Park, CA: Sage.

Hirsch, M., & Keller, E. F. (Eds.) (1990). *Conflicts in feminism.* New York: Routledge.

Loseke, D. R. (1989). Violence is "violence" . . . or is it? The social construction of "wife abuse" and public policy. In J. Best (Ed.), *Images of issues* (pp. 191–206). New York, Aldine de Gruyter.

Maguigan, H. (1991). Battered women and self-defense: Myths and misconceptions in current reform proposals. *University of Pennsylvania Law Review, 140*, 379–486.

Messerschmidt, J. W. (1993). *Masculinities and crime.* Lanham, MD: Rowman & Littlefield.

O'Leary, K. D. (1993). Through a psychological lens: Personality traits, personality disorders, and levels of violence. In R. J. Gelles & D. R. Loseke (Eds.), *Current controversies on domestic violence* (pp. 7–30). Newbury Park, CA: Sage.

Randall, T. (1990). Domestic violence intervention calls for more than treating injuries. *Journal of the American Medical Association, 264*, 939–944.

Renzetti, C. M., & Curran, D. J. (1995). *Women, men & society: The sociology of gender.* Boston: Allyn and Bacon.

Schwartz, M. D., & DeKeseredy, W. S. (1993). The return of the "battered husband syndrome" through the typification of women as violent. *Crime, Law and Social Change, 20*, 249–265.

Sherven, J., & Sniechowski, J. (1994, June 21). Women are responsible, too. *Los Angeles Times*, p. B7.

U.S. Department of Justice (1994). *Violence against women*. Washington, DC: Author.

Waldron, I. W. (1986). Why do women live longer than men? In P. Conrad & R. Kern (Eds.), *The sociology of health and illness* (pp. 34–44). New York: St. Martin's Press.

Index